risk

living by faith
in the face of fear

Shannon C. Deal

To my parents,

David & Barbara Cross

who took me with them into mission

This morning they bombed my city.

Just as my husband Carlton was about to leave for the office and I was settling down to work on this book, my daughter sent me a text. *Explosion at the airport*, it said. I turned on the television and saw images of broken windows in the terminal, and people running for cover. Carlton joined me to watch. A few moments later, as he prepared once again to leave, another text came in: *Explosion at Maelbeek now apparently, metro closing.* My husband's office is less than a kilometer from this subway station. I told him, "You'd better drive," and texted my daughter that he was taking the car. Immediately she returned, *No no stay home!* We did.

I started writing this book just over a year ago, just after the Charlie Hebdo attacks in Paris in January 2015. I hoped to finish it by August, when our eight-month furlough from our work in Brussels ended. But various circumstances combined to prevent me from completing my planned chapters on time, and I found myself still working on it in November when Paris was attacked again.

And still a week later, when the attackers were traced back to my city, Brussels. When a high terror alert shut down public venues and transportation and schools for a number of days. When traces of the escaped terrorist and signs of bomb construction were found in an apartment four blocks from where I live.

Perhaps Someone thought I needed to live this book, not just write it.

We live in a dangerous world. As I write this, the death toll from this morning's attacks continues to climb as they sift through the wreckage in the subway tunnel. Injured people fill the hallways of the Military Hospital where a friend of mine is recovering from knee surgery. The authorities warn that possibly we have not yet seen the end of these attacks.

And danger is in no way confined to Brussels. During our sabbatical in the US last year, Carlton and I found ourselves locked down in Camden Yards during an Orioles' baseball game as riots raged outside in the streets of Baltimore, following the death of a young black man in police custody. It seemed that every morning I picked up the papers in Carlton's hometown of Norfolk, Virginia, I would read of a shooting in the city. And whenever I watch the news, images from all over the world of earthquakes and plane crashes and fires, with their attendant deaths and injury and destruction, fill the screen.

Should we be surprised?

Jesus told us: *You will hear of wars and rumors of wars,* **but see to it that you are not alarmed. Such things must happen,** *but the end is still to come. Nation will rise against nation, and kingdom against kingdom. There will be famines and earthquakes in various places* [Matthew 24:6-7].

So, no, we should not be surprised or alarmed.

Should we be afraid?

Jesus also told us: *I have told you these things, so that in me you may have peace.* **In this world you will have trouble. But take heart!** *I have overcome the world* [John 16:33].

So, no, we must not be afraid.

This is all the more remarkable, considering that Jesus is not saying: "I'm telling you all the bad stuff that will occur so you can avoid it." Or, "Sit tight, hide in your house and wait it out." Nor yet, "Don't worry; if you're on my side nothing bad will ever happen to you."

Rather, he tells his disciples: *Then* **you will be handed over to be persecuted and put to death,** *and you will be hated by all nations because of me.... the love of most will grow cold, but* **the one who stands firm to the end will be saved** [Matthew 24:9,12-13].

So not only should we not be surprised, or afraid. We should be bold in the face of death itself.

It's not easy. Political rhetoric and media hype thrive on fear. Personal security—not just from terrorism, but also from disease, accident, financial loss, or any other kind of pain—is often presented as our society's highest goal. I started writing this book because of a deep inner sense that maybe this was a hidden idol that needed to be exposed, and it is an idol that could consolidate its demonic hold on an even larger number of people after today's attacks.

But Scripture reminds us that **the Spirit God gave us does not make us timid,** *but gives us power, love and self-discipline* [2 Timothy 1:7].

It tells us, "*Be strong and courageous.* **Do not be afraid;** *do not be discouraged, for the Lord your God will be with you wherever you go*" [Joshua 1:9].

It exhorts us, "*Be on your guard; stand firm in the faith;* **be courageous; be strong.** *Do everything in love*" [1 Corinthians 16:13-14].

Let's overthrow this idol, and learn to risk it all in following the One who is *the pioneer and perfecter of our faith,* the One who *for the joy set before him he endured the cross, scorning its shame, and sat down at the right hand of the throne of God* [Hebrews 12:2].

The risk is worth the reward.

Praying for boldness in Brussels and beyond,
Shannon

How to Use This Book

Dear Reader –

I am praying that this book you have picked up will give you courage to step into new risks to which God is calling you, and to give you strength to face those dangers which have come into your life unbidden.

Here are a few suggestions to help you get the most out of it:

- **Scripture Quotes:** In this book, I use a large number of quotes from Scripture. Now, I don't know about you, but I notice a bad tendency in myself to skip over these in other people's books, somehow thinking I already know the references, and therefore I barely skim them so I can get back to the author's words. I would like to urge you not to follow my poor example. The Scripture quotes are not only integral to the message of this book, but inspired by God himself, and *useful for teaching, rebuking, correcting and training in righteousness* [2 Timothy 3:16]. So rather than speeding up when you come to a Scripture quote, I would like to encourage you to slow down, perhaps to read it aloud. In this way, you can let God's Word sink in to you and change you, and whatever I say will be simply an adjunct.
- **Reading Alone or with Small Groups:** I have attempted to make each of the chapters to be short enough to read and digested at one sitting (average five pages, plus reflection questions). They are also written in groups of five, so that you could conceivably read one on each weekday. In this way, you will cover one main topic each week, and have a couple of days left over to ponder what you have read. You could also read one section a week with a small group, and then discuss it together. You will find free small group study and discussion resources on my website (shannoncdeal.com).
- **Further Reflection.** For those who want to go deeper with their reflection, a workbook form of this book will also be available, in which study and application questions will be included with space for responses. This can also be used as a topical study for an in-depth Bible study group, and will be available from the same vendors that sell this version of the book.

TABLE OF CONTENTS

designed to dare

(or, lions and teapots)

1 On Becoming a Lion

The wicked flee though no one pursues, but the righteous are as bold as a lion. [Proverbs 28:1]

Is it any surprise that terrorism produces terror? That is what it is meant to do.

In the wake of the Paris attacks on November 13, 2015, the attackers' center for planning and plotting was traced to the suburb of Molenbeek in Brussels—about three miles from where we live. Fearing that Brussels itself might be attacked, the authorities shut down the city, closing museums, concert venues, sport stadiums and anywhere else that people might gather. The metro was closed. Schoolchildren stayed home and people worked from their houses and apartments. And although this information did not become public, a European Union official confided to us that the government feared a chemical attack.

For about a week, Brussels became a ghost town.

Our Christmas market, which opened the first weekend of Advent, is normally thronged with shoppers, and the mild weather of that week should have increased the crowd. But in this season, the main people standing outside the little huts selling hot wine and holiday baubles were soldiers with machine guns.

The proprietor of our favorite local café glumly told my husband of his devastating financial losses as customers stayed home.

Our own largely Muslim neighborhood seemed eerily empty, save for the increased police patrols on the streets, and yet more camouflaged military guys.

Was this reaction any surprise? The threat hung over us like a sword on a thread. Terrorism created terror, as it was meant to. Even while nothing was happening.

Though No One Pursues...

Sometimes the fear of what **might** happen can impact our lives almost as much as—sometimes more than—the disaster itself. In the wake of recent terrorist attacks in Brussels on the airport and metro, I can predict how terror of further attacks could infect our population:[1]

- **Suspicion.** Mistrust of Brussels' large and growing Muslim minority—predicted to increase to become half of the city's population by 2030—will further isolate and alienate people whose lack of integration into the community has catalyzed the handful of terrorists now erupting in violence. Fear could result in a growth of suspicion, tarring innocent people with the brush of terrorism—and possibly fueling the very radicalism of which they are accused.

- **Blame.** Indignation over failures of security intelligence and police intervention, or lack of cooperation by governmental bodies will motivate effort to fix the guilt on someone rather than fixing the problem at hand. Fear could result in 20/20 hindsight, and accusations that undermine the ability of authorities to deal with the present.
- **Paralysis.** Warnings to citizens to "be careful" and "stay vigilant" fail to state exactly how to do that. Security points could be set up outside transport hubs like airports and metro stations, causing sluggishness and delays and increased costs. People could stop going outside, stop going to public places and events, stop taking the metro, stop going to the airport. Fear could result in a kind of panic that leads to stagnation of the city, with all personal, corporate and governmental energies directed toward complete and total security.

If such things result, the terrorists will have won. For the price of some cheap suitcases filled with nails and homemade explosives, they will have purchased alienation, accusation, and immobilization in our city. And more, for around the world, we are likely to find:

- Increased suspicion/hostility toward Muslims in other Western countries
- Thousands of refugees from the same terror turned away from safe haven, in fear of a possible terrorist hidden among them
- Worldwide reshaping of security measures to create (the illusion of) complete safety – at an immense price of time, mobility, and manpower
- The back-and-forth of blame and defensiveness played out by authorities

But as Salman Rushdie said, "There is no such thing as perfect security, only varying levels of insecurity." A tram could hit me tomorrow. (Indeed, in Brussels' busy streets this is much more likely, statistically, than being blown up by a terrorist bomb.) But fear of what terrorists **could** do—that at any moment they might strike again—is a powerful force that leads many people to hole up or run away.

> *The wicked flee though no one pursues…*

In a world without faith, without a framework for interpreting such fears, fleeing often seems the best option. Or whatever else will restore the illusion of security.

For those of us who live by faith, there is another way.

Bold as a Lion

After the Paris attacks, with Brussels on lockdown and public venues closed, churches in our city faced a decision: would they hold public services in the shadow of such a threat? Some, respecting the governmental warnings, cancelled their gatherings. But others reacted differently.

The Anglican Church located in the center of town went ahead with its regularly scheduled services, as did every Catholic parish in the city.

The International Baptist Church counts among its members many NATO employees, people who possessed awareness of the details of the threat beyond that of most citizens. Because of this, the elders decided officially to cancel services—but the pastor let the congregation know that he would still be there in the church building to lead prayer and worship informally with whoever chose to come.

The same number of people showed up as on a normal Sunday.

Our own church, which gathers most weeks in multiple neighborhood groups, went through the same discussion process with the leaders, and decided to come together as usual. Our attendance that Sunday actually rose.

> *… but the righteous are as bold as a lion.*

The choice wasn't easy. A definite air of menace haunted the streets of our neighborhood of Schaerbeek, and instead of simply buzzing up whoever rang the bell of our fourth-floor apartment, my husband Carlton stood at the ground floor door and let people in one by one as they arrived. During our Bible study, one girl's phone kept beeping with texts reporting police raids all over the city. For us, it was the first time ever that gathering carried with it a sense of threat, and we got the barest glimpse of what it must have been like for the early Christians, and for many persecuted Christians meeting today. We wondered if perhaps this was a peek into a future reality, when house groups such as ours might not be just a missional strategy, but an underground necessity.

Applying the Proverb

Look once more at the proverb quoted at the beginning of this chapter. Proverbs constitute an interesting form of Biblical literature. They are not the same as promises: do this, and that is guaranteed to happen. They are more like rules of thumb: this is the way the world as God created it usually works. But there are exceptions.

And sometimes the righteous, unfortunately, behave more like rabbits than lions.

- Listen to how Christians whisper about conspiracies to undermine our principles and freedoms, bemoaning some lost "golden age" of the past and pointing fingers of blame in all directions.

- Watch how we hover over our children, protecting them from any possible hardship or poor choices.

- Look at how strictly we separate ourselves from those with different beliefs—even those who also claim faith in Christ— so as not to be contaminated.

- Observe our attitudes towards "illegal aliens," towards refugees, towards any foreigner who might encroach on our rights or riches, or pose any danger to comfort and security.

- Notice how we choose to interact only with people who are like us—and then only with "boundaries" firmly in place in case they come close enough to harm us in some way.

Deeper and deeper we dig our burrows, out of harm's way, so we can be warm and comfortable and safe. Sometimes we even convince ourselves that our own and our family's security and protection is God's most important goal for us.

But we are not meant to be safe—we are meant to be dangerous. (At least, dangerous to the spiritual forces of evil and death.) God wants to come to his people in their fear and put in them the boldness of lions.

Think of Gideon. The oppressive occupiers of his land have him so scared that he is threshing meager portions of grain in the dead of night, lest they take it away from him. And how does the angel of the Lord greet him? *"The Lord is with you, mighty warrior!"* [Judges 6:12].

Not long after, he leads a tiny army to defeat the oppressors' massive one with nothing more than torches, pitchers and trumpets.

Think of Esther. Already, she is the leading lady in the harem of a pagan prince—hardly the place for a good Jewish girl. When her uncle asks her to speak up to her husband on behalf of her threatened people, she fears for her life. But her uncle tells her: *"Who knows but that you have come to your royal position for such a time as this?"* Asking her people to pray, she says, *"If I die, I die"* [Esther 4:14,16]. And God uses her not only to save her people, but also to defeat their enemies.

Think of Peter, cowering in fear and shame with the other disciples after the Romans had executed their master, goaded by the Jewish leaders. Jesus appears to them in the locked room where they are hiding, saying *"Peace be with you!"* [John 20:19]. Only weeks later he is boldly proclaiming the resurrection of this same Jesus, carrying the message to the heart of the Empire it would subvert, unafraid in the end to die even as his master did.

Losing Your Life to Save It

Are these people special heroes, called in a way I am not? Only if you are not part of *"whoever"* in this startling paradoxical statement by Jesus:

> For whoever wants to save their life will lose it,
> but whoever loses their life **for me** will find it. [Matt. 16:25]

In this study, you will be challenged to a great adventure. And no adventure is without risk. But what I hope you will see is that when you run those risks on Jesus' behalf, accompanied by his Holy Spirit, for his kingdom's sake and his name's fame, you will discover the truth of his promise:

> *"I have come that they may have life, and have it to the full."* [John 10:10]

We are meant to be—created to be—lions, whether people around us are fleeing from nothing at all, or whether we are surrounded by much real danger. So shed your rabbit skin, grow a mane, and begin to believe what Jesus said to his disciples before he died, before he sent his Spirit to live with them always:

> *"In this world you will have trouble.*
> *But take heart! I have overcome the world."* [John 16:33]

Reflections:

Risk must be faced with boldness.

What terrifies you the most? What are your greatest fears at this moment? Write them down as they come to you, and go as deep as you can. Below are some lists (just a few of our possible fears) to get you started:

- **Fear of violence?** (Terrorist attacks, random shootings, gang violence, serial murderers, getting mugged/raped, domestic abuse...)
- **Fear of catastrophe?** (Plane crashes, house fires, car accidents, being attacked by an animal, drowning, being buried alive...)
- **Fear of disability?** (Cancer, Alzheimer's, chronic illness/pain, disfigurement, paralysis, blindness/deafness, mental illness, epidemics like Ebola, losing mobility, getting old...)
- **Fear of loss?** (Losing your job, losing your home, losing your savings, losing your retirement, being burgled/robbed, declining property value/ investment value, never having children, never being married, never finding your purpose...)
- **Fears of 'outsiders'?** (Foreigners in your country, Muslims, illegal aliens, refugees, other races, other religions, members of cults, other Christian denominations, the people next door...)
- **Relational fears?** (Abandonment, criticism, rejection, disrespect, betrayal, being manipulated, someone being angry at you, distance/coldness, powerlessness, being alone...)
- **Fears for your children?** (Moral corruption, failing at school, not having friends, thinking the wrong things, alcohol/drugs, pornography/sex, committing a crime, not keeping up, learning disabilities, physical handicaps, emotional distress...)
- **Fear of losing control/comfort?** (Decisions taken from you, being trapped in a relationship/situation, political situation devolving, having to move, having to leave something familiar, engaging with people who intimidate you...)

Look back over your list of fears.

- Which of these things are immediately threatening you right now (are happening, or are likely to happen and soon)?
- Which of these things are quite likely to happen in the future?
- Which of these things are just a possibility?
- Now put your hand over the list, and pray, admitting to God that you are afraid of these things and that you have no control over **any** of them. The truth is that the things that we really cannot tell which of them truly **will** happen to us—even the ones that seem most or least likely.

Below is a prayer affirmation that you might want to **pray each day as you go through this study**. It is called "St. Teresa's Bookmark," because, when she died, it was found between the pages of Teresa of Avila's prayer book, written on a small piece of paper.[2]

Let nothing disturb thee,
nothing affright thee;
all things are passing,
God never changeth!
Faithful endurance attaineth to all things;
who God possesseth
in nothing is wanting;
alone God sufficeth.

2 Designed for Good Works

For we are God's workmanship, created in Christ Jesus to do good works, which he has prepared beforehand for us to do. [Ephesians 2:10]

THÉology

Here is a little song that helps me to apply this verse to my life:

I'm a little teapot, short and stout,
Here is my handle, here is my spout,
When I get all steamed up, hear me shout:
"Tip me over, pour me out!"

Maybe this metaphor helps me because I am strangely attracted to teapots. In my collection, I have teapots of all shapes and sizes: tall graceful teapots; round squatty teapots; teapots shaped like a piano, a pumpkin, a pub. They all, however, have a handle and a spout, and all of them can be used to serve out that delightful beverage, which as Gladstone said, "warms you when you are cold, cools you when you are heated, cheers you when you are depressed, and calms you when you are excited."

Each one of my teapots was crafted as a work of art by some pottery, which designed it to be both aesthetically pleasing and practically useful. And that is what this verse says about us as well.

Scripture often describes us as pots created by the Potter for his purposes: *You, Lord, are our Father. We are the clay, you are the potter; we are all the work of your hand* [Isaiah 64:8]. Here in Ephesians 2:10, we actually can distinguish **three** different creative endeavors that the Potter goes through to make sure that we are fit to bear the brand of his workshop.

Created Twice

The first is that *we are God's workmanship.* This word *workmanship* could also be translated "artistry" or "masterpiece." Each one of us is a masterful work of art, specially designed by God with strengths and preferences, gifts and talents, physical, mental, and emotional attributes as unique to us as the fingerprints he carved with love. Together as a Body, we form an oeuvre of fantastic breadth and virtuosity that should make us stand openmouthed in awe before the Artist.[3] As the expression of a Designer, you are worthy of any display. As the Psalmist says: *You created my inmost being; you knit me* together in my mother's womb. I praise you because I am fearfully and wonderfully made [Psalm 139:13-14].

But probably, you don't always feel like a designer piece. You are, as I am, aware of the faults and flaws and cracks and chips that weaken you. You are embarrassed about the dirt and grime that hide your colors. You aren't sure that you are worth all that much, really; certainly not the going price for a masterpiece. Sin and weakness and age and brokenness will do that to you.

And that is where God's second creative endeavor comes in, when we are *created in Christ Jesus.* This is the redemption of God, where we are not just hosed off and patched up, recycled like junk picked out of the trash, but completely made new through Christ's righteousness. It starts with our spirits, but spreads much further. For we are the beginning of a totally new creation. As Paul tells us: *I consider that our present sufferings are not worth comparing with the glory that will be revealed in us. For the creation waits in eager expectation for the children of God to be revealed* [Romans 8:18-19]. One day, even our bodies will be remade in perfection, to inhabit the New Heavens and Earth recreated in Christ. No flaw will remain.

And Yet a Third Creation

And is this where it ends? Are we delicate porcelain pieces made to sit in protective glass cases, for our beauty to be admired? That's what you do with works of art, isn't it?

The third creative endeavor of God in this verse reveals that we have a much greater purpose than simply revealing his artistry. We are made to **do** something. And the great thing is, that not only are we purposely designed so that we can do these things called *good works*, but he also *prepares beforehand* the good works that we are to do.

So, if I am a little teapot (short and stout), I have been made with a handle and a spout so I can pour out refreshing tea. The Potter himself measures the leaves and adds the boiling water and lets it brew, so that I am a vessel of comfort and warmth and refreshment and energy to all for whom I am poured out. He makes the pot, and then he makes the tea. And, as anyone who truly loves tea will tell you, this also is an art.

In China, the most prized teapots are made with unglazed clay from the YiXing region. A tea importer told me that each pot retains the flavor of the tea that it holds; for this reason, a different pot is used for each different blend of tea, whether green, red, black, yellow, or white. So it is with the works God prepares for each of us; while all are meant to pour out good works on the world around us, those good works will taste different depending on which brew the Spirit has chosen specially for us. (Perhaps you are not even meant to dispense tea; perhaps you are a coffeepot. Or a water pitcher. Or a wine carafe.)

Fragile Vessels Put to Use

One problem with teapots and other such vessels: they tend to be fragile. And it is true that if we use a teapot for a risky purpose that it was not created to serve—such as kicking it around as a soccer ball—it will not last for long.

Because of that fragility, some collectors never use their pots, but rather leave them in a protected display. But how can a teapot that has never brewed tea be worthy of the name? I believe teapots are created to be used, and when I host people, I enjoy choosing the right pot(s) to serve those particular guests. There is a risk that they may be broken—chipped or cracked or dropped—but the joy of service is worth the risk.

It is a dangerous world when you feel you are fragile. Maybe you feel you were made with flaws to begin with, and have trouble recognizing your own worth. Maybe you fear you have only been patched, not remade, and any hot water will burst you. Maybe you are afraid to be taken out of the cupboard, to do and dare.

But who are you, the teapot, to argue with the Potter who has designed you and wants to fill you to the brim to be poured out? Isaiah warns us: "Woe to those who quarrel with their Maker... Does the clay say to the potter, 'What are you making?' Does your work say, 'The potter has no hands'?" [Isaiah 45:9].

God assures us that he has made us to do his works, and that he has also made the works for us to do. We can accomplish what he has set out for us because the fit is perfect. We need merely be willing to risk being taken off the shelf to be satisfied in being poured out in service, fulfilling the purpose for which we were fashioned.

Choices for Courageous Challenge

These good works always involve a choice. Sometimes this choice is a deliberate one to lean into a new purpose to which God is calling you. Maybe you feel that God is leading you to do something because of a particular strength he has given you, like using your gift of teaching English to those who are just learning to speak it. Other times he calls us to step out and do things for which we feel unequipped, to do them in weakness. Or you are called to use your strengths, but in an uncomfortable setting or with people who make you nervous—like teaching English to refugees in a homeless shelter.

We see this kind of choice given to Abram, when he is called to leave his home, or to Peter, invited to step out of the boat and come to Jesus over the water. We might call these choices **Practical Catalysts,** since you must make the choice to step into them and do them, to lean into a calling to good works for which God is equipping and sending you.

At other times God just puts the good works in your path in a way you **must** deal with—as when your child is diagnosed with learning difficulties, or your spouse develops Alzheimer's. Even then, you have a choice: whether to feel like a victim, complaining, escaping or minimizing difficulties, acting like a martyr or hero; or to engage the challenge with courage and even joy as one more good work designed for you by God.

Ruth faced such a choice when she confronted the need of her mother-in-law Naomi. So did Job, as he refused to curse God in his calamity. The choice to embrace the challenge of difficult or risky situations in which God has placed you we might call **Providential Catalysts,** since God puts them in our path, and our choice is **how** to deal with them.

Paul knew this feeling of challenge, from both stepping out toward a calling and confronting formidable good works put in his path. But he also knew that God, who made both us and our good works, could also give us the resilience to be tipped over and poured out—even in difficult circumstances:

> "But we have this **treasure in jars of clay** to show that **this all-surpassing power is from God and not from us.** We are hard pressed on every side, but not crushed; perplexed, but not in despair; persecuted, but not abandoned; struck down, but not destroyed... **Therefore we do not lose heart...** For our light and momentary troubles are achieving for us **an eternal glory that far outweighs them all.**" [2 Corinthians 4:7-8, 16-17]

Reflections:

Think about yourself as **a unique creation of God,** different from every other person he has created.
- What three words would you use to describe your personality?
- What would you say are your two most prominent strengths?
- What have you always loved to do, ever since you were little?

Some of us have a hard time thinking of ourselves in this way, because we are so focused on what is wrong with us.
- Do you tend to focus most on your physical flaws, intellectual limitations, lack of abilities, relational difficulties, or spiritual failings? What, specifically, most makes you feel like trash rather than a treasure?
- **What would it mean to you to truly believe that you are "made new" in Christ?** For now? For the future?
- In what way might your flaw or failing actually be part of his purpose for you in this world?

What new thoughts or feelings does the idea that **God has crafted works specifically for you to do** inspire in you? How does it put your strengths and weaknesses in perspective? How might it renew your purpose?

Risk involves choice.

In this chapter, we looked at **two choices** you might have to make regarding these good works and the risk they involve:
- When you look back at the things you fear from the last chapter, do any of them relate to a **Practical Catalyst** you fear stepping into, or to a **Providential Catalyst** you either fear facing or are facing presently?
  - How have you tried to avoid or sidestep taking on new risks and challenges God might be calling you to?
  - How have you tried to escape or minimize the risky challenges God has put in your life already, or indulged in being the martyr or hero because of them?
- How might perceiving these as "good works created by God specially for you" change your attitude toward the risks they entail? Spend some time praying through these attitudes.

3 Provision, Renewal, and Risk

In a well-furnished kitchen there are not only crystal goblets and silver platters, but waste cans and compost buckets—some containers used to serve fine meals, others to take out the garbage. Become the kind of container God can use to present any and every kind of gift to his guests for their blessing. [2 Timothy 2:20-21, The Message]

Vessels for God's Righteous Works

Visiting the stunning glass collection of the Chrysler Museum of Art in Norfolk, Virginia, I marveled at a delicate 17th century goblet that had miraculously survived intact for over four centuries. Its clear blown-glass bowl had been diamond-engraved with a dainty foliage pattern, and the graceful stem embellished with two elegant turquoise-colored wings.[4] One could imagine some Flemish nobleman or wealthy Dutch trader of the time setting this exquisite object, filled with the finest wine, in front of an important guest in order to indicate the honor in which he was held.

In the above verses, Paul is exhorting Timothy (and us) to become the kind of vessels God can use to serve blessing to others, *"made holy, useful to the Master and prepared to do any good work"* [v. 21, NIV].[5] To do this, we must first make sure we are clean of any kind of filth or rubbish that would make it impossible for God to use us for serving the good stuff; as Paul says in verse 22, *"Flee... evil desires"*. By confessing and turning away from such sin we hold ourselves ready for God to use us, to set us in front of his guests full of fine wine.

The wine that God would like to serve from us is nothing less than the fruit of his righteousness, his gracious works in the world. These works might be categorized into two main genres: Provision and Renewal.[6] Provision flows out of his great work of Creation as God continues to meet the needs of the universe and the beings he has created. And Renewal pours from the floodgates of grace opened by Jesus' work of Redemption, starting with purified people reconciled to God and ending with the rebirth of the whole cosmos.

We have already seen in the last chapter how God's great works of Creation and Redemption in the world have authored our own design and deliverance. Now he invites us to be partners and vessels in pouring out and revealing what he is doing in the world to the people and places around us.[7]

Participating in Provision and Renewal

God invites us to participate in his work of Provision not only by providing for our own needs through the work we do, but for those of others: *Anyone who has been stealing must steal no longer, but must work, **doing something useful with their own hands,** that they may have something **to share with those in need*** [Ephesians 4:28]. In this command, we can see both the dimensions of repudiating acts that make us unfit vessels, and of embracing the service to which God is calling us. We are to turn our backs on the sin of stealing, which takes from others to meet our own needs. Instead God offers us the honor of *doing something useful with [our] own hands.* And then, instead of taking from others, he gives us the purpose of sharing with others who because of their needs might be tempted to steal.

He also invites us to participate in his work of Renewal regarding both people and place. Paul uses a metaphor of renewal rooted in God's work of Provision when he says of the Corinthians: *I planted the seed, Apollos watered it, but God has been making it grow. So neither the one who plants nor the one who waters is anything, but only God, who makes things grow. **The one who plants and the one who waters have one purpose,** and they will each be rewarded according to their own labor* [I Corinthians 3:6-8]. It is clear here that the work of renewal in the hearts of the Corinthian church members is God's—but Paul and Apollos both have had a significant part to play in it.

In a world where God says, "*I am making **everything** new!*" [Revelation 21:5], places as well as people are in need of restoration. Isaiah the prophet, calling God's people to justice, says of those who *spend [themselves] in behalf of the hungry and satisfy the needs of the oppressed* [58:10]:

> *Your people will rebuild the ancient ruins*
> *and will raise up the age-old foundations;*
> *you will be called **Repairer of Broken Walls,***
> ***Restorer of Streets with Dwellings.*** [v. 12]

Many of us have heard this as a call not just for Old Testament Jews, but also for those of us looking around at degraded slums and corrupt or broken systems in the cities where God has placed us. We take to ourselves the call of the prophet Jeremiah to the people in exile in Babylon: *"Seek the peace and prosperity of the city to which I have carried you into exile. Pray to the Lord for it, because if it prospers, you too will prosper"* [Jeremiah 29:7].

This is the wine God wants to serve from his precious, clean goblets to the world, inviting people and cities and nations as his honored guests to taste his goodness through the *good works* of his people. But there is one problem with this—for the goblets.

Stepping into Need and Brokenness

Serving is risky. (We thought about this a little before, but think more deeply.)

Being willing to be a vessel of God for Provision means stepping into areas of **need**. Now, there is nothing wrong in itself with need—it is the way God created us, and it should keep us coming back to Him as Provider in increasing gratitude. And from the beginning, he gave us a part to play in our own provision as gatherers in his garden. But sin arises at the point where **people want to meet their own needs apart from God**, in ways not sanctioned by him.[8]

Because of this sin tendency in both yourself and others, working with God in Provision to meet the needs of others necessarily entails some risk, not least to your personal resources and comfort. Imagine yourself in these situations:

- Your four-week-old baby cries with colic between 4:00 and 6:00 PM daily. No matter how you modify feedings, you end up pacing the room, jiggling him up and down, for the whole time. Your patience is creeping toward irritation with him— when is this going to end? —and also with your spouse, who could certainly get home earlier to give you a break...
- Your aging mother is dependent upon help from you for her functioning in daily life—but she is also sharply critical of how and when that help is given, while resisting help from supplemental sources.
- That homeless guy sits on the corner every day with a sign that says: WILL WORK FOR FOOD. Is it just a pity scam to get people to give him money? How are you supposed to respond to his apparent need?

Being willing to be a vessel of God for Renewal means stepping into areas of **brokenness.** Inherently, brokenness in the world has been caused by sin, whether the sin of a specific person, or the sin of a group or nation, or simply the sin that cracked the cosmos at the

Fall. Because of this, working with God in Renewal to reconcile people to God and each other, and to restore in places some reflection of God's kingdom, intrinsically carries risk with it as you cross these crevasses. Imagine yourself in these situations:

- A couple you are friends with has separated with a great deal of rancor, and each of them is trying to get you on their side. Whenever you try to help one see or remember the good in the other, you are met with a cold response. It is exhausting, and you wonder: will you lose both friends?
- Your teenage daughter is struggling with severe social anxiety, and every morning is a battle to get her out the door to school. You personally have shown up late to work multiple times because of this problem, and your boss is not happy about it. Every day you have to evaluate the battle, and whether she should just stay home this time. It is even more disconcerting to discover that her psychologist blames the problem on you.
- You are helping lead a Bible Study run by an urban church, reaching out to women in a tough neighborhood. Once you get there each week, in the room with the ladies, you love it... But the problem is parking your car and running the gauntlet of the dangerous street you have to walk down to get there, keeping your eyes on the sidewalk as you pass the hostile glares of guys hanging out on the steps of broken-down houses.

Jesus was not ignorant of the risks that he asks us to run in His Father's service. As he sent out his disciples to proclaim the kingdom of God and heal the sick, he told them: *"I am sending you out like sheep among wolves... You will be hated by everyone because of me, but the one who stands firm to the end will be saved"* [Matthew 10:16,22]. We are fragile goblets set before sometimes ungrateful guests. But the Master promises us that he will preserve us far beyond a mere four centuries, to eternal life.

Reflections:

What would God have you repudiate and turn your back on so that you can be a worthy vessel to serve his grace to others? Take some time to confess and accept his cleansing.

Now take a moment to think of how God has blessed you through his works of Provision and Renewal. Who are some of the people he has used to serve you in these areas?

Partnering with God involves risk.

Think about how you can partner with God in his work of **Provision:**

- How do you, in your daily work or activity, contribute already to providing for others? (This may be in intangible ways— emotionally, intellectually, spiritually—as well as in tangible, physical ways.)
- In other words, what **needs** are you meeting for others? What risks do you face as you do this?
- What other needs do you see around you that you sense God calling you to help meet? What risks might be keeping you from doing this?

Think about how you can partner with God in his work of **Renewal:**

- How do you, in your daily work or activity, contribute already to the renewal of God's world? This could be through creating order from disorder, fixing broken objects or degraded environments, care resulting in healing and restoration, solving problems, facilitating discovery of knowledge and truth, humanely improving systems, negotiating reconciliation, sharing your faith, and many others...
- What **brokenness** do you observe in the **people** around you? Think first of the people closest to you, such as your family, and then move out to others. What is the role God is calling you to, personally, in dealing with this brokenness?
- What **brokenness** do you see in the **place** where you live? This may be environmental, systemic, interpersonal, or a number of other kinds. How is God calling you specifically to engage with this brokenness?
- What risks might be keeping you from being God's agent of Renewal among the people around you and in the place where he has put you?

4 Risk and Recklessness

> *"The wise fear the Lord and shun evil,*
> *but a fool is hotheaded and yet feels secure."* [Proverbs 14:16]

Riding the Tiger

> There was a young lady of Niger
> Who smiled as she rode on a tiger;
> They returned from the ride
> With the lady inside,
> And the smile on the face of the tiger.

I want to make it clear right from the beginning that not every kind of risk is good and laudable.

The risks we need to run are the ones we step into **because we are called by God to do so.** As we saw in the last chapters, these may be faith choices he calls us to make, or situations that he places us in by his sovereign will—stepping into risk through Practical or Providential Catalysts.

But risks that we run because we are hotheaded and feel invincible (as in the proverb above) are just recklessness. This is one of the characteristics listed in 2 Timothy 3:2-4 of the godless in the last days: *People will be lovers of themselves... boastful, proud... without self-control... treacherous, **rash**, conceited, lovers of pleasure rather than lovers of God...*

Proverbs has quite a lot to say about the dangers of recklessness and the wisdom of prudence:

- *"All who are prudent act with knowledge, but fools expose their folly."* [13:16]
- *"The wise store up choice food and olive oil, but fools gulp theirs down."* [21:20]
- *"The wicked put up a bold front, but the upright give thought to their ways."* [21:29]

To act with no forethought, to waste resources, to indulge in false bravado... these are not the ways of the wise. In this broken world, we are meant to exercise prudence. If you live in a place where scorpions are common, it is a good idea to shake out your boots before putting them on. If you want to raft on the river, it is a good idea to put on a life jacket first. If you live in a bad neighborhood, it is a good idea to lock your doors (and maybe in a nice one too). In other words: don't ride tigers.

There is always a segment of society that finds risk a rush, an adrenaline flood that can be addictive. Extreme sports like motocross, rock climbing, or skateboarding can fuel this fire—perhaps without the prudent precautions of helmets, ropes or pads. Sometimes the risk-addict experiments with the darker side of daring: illicit sex, alcohol and drug abuse. Or maybe it's just driving far above the speed limit. Many of these thrill-seekers are young, in their teens and early twenties, a time in life when risk-taking peaks.

But not all of them.

The Riskiest Behavior

Think of the middle-aged man who throws everything away—his wife, his kids, his property—for an affair with a younger woman. Think of the woman who racks up tens of thousands in credit-card debt in a compulsion to have the latest clothes, the designer kitchen, the new stuff everyone else has. Think of the guy who figures out a sneaky way to siphon off a couple pennies of every online transaction at his company, in order to line his pockets. Think of the lady who lies constantly about her experiences and abilities to impress friends and strangers.

It is not only the young who try to ride tigers. The most tempting and dangerous tiger we ride is called SIN. Sin is the riskiest behavior of all.

Whenever we engage in sinful behavior, we are operating in opposition to the instruction manual that came with us when we were made. To return to our earlier metaphor, it is like playing soccer with a teapot. Eventually, it will break us.

Sin is an attempt to meet legitimate needs that God has made us with—whether for intimacy, or possessions, or respect, or novelty and excitement—but it seeks to meet them **my way**. It shows that I am greater than the way God has made the world to work—that I am in control of my own world.

Look at Eve in the Garden. There was a clearly stated risk inherent eating the fruit of the Tree: *"You are free to eat from any tree in the garden; but you must not eat from the tree of the knowledge of good and evil, for when you eat from it **you will certainly die"*** [Genesis 2:16-17]. The resources to meet the need for food God had bountifully given; there was no need to eat from **this** tree. But the serpent both negated the danger ("*You will **not** certainly die*") and pointed out that eating the fruit would also meet another human need: that of wisdom. After all, God-planted desire for knowledge is what motivates us to learn and to discover.

But Eve and Adam choose to meet the need to eat and the need to know in a way not sanctioned by God, in spite of the risk: *When the woman saw that the fruit of the tree was **good for food** and pleasing to the eye, and also **desirable for gaining wisdom,** she took some and ate it. She also gave some to her husband, who was with her, and he ate it.* They relied on their own judgment and assessment of the risk, and determined that this was the best way to meet their need.

Proverbs tells us: *Those **who trust in themselves are fools,** but those who walk in wisdom are kept safe.* [28:26]

Self-reliance is at the root of this kind of risk. And it is not a safe bet.

The Sin of Self-Reliance

Self-reliance was also the temptation that Satan held up to Jesus much later in a dare to risky behavior:

*Then the devil took him to the holy city and had him stand on the highest point of the temple. **"If you are the Son of God,"** he said, **"throw yourself down.** For it is written: 'He will command his angels concerning you, and they will lift you up in their hands, so that you will not strike your foot against a stone.'" Jesus answered him, "It is also written: 'Do not put the Lord your God to the test.'"* [Matthew 4:5-7]

What is Satan trying get Jesus to do here? He is tempting Jesus to go out on his own hook and dictate to the Father what he must do to validate his mission. He wants Jesus to "claim God's promise" and presume on his own certainty that God needed him to accomplish his purposes, in order to make God invalidate natural law and save his life in a spectacular way.

But Jesus knew this was not the way. As Son of God, he served his Father, rather than the reverse. In John 5:19 he says, *"Very truly I tell you, the Son can **do nothing by himself;** he can do only what he sees his Father doing, because whatever the Father does the Son also does."* (If the Son of God himself says this, how much more should we?) And so, he matches Satan's twist of Scripture with a verse of his own from Deuteronomy 6: "*Do not put the Lord your God to the test.*" God is not a genie in our pocket, on hand to do all our bidding. He is the Lord of the universe, and we are meant to do his.

Risk and Rescue

But sometimes our Father **does** call us into risk, even into things that might be considered reckless if they were not for his sake. This is not because we are invincible, but because He is. If we look at that Psalm misquoted by Satan, we will see that it is dependence on the Father that is our source of safety, not self-reliance:

> Whoever dwells in the shelter of the Most High
>> will rest in the shadow of the Almighty.
>
> I will say of the Lord, **"He is my refuge and my fortress,**
>> **my God, in whom I trust."** ...
>
> **If you say, "The Lord is my refuge,"**
>> **and you make the Most High your dwelling,**
>
> no harm will overtake you,
>> no disaster will come near your tent.
>
> For he will command his angels concerning you
>> to guard you in all your ways;
>
> they will lift you up in their hands,
>> so that you will not strike your foot against a stone. [Ps. 91:1-2,9-12]

When our Father calls us to risk for him, then he will also be our refuge and our rescue. The complicated factor is that while God calls all of us to risk on his behalf, he does not call all of us to the exact same risks. Some he calls to risk in a foreign country; others he calls to risk in our hometown neighborhoods. Some calls to risk involve daring, courageous choices to go and to act. Others involve embracing an imperative situation that you would never choose on your own, in the midst of which God calls you to rest in him as refuge. Whatever the risk he calls us to for his sake, he calls us to face with him in trust, rather than in self-reliance.

Jesus knew the truth of this even as he obeyed the Father through death to resurrection:

> For whoever wants to save their life will lose it,
> but whoever loses their life **for me** will find it.

Reflections:

Risk + self-reliance = recklessness.

A good **example of this kind of recklessness** is found in Jesus' parable of the Two Sons, in the description of the **Younger Son** [Luke 15:11-14]:

- *"There was a man who had two sons. The younger one said to his father, 'Father, give me my share of the estate.' So he divided his property between them. Not long after that, the younger son got together all he had, set off for a distant country and there squandered his wealth in wild living. After he had spent everything, there was a severe famine in that whole country, and he began to be in need".*

- In Jesus' time, for a son to ask for his inheritance in this way was tantamount to saying to his father, "You are dead to me." The son co-opts the father's resources as his own, and relies on himself to meet his own needs and shape his own reality as he sets off on his wild adventure. But the reckless risk does not turn out well, as he loses everything his father has given him.

When you read this story, **how do you relate to the Younger Son?**

- What are some ways in which you appropriate resources from God as your own, and spend them on your own gratification?
- What are some needs that you feel like you deserve to have met, in whatever way works?
- In what areas of your life are you inclined to excess, and "wild living" (even secretly)? How do you justify these to yourself?

Think more deeply about this statement: **Sin is relying on myself to meet my needs apart from God.** We have many needs, ranging from food and shelter, through intimacy and rest, to identity and purpose. God has provided legitimate ways for these needs to be met: for example, we are meant to gain our bread through working, and not through stealing.

Now think through how this works in your own life:

- What sin pops up most often when you are confessing? What need is that sin trying to meet?
- What danger do you face if you continue to meet your need in this way? What will it do to you, your relationships, your resources?
- How could you choose instead to trust in God in the face of your need? What are legitimate ways he has provided to meet it?

5 The Risk of Playing It Safe

Then the man who had received one bag of gold came. 'Master,' he said, 'I knew that you are a hard man, harvesting where you have not sown and gathering where you have not scattered seed. So I was afraid and went out and hid your gold in the ground. See, here is what belongs to you.' [Matthew 25:24-25] **Read Matt. 25:14-30.**

Called to Gamble

God calls us to gamble.

No, this doesn't mean you should pack up your bags and head to Vegas. Rather, we are meant to assess the resources he has put in our hands and take the chance of investing them in ventures that will pay off in glory and fame for our Master.

That's what the first two servants did in this famous parable of Jesus, known as the Parable of the Talents. A "talent" was a weight of gold equal to about twenty years of pay for a day laborer—a significant amount of money to entrust to slaves who had no property but what was given them by the Master. To one of these slaves, the Master gives five talents; to another, two; and to another, one—*each according to his ability*, the text tells us. In a parallel passage in Luke 19, he tells them, *"Put this money to work until I get back,"* so there is no doubt what he wants them to do with it. And when he does get back, the entrepreneurial endeavors of the first two servants have doubled his resources.

To do this, they would have had to buy commodities and trade them in the market, things like livestock, grain, and spices. This was not without significant risk. The quality of the product could vary, transportation was unreliable, and caravan-robbing bandits always threatened profit. But it was the ability to manage such complicated systems of commerce that determined the success not only of wealthy businessmen, but the might of ancient kingdoms and empires.

Burying the Talent

The third guy, holding twenty years' worth of pay in his hands, thinks: *No way. What if I buy barley and it goes moldy? What if I purchase camels and they get sick? What if I invest in frankincense and it gets stolen? The Master will be mad, if I lose all this money.*

Besides—the Master is capricious and not really fair. Look at the resources he gave those two other guys, and how little he gave me. [The twenty years' pay starts to look like a pittance, now.] And we don't even know when he's coming back! What if all the capital is out on commodities when he arrives? I won't have any of it to show him. He will only be angry.

And then there are those rumors about him. I have heard it said that the Master is actually a shyster, stealing the produce of other people's fields. He is a hard man, out to profit from everyone! Perhaps he gave me this money just to have an excuse to lower the boom on me, to take advantage of me too. Maybe he's just waiting for me to embezzle it, so he can slap me into prison.

Well, not me, no sir. I'm not to be taken in by his so-called expressions of trust. The only way to deal with a sly customer like that is to call his bluff.

I'll play it safe. I'll bury his money in the ground.

He can't say anything to that, can he? I won't take the chance of losing it. I won't take the bait of stealing it. When he comes back, I'll just hand him the whole bag—safe and sound. I can protect the money, all right. And by protecting the money, I protect myself. Just watch me.

Except the servant's ploy to play it safe doesn't end up that way. The Master, hearing the servant speak this slander to his face, this insult to his trust, takes the talent he has and gives it to one of the gamblers. And he throws that *worthless servant* out of his house, out in the dark, with nothing.

Playing it safe can turn out to be very risky.

I Knew You Were a Hard Man...

We saw in the last chapter how self-reliance can lead to recklessness, to risk not rooted in trusting God, but in meeting our own needs in our own ways. But the opposite can be true. A lack of trust in God—a perception of him as vindictive, capricious, uncaring, or just far away—can lead us to eschew the risks he calls us to, and embrace another form of relying on ourselves: self-protection.

Look at how the servant describes the Master: *a hard man.* Some of us feel this way about God. Maybe it is because you are disappointed with the circumstances he has brought into your life at various times. You question: how could He let my mother die of cancer? How could he let **me** get cancer? You think: if this is what he does to his unsuspecting children, what else might he do if I **really** gave him the go-ahead to direct my life? You feel like God is unfair and arbitrary, taking away from you the very things you most treasured, sending you places you never wanted to go, inflicting your life with trouble.

Or perhaps you felt like God abandoned you in distress, like he has been uncaring and far away. You prayed and prayed and nothing happened. You failed the crucial exam. Your husband lost the job, or didn't get the job. Your wife never changed. Where was God for you when you needed him most? Why was he silent?

Or maybe you perceive God as hard in his judgment of you. I have lived here myself. Back in the 90's, my husband and I were given the opportunity to move into an amazing chalet house in the Jura Mountains in France, for a very reasonable rent. But a couple months after we moved in, our landlord, who had been working overseas, lost his job, came back, and moved into the granny flat in the basement. He was angry over his situation, and it wasn't long before his anger found a focus in me.

Every day he found an excuse to come upstairs to the main part of the house and check out my housekeeping. If the cats had vomited on the welcome mat, if there were rings around the bathroom sink, if the dishes were left unwashed—he took note. Then he went back downstairs and wrote angry emails to my husband about me.

As you can imagine, this situation caused me much anxiety for the one year we lived there. But it helped me realize something. I saw God the same way as I saw my landlord: as someone who lived in my basement and constantly popped up to see how I was blowing it. That year, while studying Galatians, I realized how much of my life was spent in self-protective excuses and self-justifying behavior toward God and others, and how little I understood God's grace. (I further realized that I had misidentified the accuser who was living in my mind's basement—and I started to send him off to face the **real** landlord of my life.) It is no accident that during that same year, as I began to become free of my perceptions of God as *a hard man,* I rediscovered Ephesians 2:10, and the adventurous purpose God has in mind for me.

When we are disappointed with God, when we feel like he has *harvested where he has not sown* in our lives, we will retreat to our own resources, to a form of self-reliance called **self-protection.**

Relying on Self-Protection

The weird thing is that we can make a virtue out of this, just as the servant in the parable does. He proudly brings back the dirt-covered sack, presenting it as though he had done exactly what he was meant to do. We can say, "Look at all the bad stuff I **haven't** done!" But accusing the Master of being a *hard man* becomes a self-fulfilling prophecy, and the servant finds that hardness is what he ends up receiving.

On the other hand, when we look at the response of the Master to the other servants, joy and grace abound as he invites them to *share their master's happiness*. Far from wanting to take what was theirs, he encourages them to share what is his. The rewards of building his kingdom become their rewards as they sit at his banquet table, live in his house, share in the satisfaction of spreading his name and renown. Rather than a *hard man*, these servants find their Master a bountiful giver, even as he invites them into further responsibility.

The Master says to the third servant: *You should have put my money on deposit with the bankers, so that when I returned I would have received it back with interest.* Merely to dare a little with the given resources would have been acceptable, to have just a small rate of return on the investment would have pleased him. Grace was available even to this man of little capacity, if only he trusted it.

But his fear made him rely only on himself, not only to protect the resources he had been given, but also to protect himself from the Master he saw as hard.

When we are afraid, as fragile vessels, of how God will put us to use, of how he would handle us—when we do not trust him—we start to protect ourselves. We would rather stay on our safe shelves where we think nothing can chip or blemish us. But we might find that the shelf is not as safe as we think it is.

Reflections:

Investing resources involves risk.

Think back through the parable of the Talents:

- How do you think you would have responded if you were the guy in the story? More like the first servants, or more like the last one?
- Why was the Master not happy just to have his money kept safe? What was wrong with burying the talent? How did this contradict the mission the servants had been given?
- How might the Master have responded if the servant had invested some of the money and lost it? Would he have been upset, or happy that the servant had made the attempt?
- Which was worse—the servant's lack of action, or his bad attitude toward the Master as a *hard man*?

Lack of trust results in self-protection.

In Jesus' story of the Two Sons, we can see this same kind of attitude—seeing the father as stingy and begrudging—in the Older Son:

- *"The older brother became angry and refused to go in. So his father went out and pleaded with him. But he answered his father, 'Look! All these years I've been **slaving for you** and never disobeyed your orders. Yet **you never gave me even a young goat** so I could celebrate with my friends.'"* [Luke 15:28-29]
- How does this compare with the third servant in the other parable? In self-perception? In perception of the father? In action?

How do you relate to the Older Son?

- How do you feel God is withholding from you, or being unfair to you?
- Do you feel like you deserve more than he is giving you? That others are deserving less, and receiving more?
- Does your service for God feel like drudgery—slavery even? Do you feel a bit jealous of Younger Brother types who get to go wild?

five habits of
self-protective people

(or, buried bags)

6 Creating Security Systems

Unless the Lord builds the house, the builders labor in vain.
Unless the Lord watches over the city,
  the guards stand watch in vain. [Psalm 127:1]

Two things I learned from watching the *Jurassic Park* movies:

One: Dinosaurs are pretty scary.
Two: No security system is completely fail-safe.

The era when people left their doors unlocked is over. Now most of us not only lock, but also set an alarm when leaving, and perhaps when going to bed. This is a prudent thing to do, because you never know when dinosaurs—or other predators—might attempt to enter your house. (See Item One, above.)

But it is also worth keeping in mind Item Two.

The Limits of Prudent Systems

The first habit of self-protective people is creating security systems. If we are afraid that we will lose something we have—whether it is our possessions, our money, our family, our emotional well-being, our self-image, our home's market value—we want to build a fence around it to keep the dinosaurs out. These fences might be literal security systems, or they might be emotional or social walls designed to repel intruders from taking what is ours.

In a very real sense, many of our houses have become more like medieval fortresses than ever before (if somewhat less drafty). We may not have a drawbridge, but we do have intercoms and entry cameras. We may not have guards patrolling crenellated walls, but we do have motion-sensor floodlights and alarms on the windows. We may not have soldiers with swords at the ready, but we have a direct line to the police station. We may not have a keep to which we may retreat in need, but we might have a panic room.

Of course, to take reasonable precautions is wise in our broken world. We have lived in what is considered a "bad neighborhood" of Brussels for the past several years.[1] But during the only act of home aggression we have experienced in the area, rocks thrown through two bathroom windows failed to trigger the motion sensor of our security system, even though it was armed. In other words, all our precautions, while prudent, may not be enough, and that is not where our confidence should rest.

Following the bombings in Brussels, it was decided that security should be stepped up in the departures hall of the airport. We already had armed military standing guard there following the Paris attacks, but clearly that was not enough. Now people have to pass through security not only before going to their gate, but also before entering the airport building itself. But as an official from IATA pointed out on TV, this precaution only moves the crowd of vulnerable people to the outside of the airport, where they are once more susceptible to attack. In order to have **complete** security, the whole airport would need to be closed.

As our opening verse reminds us: *Unless **the Lord** watches over the city, the guards stand watch in vain.* Zephaniah 2:14-15 paints a haunting picture of Nineveh, the capital of Assyria, as it would be in just a few short decades after his prophecy:

Flocks and herds will lie down there, creatures of every kind.
The desert owl and the screech owl will roost on her columns.
  Their hooting will echo through the windows,
  rubble will fill the doorways,
  the beams of cedar will be exposed.
*This is the city of revelry **that lived in safety.***
*She said to herself, **"I am the one! And there is none besides me."***
  What a ruin she has become, a lair for wild beasts!

This projection of the superpower city of their world would have been almost unimaginable to Zephaniah's audience. But Nineveh's walls were so high! And its buildings so impressive! And its armies so powerful! Nevertheless, *the city of revelry* that had felt so safe, relying on her strong fortifications, was in a few years defeated by Babylon and reduced to this state.

Keeping Others In and Out

Sometimes we rely for our children's safety on the security systems that we have created for them. We rely on the gates we erect to keep the toddler away from the fire and from falling down the stairs. We put our confidence in the child-locks on cupboard doors and the child-proof caps on bottles to keep our children from ingesting poisons. We trust that the firewall we have erected on the Internet will never let pornography through, and that the filter on the TV will protect them from seeing destructive programming.

And while these precautions are wise, sometimes we trust them so much that we don't even try to teach our toddlers to obey us when we say, "Don't touch that"—because there is nothing dangerous in reach. We don't have to help our children learn to choose to say "No" to temptation, because we think temptation has been eliminated. But this becomes a big problem when the security system breaks down, or when they wander off someplace where the walls do not exist.

We also rely for our emotional safety on "boundaries" that we have erected with people to protect ourselves. Now, hear me out—there are definitely emotional boundaries in relationships that are vital and healthy. We all need to be able to differentiate ourselves from others, to see ourselves as individuals made uniquely and loved by God, and not dependent for our self-assurance on the opinions or feedback or demands of people around us. We also need to be able to set aside private time apart from others for rest and prayer and meditation. Such strong boundaries are especially necessary in dealing with controlling or abusive people.[2] These are not what I am addressing.

Rather, sometimes the walls we erect against others are simply so that we don't have to deal with their junk—or ours—which we then mislabel as "boundaries." I was once in a Bible study with three other women in which we were attempting to deal with some of our core issues. One of the women began to talk about conflict with her husband, and to explore how she might be contributing to it—a healthy thing for any of us to do. But the other two women began to say to her, "Well, you should just put up some boundaries," and proceeded to outline strategies that focused not on repentance and character change, but on her husband's foibles and flaws. This made me uncomfortable. Isn't part of the purpose of marriage to allow God to let our rough edges rub together so they can be smoothed away? Shouldn't my first response be, "How does God want to shape me in this?" rather than, "Put up boundaries"?

"Boundaries" may also be an excuse we use to avoid our responsibilities toward family members, particularly our parents. It is not always easy to be around aging parents, especially if they are people who are critical and unappreciative, or self-absorbed, or stubborn, or suffering from some of the nastier effects of dementia on their personalities. At the same time, the fifth of the Ten Commandments tells us to *"Honor your father and your mother"*

[Exodus 20:12]. This does not mean you need to let them control you, belittle you, or mistreat you. In fact, you are honoring them to call them out, without anger, on sinful behavior that damages them as well as you.

But it does mean treating them with respect as the people God used to bring us into his world, and as people made in God's image. We are also responsible, as far as we can, to make sure their needs are met and they are not destitute or suffering: *If a widow has children or grandchildren, these should learn first of all to put their religion into practice by caring for their own family and so repaying their parents and grandparents, for this is pleasing to God* [1 Timothy 5:4].

Fending Off the Fearsome

Another form of this habit can be seen in how we protect ourselves from outsiders we perceive as dangerous to our own self-interest. We work hard to keep groups of people out of our neighborhoods that are perceived as bringing down property values, as well as businesses—even necessary ones, like water treatment plants—that might be considered undesirable or unsightly. We fret and worry over "illegal aliens" who will take jobs from citizens, and support tougher laws that will make it easier to deport them and harder for them to get papers, that will strengthen our borders and protect our social services. We turn away thousands of refugees who have suffered horrors under a terrorist regime on the chance that one of them might be a bomber in disguise.

We forget, maybe, how God is described to his people in Deuteronomy 10:18-19: *He defends the cause of the fatherless and the widow, and **loves the foreigner residing among you, giving them food and clothing. And you are to love those who are foreigners, for you yourselves were foreigners in Egypt.***

When we see God as one unconcerned for our safety, a *hard man* who wants us to learn the hard lessons of fending for ourselves in the world, we are likely to rely on our personal security systems as our protection. We miss out on *the Master's happiness* we could share, if only we were to rest in the safety that ultimately is found only in him.

Living in a bad neighborhood, I do lock my doors against the dinosaurs at night. But I am convinced that the protection that we experienced during five years in that first house came not from the alarm system, but from the God who watched over us, who blessed us as he gradually broke down the walls in our own hearts toward the foreigners who inhabited the streets around us. And so, even on nights when sirens are blaring outside—even when a sniper's helicopter was hovering overhead in search of an escaped terrorist bomber—we can say with the Psalmist:

> *In peace I will lie down and sleep,*
> *for you alone, Lord, make me dwell in safety. [Psalm 4:8]*

Reflections:

"Who can hope to be safe? who sufficiently cautious?
Guard himself as he may, every moment's an ambush."
(Horace)

Safety does not depend on walls.

While it is prudent and wise to take reasonable protective precautions, we are also told in Scripture that *everything that does not come from faith is sin* [Ephesians 14:23]. Consider these proverbs:

- *Those who trust in themselves are fools, but those who walk in wisdom are kept safe.* [Proverbs 28:26]
- *Fear of man will prove to be a snare, but whoever trusts in the Lord is kept safe.* [Proverbs 29:25]
- What do these proverbs suggest about the attitude we are to have toward the protective measures we put in place?

Dwight Eisenhower said, "If you want total security, go to prison. There you're fed, clothed, given medical care and so on. The only thing lacking... is freedom."

- **How much are you preoccupied with your physical security**? What measures do you trust for it? (E.g.: alarm system, owning a firearm, carrying pepper spray, avoiding "dangerous" areas...)
- How would you respond if the Master asked you to live in a dangerous place or to give up your means of protection? Would you see him as a "hard man," unconcerned for your safety? Or would you be able to trust him? (Not that he is, necessarily—I'm just asking you to imagine.)

Pope Francis said, "A person who thinks only about building walls, wherever they may be, and not building bridges, is not Christian."

- **Who are the people in your life that you have walled out**? (Begin with those who are close, like family and friends, and work through to people like foreigners and "sinners.")
- **How might God be calling you to change from a "wall-building" attitude to "bridge-building" mode with these persons?** What would that change in how you relate to them?

For some of these people, there may be forgiveness and boundary issues that need to be addressed to lay foundations for bridges. Who could you approach to help you work through this?

7 Stockpiling Resources

The wealth of the rich is their fortified city;
they imagine it a wall too high to scale. [Proverbs 18:11]

The young wife creatively stacks the 16 cases of barbeque sauce (12 bottles to a case), and in front of it piles 60 boxes of instant coffee, 25 pints of strawberry yogurt, 50 frozen dinners, and 40 ears of corn in an artistic pyramid. The young husband photographs today's haul, his wife's win in the game of shopping, to put in her album. Alight with enthusiasm, she brags that this whole caboodle has cost her under a dollar, in a segment of the U.S. TV show *Extreme Couponing.*[3]

Sounds like a great deal. But tell me—how do two people ever use up 192 bottles of barbeque sauce?

The Bomb Shelter in the Basement

People have always stockpiled resources. In old agrarian economies, it was necessary to store up the bounty of summer to get through the lean winter. People developed methods of preserving fruit and vegetables, salting and smoking meat, turning milk into cheeses, drying fish. The ant, in Proverbs, is held up as an example of prudence for the way *it stores its provisions in summer and gathers its food at harvest* [6:8].

In the wake of worldwide recession, interest in stockpiling has grown, whether it be in material goods or in the means to buy them. Some of this is helpful; certainly it makes sense to buy things you know you will use ahead of time, when they are less expensive, or to prep meals for the freezer so you are not tempted to eat out so much. But some of it can be simply a "bomb shelter" mentality: a sense of security that no matter what comes, I still have 191 bottles of barbeque sauce in my basement.

Another U.S. TV show, *Hoarders: Buried Alive,* shows people whose extreme anxiety has led them to keep all kinds of things in excess.[4] Sometimes these are "great deals" they have found at flea markets or garage sales or online, things that will purportedly save them money and they will use "someday." Sometimes it is just garbage. A psychologist on the show tries to help these people, and invariably finds that their tendency to hoarding began with a significant loss in their life, such as a death or divorce. Often, too, they were deprived of things in their past, and like Scarlett O'Hara, have vowed, "I'll never be hungry again."

The examples I have given so far are extreme ones. But look through these stockpiling behaviors to see if you recognize any in yourself, and evaluate to what degree they are related to a sense of comfort and security for you:

- Indulging in "retail therapy" when life is stressful, looking for that one perfect thing would fill the void and soothe me.
- Racing so I am the first to buy whatever new technology comes out.
- Compulsively purchasing the next new piece of equipment (musical instrument, sports shoes, fishing tackle, sewing machine, etc.) that I must have to enhance my hobbies.
- Spending lots of time and money on collections, looking for that rare whatever-it-is I am still missing.
- Decorating to the nth degree till my home is magazine-worthy (except that it is never quite done).
- Getting excited about new shelving and storage systems that will help me organize all the stuff I have been stockpiling.

Once more, there is nothing wrong with having things and enjoying them as God's gracious gifts to us, with gratitude for all of his bounty. But when getting them, having them and keeping them become our source of comfort and security, a major focus of our efforts, we are lavishing our love on stuff that can't love us back. Sometimes we even alienate the people that do love us because we feel they are not properly respecting these possessions.

Wobbly Walls of Wealth

For some, self-protection is less about stuff and more about the power to buy or control it: in other words, money. The proverb at the beginning of the chapter says it all. Like an ancient fortified city, we stockpile more and more and imagine that it makes us invulnerable. However, we saw how well that attitude worked out for Nineveh, with its literal walls, in the last chapter...

Once again, the world's wisdom of self-protection tells us that this is a good thing to do. Financial advisors used to say that we should have three to six months' worth of expenses saved up in the bank for a rainy day. Now, in the wake of financial crisis, the new revised advice is to have a year's expenses or more saved up. Fear of what **could** happen motivates hoarding of as many resources as possible.

To be sure, the habit of saving is a good one. Scripture encourages such prudence, rather than wasting our resources. But when our **reliance** is on our own stockpile, when it makes us misers, gloating over our gains, grudging and grasping lest someone take away what is rightfully ours—that is when we know that prudence has morphed into self-protection.

Jesus tells a story that should give us pause, in Luke 12:13-21. Read through this narrative aloud, emphasizing the word "**I**":

> "The ground of a certain rich man yielded an abundant harvest. He thought to himself, 'What shall I do? I have no place to store my crops.' Then he said, 'This is what I'll do. I will tear down my barns and build bigger ones, and there I will store my surplus grain. And I'll say to myself, "You have plenty of grain laid up for many years. Take life easy; eat, drink and be merry."' But God said to him, 'You fool! This very night your life will be demanded from you. Then who will get what you have prepared for yourself?' **This is how it will be with whoever stores up things for themselves but is not rich toward God.**"

Was it wrong for him to have an abundant harvest? Of course not! God gave it to him. But instead of gratitude and generosity—being *rich toward God*—the harvest was **his**, a bastion against personal poverty for many years to come, and a guarantor of comfort and ease. But as Jesus says, rather ironically, in the introduction to this parable: *Life does not consist in an abundance of possessions.* In fact, this man with such an abundance of possessions would lose his life that very night. The Message interprets Jesus' punchline: *"That's what happens when you fill your barn with Self and not with God."*

> *Whoever wants to save their life will lose it…*

James, Jesus' brother, warns those who are rich in this world—a category that surely includes us—that this is not just some story:

> Now listen, **you rich people**, weep and wail because of the misery that is coming on you. Your wealth has rotted, and moths have eaten your clothes. Your gold and silver are corroded. Their corrosion will testify against you and eat your flesh like fire. **You have hoarded wealth in the last days** [5:1-3].

Hoarding Against the 'Hard Man'

After telling his parable, Jesus turns to his disciples, men who were less concerned about where to store their wealth than where their next meal was coming from. But he goes to the heart of both problems when he tells them, in Luke 12:22-26:

> "Therefore I tell you, **do not worry about your life**, what you will eat; or about your body, what you will wear. For life is more than food, and the body more than clothes. Consider the ravens: They do not sow or reap, **they have no storeroom or barn;** yet God feeds them. And how much more valuable you are than birds! Who of you by worrying can add a single hour to your life? Since you cannot do this very little thing, **why do you worry about the rest?**

Do you see your Master as a *hard man* who, rather than providing for you lavishly, is out to *harvest where he has not sown and gather where he has not scattered seed*? Out to take things away from you? If so, you are likely to rely on your own ability to stockpile the resources that will allay your *worry about your life* so you feel safe from want.

Jesus assures us that we have nothing that God did not provide, and that he can be relied on. And he invites us to share in a greater treasure: **"Do not store up for yourselves treasures on earth, where moths and vermin destroy, and where thieves break in and steal.** But store up for yourselves treasures in heaven, where moths and vermin do not destroy, and where thieves do not break in and steal. **For where your treasure is, there your heart will be also**" [Matt. 6:19-21].

Dietrich Bonhoeffer comments on this text: "Earthly goods are given to be used, not to be collected. …the disciple must receive his portion from God every day. If he stores it up as a permanent possession, he spoils not only the gift, but himself as well, for he sets his heart on accumulated wealth, and makes it a barrier between himself and God. **Where our treasure is, there is our trust, our security, our consolation and our God. Hoarding is idolatry.**"[5]

Jesus' parable calls to mind Ecclesiastes' lament: *For a person may labor with wisdom, knowledge and skill, and then they must leave all they own to another who has not toiled for it. This too is meaningless and a great misfortune* [2:21]. Even worse is when you spend your time piling up, caring for and protecting your possessions, and when you die, your grandchildren curse your name as they throw out 163 mummified bottles of barbeque sauce from your basement stash. Let's fill our barns with God instead.

Reflections:

Wealth does not guarantee security.

When you look over the bulleted list on page 50, do any resonate with you? How do you seek comfort by accumulating possessions?

Dietrich Bonhoeffer writes, "Earthly possessions dazzle our eyes and delude us into thinking that they can provide security and freedom from anxiety. **Yet all the time they are the very source of anxiety.**"[6] What are some ways in which you have found your possessions or your wealth causing you anxiety?

- Protecting them? (From damage, theft, devaluation...)
- Maintaining them? (Cleaning, repairing, upgrading...)
- Storing or displaying them? (Finding adequate space or systems to deal with increasing numbers of possessions...)
- Replacing or adding to them? (Keeping up with trends and advances, building additions, collections or "stashes" ...)
- Disposing of them? (Re-decorating, basement or attic filling up with discards, going to the dump...)

And how much money do you feel like you would need to have in order to feel really secure? Really? Are you sure?

Paul says: *Command those who are rich in this present* **world not to be arrogant nor to put their hope in wealth, which is so uncertain,** *but to put their hope in God,* **who richly provides us with everything for our enjoyment.** *Command them to do good,* **to be rich in good deeds, and to be generous and willing to share.** *In this way, they will lay up treasure for themselves as a firm foundation for the coming age, so that they may take hold of the life that is truly life.* [1 Tim. 6:17-19]

- What difference would it make to you to regard your possessions and your wealth as "bags of gold" entrusted to you by the Master, rather than your own personal possession?
- How does that change your attitude to their **loss**? How does it change your attitude toward **sharing** them? How does it change your **definition of investment**?
- How might God want you to use the resources he gives you to *share in the Master's happiness,* not just personal gratification?

8 Planning and Controlling

The Lord knows all human plans;
he knows that they are futile. [Psalm 94:11]

I wrote Bible lesson plans for our church for a long time, both for myself and other teachers. As I did, I would think strategically about things that could go wrong: What if they don't understand this concept? What if someone asked that question? What if we can't get those materials? What if the teacher doesn't want to do it this way? Every question led to a new detail, another paragraph, a contingency plan, an explanation, an alternate activity. These went on and on for pages. I didn't even realize this overly detailed, perfectionistic tendency in myself until my team members pointed it out to me.

Even worse was the fallout when my meticulously designed plan would go wrong. When I showed up to teach with a perfectly prepared PowerPoint and found that the video projector bulb was burnt out. When creative materials I needed had been left behind on my kitchen table. When the room where we were meeting was double-booked and we had to cram into some place with not enough chairs for everyone. I would throw a mini-tantrum, all the Biblical principles on *rest* and *grace* and *freedom* I had come to teach out the window.

(Guess which one of these self-protective habits is most mine?)

The Illusion of Invincible Ingenuity

As with the previous habits, I am not implying that planning in and of itself is useless. Proverbs 21:5 tells us: *The plans of the diligent lead to profit as surely as haste leads to poverty.* Slap-dash efforts in the work and purposes God has for me are not more holy; they are just more lazy and unwise. The problem creeps in when The Plan is the **source** of my security, when my ability to think ahead through every contingency and around every roadblock is my fount of confidence, when I forget that God has his own purposes for me and for my work.

Proverbs has much more to say about this:

- *In their hearts humans plan their course,*
  but the Lord establishes their steps. [16:9]
- *Many are the plans in a person's heart,*
  but it is the Lord's purpose that prevails. [19:21]

These proverbs sound the same at first, but notice the interesting subtle differences. In the first proverb, we see the difference between looking at a map (our plans), and the actual walking of the path (God's determination of each individual step). The plan and the actuality of carrying it out may not coincide, by God's design. He has his own purposes for us, personally. More than once God has used the frustrations of my own teaching plans to drive deeper in my heart the application of those selfsame truths, by making me walk them out in ways I had not foreseen.

By contrast, in the second proverb, we see the difference between our little plans and God's big ones. We may think we have our own interests, or God's, at heart as we construct our schemes; but God sees the big picture, his purposes at large in the world. I may think that I have determined the message people need to hear, and the best way to teach it, but God knows what is needed in the community, and his purposes prevail—even through the very obstacles I encounter, even as my plans crumble to pieces.

James warns us against trusting all to our own plans [4:13-16]:

Now listen, you who say, **"Today or tomorrow we will go to this or that city, spend a year there, carry on business and make money."** *Why, you do not even know what will happen tomorrow. What is your life? You are a mist that appears for a little while and then vanishes.* **Instead, you ought to say, "If it is the Lord's will, we will live and do this or that."** *As it is, you boast in your arrogant schemes. All such boasting is evil.*

Look at all the things we think we can control by our plans:

- **Time** (*today or tomorrow*)
- **Purpose** (*we will go*)
- **Place** (*this or that city*)
- **Goals** (*carry on business*)
- **Benefits** (*make money*)

Think of all the ways we strategize about these objectives. We visualize the end goals, work out all the contacts we will need, amass all our resources. We think we have the end in sight and under control. We may even do this in the name of "ministry," unaware that the kingdom we are building is actually our own.

In reality, James suggests, in a text echoing his brother's teaching in Luke 12, we cannot even control the first variable—*what will happen tomorrow*. As the verse at the beginning of this chapter tells us, our plans are ultimately *futile*. To boast about them, as though we were our own gods, in control of our own fate and secure in our well-planned strategies, is to repeat the evil of the Fall.

Playing the Puppet-Master

Even worse, we often think we can control other people, make them part of our plan. We not only develop perfectionistic plans for ourselves, but also models of how others should be and behave. Then we try to make them conform to our own plans by manipulating, micromanaging, nagging or bullying them. Whatever means we use to control others, it is for the relief of our own anxiety and insecurity that cannot let the other person be a loose cannon in our ordered world.

In a work or ministry environment, where all of the elements of James 4:13 are in play, others may be seen as blocks to any or all of our schemes, especially if we are the person in charge of making those plans happen. We can over-check details with employees or colleagues, micromanaging each step of the plan, never allowing deviation. We can throw fits when things are not done our way, make demands of extra time and effort to accommodate our schedule and standards.

Self-protection can also be seen in the way we control our children, especially if we have made them into an extension of our own ego boundaries, indistinct from ourselves. Parents hover over kids, ready to prevent or correct any behavior that might be dangerous, disappointing, or disapproved. It might be by sitting with them through every homework session so they won't make any mistakes. Or in dissuading them from taking an Arts degree in college because it won't make them money. The children find themselves constantly urged to "Be careful!" as their actions are controlled by the anxieties of their parents. We have never needed more the injunction of Paul: *Fathers, do not embitter your children, or they will become discouraged* [Colossians 3:21].

We can also construct in our minds the ideal vision of who and what our spouse should be, and then go about sculpting them into that image. Sometimes these efforts are transparently abusive or coercive. Other times, they are subtler. See if you have ever used any of these controlling techniques:

- Expecting mind reading, or often complaining of being misunderstood
- Nagging, and then justifying it as a "reminder"

- Exaggerating situations into black and white, to make yourself a victim
- Using the silent treatment or pouting to change behavior
- Constantly correcting things the other says or does (either in front of others or as soon as you get them on their own)
- Using pity or guilt to motivate desired actions
- Tit-for-tat trades: "Well, I'll do that as soon as you start..."
- Making an accusation that provokes a defensive response, then using the response as a justification for the accusation

The crazy thing is that in our fear, we end up creating exactly what we want to avoid. By controlling the people we love so we do not lose them, so they are shaped into our ideal, we may end up driving them away.

Dietrich Bonhoeffer, in his classic *Life Together,* speaks of this tendency also in our Christian communities, as in all relationships:

"Human love...seeks direct contact with the other person; **it loves him not as a free person but as one whom it binds to itself.** It wants to gain, to capture by every means; it uses force. It desires to be irresistible, **to rule... Human love constructs its own image of the other person, of what he is and what he should become. It takes the life of the other person into its own hands.** Spiritual love recognizes the true image of the other person which he has received from Jesus Christ, the image that Jesus Christ himself embodied and would stamp upon all men."[7]

Machinations of Distrust in the Master

When we see our Master as a *hard man* who either is far away, allowing his world to operate on its own, or as having capricious plans that we cannot trust, it becomes up to us to protect ourselves by controlling our own world. We must make our own plan, follow it slavishly, and conform all those around us to our own will. But in doing so, we miss out on *sharing our Master's happiness* as we seek for his good and perfect will to operate in our life and character, in our world, and in the people around us.

May we all repent of our self-protective plans and instead do as the Psalmist suggests: **Commit your way to the Lord;** *trust in him and he will do this: He will make your righteous reward shine like the dawn...* [37:5-6].

Reflections:

Control is only an illusion.

Guess who said the following quote?

> "I will say that I cannot imagine any condition which could cause the ship to founder. I cannot conceive of any vital disaster happening to this vessel. Modern shipbuilding has gone beyond that."

If you guessed E.J. Smith, the captain of the Titanic, you are right...

Review the two proverbs at the beginning of the chapter.
- Can you think of a time when it seemed like your plans were frustrated, but you personally learned or gained something that you would not have otherwise, as in the first proverb?
- Can you think of a time when your plans didn't work out, but the benefits to those around you or in the long run were greater than if they had, as in the second proverb?
- What does this tell us should be our attitude to the plans that we make as we trust the Master? How does it impact our strategy as we gamble the gold he is calling us to invest on his behalf?

Who are the people in your life that you are most likely to try to control?
- What makes you think you need to control them? What do you fear would happen if you did not?
- What methods do you most often employ to try to control them? (Have a look back at the list on pages 56-57.)
- How successful have these methods been in preventing the outcomes you fear?
- How have they impacted the emotional tone of your relationship?
- How would it change your relationship—and your anxiety—if you were to free them, even to fail? What would it take to trust that the Master loves them even more than you do, and can redeem them to be the people he made them to be (as he has with you)?

So far, which of the three habits of self-protective people that we have looked at are most characteristic of you?

9 Distracting Ourselves with Pleasure

Woe to you who are complacent in Zion,
* and to you who feel secure on Mount Samaria...*
You put off the day of disaster and bring near a reign of terror.
You lie on beds adorned with ivory and lounge on your couches.
You dine on choice lambs and fattened calves.
You strum away on your harps like David and improvise on musical
* instruments.*
You drink wine by the bowlful and use the finest lotions,
* but you do not grieve over the ruin of Joseph.* [Amos 6:1,3-6]

Sometimes what we bury in the sand is not only the talent our Master gave us, but our own heads.

Often it feels easiest to ignore the dangers that are out there, to numb and anesthetize ourselves from the effects of fear and anxiety by self-soothing behaviors. Fortunately (or not) for those of us in the wealthy West, we have the means at our disposal to insulate ourselves in this way, to fool ourselves into thinking that if we feel good everything is good. The suffering of others is considered irrelevant, the brokenness of the world plastered over.

As Bruce Dawe, a celebrated Australian poet, puts it:

> How to go on not looking
> despite every inducement to the contrary...[8]

Alleviating our Anxieties

Unlike the previous self-protective behaviors, this one does not directly address the source of our fears, but rather soothes the feelings that stem from them. Ironically, the very self-soothing means we abuse are a gift from God. Let's look at just one: the hormone oxytocin, a powerful stress reducer that gives a feeling of calm when it is released in the body. It is associated with warm affectionate physical touch, whether by sexual contact or simple hugging, creating bonding and trust between people. Mothers and babies flood with this hormone through contact following childbirth and in breastfeeding. Stroking a pet releases it in both the animal and the owner. Even eating stimulates oxytocin through activating touch receptors in the mouth and small intestine.[9]

This hormone was designed by God to make us feel warm and safe, cared for and connected in our relationships with others. I believe it was also meant to help us trust and connect with the Heavenly Father, who has given us *every good and perfect gift* [James 1:17]. But it is easy for us to divorce this gift and others like it from the Father, using them instead as a damper for our own anxious feelings.

To be sure, anxious feelings are often as much or more of a problem than the dangers they seek to avoid. Anxiety disorders are prevalent in our society; the National Institute of Mental Health estimates that some 40 million Americans over the age of 18 suffer from them—and a rising number of people under that age. These include panic disorder, OCD, social anxiety, and others. For many of these people, worry and tension plague them even if they can recognize logically that no real danger threatens them. And they will do just about anything to make the feelings of fear subside. (I know this, because I struggle with anxiety myself. It is one of the reasons I began studying the topic of fear in Scripture, resulting in this book.)

Anesthetizing Stress

Even for people who do not suffer from an actual anxiety disorder, escape from feelings of worry and a sense of stress can become a major goal in life. In this, we subvert the natural mechanisms God has placed in our lives to reduce stress and draw us to himself—warm relationships, simple pleasures—and focus on them to the extent that others in our lives exist to make us happy, and pleasure is used as a tool of escape.

Addictions are the most obvious example. Neurologists think that the oral stimulation of smoking, with its oxytocin release, may be more addictive than the nicotine that gets blamed. Sexual addictions push the button of pleasure hormones in the brain over and over, creating a temporary sense of well-being and relaxation that is divorced from an authentic two-way relationship with another human being. But in between, the addict feels empty because the real bond is absent, and craves only the next high.

The brain is made so that oxytocin is not only released on actual physical contact, but also when looking at or thinking about the object of our affection. No wonder so many women escape into the fantasy of romance novels, imagining themselves the sole object of an idealized man's ardor and attentions. Since eating also imparts the effects of oxytocin, the idea of "eating for comfort" is a real phenomenon. In a society where candy bars are sold next to every cash register, we can quickly comfort ourselves into obesity (and its accompanying health issues) if we eat every time we feel anxious or stressed. And, remember, oxytocin is only one of the many means of pleasure and comfort God has given us that we might use as a mask for anxiety and insecurity.

Often, people abuse alcohol and drugs (including things like painkillers and over-the-counter weight loss products) to reduce their sensations of anxiety for a time. But this self-medication never resolves the underlying issues, and often masks the symptoms of a disorder—or even makes them worse, since alcohol and many other drugs actually induce anxiety. In spite of this, many people believe that drinking or using drugs is an effective way to curb their symptoms.

This is not to say that people with an anxiety disorder should forgo medication under a doctor's supervision. For many people, pharmaceuticals that God has allowed people to discover are his gift to help them re-enter life after crippling anxiety. But even when medicine helps alleviate the symptoms that stress us, we should never treat the medicine as God—that is, it should never be the number one thing we trust to keep us safe, secure, and sane. Rather, it should be a resource we thank Him for daily as it helps us step out in the purposes He has for us without fear.

Closing Our Eyes in Complacence

We do not have to be addicted to pleasures or diagnosed with an anxiety disorder, however, in order to embrace this habit of self-protection. For many of us, comfort becomes a way to keep ourselves blind to the brokenness and injustice around us, to say, "I'll think about it tomorrow." Bruce Dawe describes this in his poem, "The Not-So-Good Earth," in which a family watches a TV miniseries about suffering and starving people without a glimmer of empathy:[10]

> For a while there we had 25-inch Chinese peasant families
> famishing in comfort on the 25-inch screen...
> digging for roots in the not-so-good earth
> cooking up a mess of old clay
> and coming out with all those Confucian analects
> to everybody's considerable satisfaction...

That was the situation Amos described in the text at the beginning of this chapter. Oppression and injustice were rampant among the Israelites of Samaria, but those in power chose to focus on their own pleasure and comfort rather than address the situation. Amos makes it clear that burying their heads in the sand will not delay the outcome: *This is what the Lord says: "As a shepherd rescues from the lion's mouth only two leg bones or a piece of an ear, so will the Israelites living in Samaria be rescued, with only the head of a bed and a piece of fabric from a couch"* [Amos 3:12]. The ivory beds and couches on which they lounged, complacent in their own comfort, will be no more.

We saw earlier that God calls us to participate with him in his works of provision and restoration in the world. When we choose to ignore the purposes he calls us to and puts before us, and focus only on our own comfort, we are burying the talent he gives us in the ground along with our heads. We may be able to distract and convince ourselves that "It's not my problem," but in the end we end up out in the cold, as the problems we ignore come to fruition around us. The Master wants us to invest our resources in the world around us, to expand his kingdom. And ironically, it is only by doing this that we truly will *share in his happiness.*

In Matthew 25:31-46, Jesus tells another parable right after that of the Talents. In it, the righteous are commended for spending their resources on the poor and needy of the world, and told that in doing this—far from wasting them—they had used them for the King himself. When he turns in judgment to those on his left, they complain, *"Lord, **when did we see you** hungry or thirsty or a stranger or needing clothes or sick or in prison, and did not help you?"* [v. 44]. They had been "not looking, despite every inducement to the contrary," as they spent the resources they had been given on their own comfort and pleasure. In doing so they fail to notice the King in his distressing disguise—and wind up receiving his judgment.

1 Peter 5:7 reminds us of the most powerful stress reliever of all: *Cast all your anxiety on him because he cares for you.* Not only is he *the Father of compassion and the God of all comfort, who comforts us in all our troubles,* but he does this *so that we can comfort those in any trouble with the comfort we ourselves receive from God* [2 Corinthians 1:3-4]. Why should we rely on our own comforts when his is so abundantly available to us?

Reflections:

Hiding from fear does not make you safe.

How would you rate your normal stress/anxiety level on a scale of 1 to 10?

- **What kinds of things do you normally do to alleviate your stress or anxiety?** (Medication, reading, watching TV, playing games, eating, exercise, meditation/prayer, drinking alcohol, taking a bath, getting a massage, talking to a friend/counselor, etc.)
- Remember what 1 Timothy 6:18 says: **God... richly provides us with everything for our enjoyment.** Which of these things do you feel you can accept with gratitude as a gift from God—a way that he is *comforting you in all your troubles*? How do you enjoy him more by engaging in this activity or using this means of reducing stress?
- Which of these means of stress-reduction do you feel you overuse, or depend on too much? Or to which do you perhaps even experience a degree of addiction? How does this impact your overall sense of stress and anxiety (as compared with the short-term alleviation of it)?
- How would God call you to find comfort primarily in him rather than your stress-relieving techniques?

Complacency in comfort does not mean you are safe.

Our society can be quite complacent about trouble as long as we are not experiencing it. We can even justify others' suffering and our lack of compassion based on their wrong beliefs or poor behavior.

- What examples of this complacency do you see in society around you? In your church? Among your family and friends?
- **How prone are you to getting sucked in to this complacency?**
- When was the last time you noticed Jesus in his "distressing disguise"—as one of the hungry, the poor, the sick, or a stranger—in the city or town where you lived? How likely are you to avoid these people and the areas where you might see them?
- What could you do practically to look for Jesus on your streets? To invest some of the resources entrusted to you in *the least of these*? How could that help you to *share in his happiness*?

Think through the four habits we have discussed already. **Which one is the Holy Spirit pointing out to you as your most characteristic one?**

10 Justifying Ourselves

The sluggard says, "There's a lion outside! I'll be killed in the public square!" [Proverbs 22:13]

"The dog ate my homework."
"The traffic was terrible."
"I never got your message."
"My computer crashed."

Excuses, excuses. We are all so good at them. They help get us off the hook when we haven't done what we were expected to do. And they justify our inaction when we don't want to do something we should be doing. The proverb above pokes fun at our propensity to excuses. The sluggard doesn't feel like doing the work he is supposed to do, so he makes up a reason why it is too risky, impossible to carry out. The odds that there really is a lion in the public square are rather low—but there **might** be one. You just can't take any chances.

Where each of the other habits of self-protective people that we have looked at contain an element of prudence that has been twisted—good boundaries, wise saving, thoughtful planning, enjoyment of God's gifts—this habit is simply sin. Self-justification is **never** wisdom; it is always an attempt to lay claim to righteousness we do not have, to excuse what we have or have not done.

Excusing our Sins of Omission

We tend to think of sin as doing things we are not supposed to do: stealing stuff, or telling lies, or blowing up in anger, or thinking bad thoughts. But just as often—possibly more often—sin is **not** doing things we are supposed to do. The theological terms for these are sins of **commission,** and sins of **omission.** James, just after his warning to ambitious planners, further cautions us against the dangers of doing nothing: *If anyone, then, knows the good they ought to do and doesn't do it, it is sin for them* [4:17].[11]

Fear is no excuse.

Of course, this excuse is exactly what the servant tries out in the Parable of the Talents. Let's look at it again: *"Master, I knew that you are a hard man, harvesting where you have not sown and gathering where you have not scattered seed. **So I was afraid** and went out and hid your gold in the ground. See, here is what belongs to you"* [Matthew 25:24-25].

At first glance it seems that what the servant is afraid of is losing the money, and that's why he buries it. But the money is not his; there is no personal loss if his investments do not pay off. Rather, his fear is of the Master, whom he perceives as an ungracious and unjust man, and his excuse for not having invested the resources entrusted to him reveals this underlying attitude.

Immediately after his excuse for inaction, he justifies his choice as he hands over the dirty bag, brushing off the clods from its interment in the ground. You can tell he feels pretty good about himself for having kept the money safe, as he says, *"See, here is what belongs to you!"* He hasn't stolen the money, as other servants might do. He hasn't done anything wrong—because he hasn't done anything at all!

We also are pretty creative with excuses to protect ourselves from why we haven't done *the good we ought to do.* Some of these, as in the proverb above, have to do with fears of what **might** happen:

- If I give that homeless guy some money, he will probably just spend it on alcohol. (So I will just pretend I don't see him.)
- If I answer the phone when that depressed friend calls, she might keep me on too long and disrupt my plans. (So I will screen all her calls.)
- If I take that pregnant teenager into my house, it might give my own kids the idea that it's okay to have sex before you're married. (So I won't.)
- What if I make a monthly pledge to support that missionary, and then I lose my job? (I'd better save up that money in case.)
- What if I sign up to care for babies in the church nursery once a month, and then no one else does? (I can't afford that kind of commitment.)
- What if I let my kid make friends with the next-door neighbors and they learn a bad word? (I'll tell them we don't play with that kind of person.)

The truth is, that every fear we let keep us from doing something that the Holy Spirit is prompting us to do is actually an accusation against God that He is a *hard man.* We fear that He somehow likes us to suffer loss, so we don't give. We fear that He cannot provide or will be stingy with us, so we aren't generous. We fear He won't protect us, so we avoid possible danger. We fear He will make us do something we will hate, something that will make us miserable, so, like Jonah, we run the other direction. The fears we express openly as excuses only hide this more insidious fear.

Justifying our Crooked Consciences

But then, when our consciences remind us, "You should have done that…" we are in a bind. We have to justify ourselves—straighten out our crooked consciences—by whatever means possible.

One way we do this is by **lowering God's standards to our own**. We edit and re-interpret Scripture so that it is possible for us to master it. Forgiveness is a command—but not when someone has done something to you like my mother did to me. Sure, you should love your neighbor—but that doesn't mean I have to actually **talk** to those Muslim people who moved in next door, does it? We edit commands to care for the poor by how much they deserve it, whether or not they are Christians, whether or not they are legally resident, whether they are someone else's responsibility, and so on— until there is no one left in the category that we must care for.

We spiritualize the commandments of God concerning our actions towards our possessions and neighbors, until giving becomes keeping, going becomes staying, and loving becomes ignoring. We bury the talent, because that is much easier than actually investing it, and then fool ourselves that that is what the Master was looking for all along.[12]

Another way we justify ourselves is by **exaggerating our own righteousness.** The simplest way of doing this is by comparing ourselves with someone else, of course. I'm a lot less stingy than my best friend, and he's a Sunday School teacher. I might have a bad temper, but at least I don't take God's name in vain like my colleague. I may not be a perfect wife—but then you should see my husband.

We may also redefine our actions to make them look like we have actually done something good when all the time we have failed to do what God commands, as the servant does when he presents his buried gold. Jesus condemns this kind of self-justification in Matthew 15:4-7: *"For God said, 'Honor your father and mother'… But you say that if anyone declares that what might have been used to help their father or mother is 'devoted to God,' they are not to 'honor their father or mother' with it… You hypocrites!"*

Failure to Love

This leads us to consider one of the biggest of all the sins of omission: failing to love other people as God has loved us. The apostle John returns to this theme incessantly, knowing it to be of paramount importance:

> For this is the message you heard from the beginning: We should love one another...We know that we have passed from death to life, because we love each other. **Anyone who does not love remains in death...** This is how we know what love is: Jesus Christ laid down his life for us. And we ought to lay down our lives for our brothers and sisters. **If anyone has material possessions and sees a brother or sister in need but has no pity on them, how can the love of God be in that person?** Dear children, let us not love with words or speech but **with actions and in truth.** [1 Jn. 3:11,14,16-18]

This sin of omission—not loving others—is indicative of an even greater sin: not loving God. For one of the primary ways we show our love for God is in the way we love others, as Jesus describes for us in the Parable of the Sheep and the Goats [Matt. 25]. John also is direct about this: "Whoever claims to love God yet hates a brother or sister is a liar. **For whoever does not love their brother and sister, whom they have seen, cannot love God,** whom they have not seen" [1 John 4:20].

God is satisfied with us if we even take baby steps toward doing the things he has asked us to do, even if we are afraid to dare greatly to begin with. The third servant was given fewer resources to invest, because the Master knew his capacity was less. He was not expected to be as daring as the one who had five talents. If he had just put it in the bank, where it would earn a meager amount of interest, he would have been at some level obeying his Master's command to put the money to work. And surely the experience of sharing his master's happiness would make him a braver investor the next time. God loves a cheerful giver.

So let's ditch the pitiful excuses and the flimsy self-justifications, knowing that they are poor protection when we are measured against God's standards. As John reminds us: If we claim to be without sin, we deceive ourselves and the truth is not in us. If we confess our sins, he is faithful and just and will forgive us our sins and purify us from all unrighteousness [1 John 1:8-9]. Hadn't we better let Jesus justify us?

Reflections:

Self-justification is self-deception.

Why do you think I stated so strongly that "self-justification is sin"? Why is this habit not just a form of "twisted prudence" like the rest?

What is something that you know you should have done in the past week that you did not do (a sin of omission)? We are not talking here about social obligation, or even duty/responsibility, so much as our **failure to love others in the ways God was prompting us to do,** like:

"*I should have apologized to him.*"
"*I should have called her to see how she was doing.*"
"*I should have listened when they tried to confront me.*"
"*I know God wanted me to volunteer to help, but I didn't want to.*"
"*I should have actually prayed for him after I said I would.*"
"*I shouldn't have walked away when I noticed she was struggling.*"

* What do you know God wanted you to do that you didn't?
* What kind of excuses are you tempted to offer for not doing it?
* What is the fear on which they are based?
* Can you be honest about this before God and admit your failure? Can you believe that he forgives and accepts imperfect you?

Consider the two ways we try to justify ourselves before God:
* How do you find yourself **lowering God's standards** so that you can meet them? By limiting who you are meant to love? By spiritualizing Jesus' commands so they need no real action? How else might we redefine God's standards?
* How do you find yourself **exaggerating your own righteousness**? By comparing yourself with other people? By redefining your actions? How else might we exaggerate our righteousness?

This habit of self-protection actually pairs very well with any of the other four as we justify **why** we have to implement them:

"*I'm just drawing my boundaries tight so he won't hurt me.*"
"*I can't do a donation to the mission fund this year because I need to be wise about my retirement plan.*"
"*I'm not trying to control you; I'm just being responsible.*"
"*After all I do, I deserve to have some fun...*"

How do you see yourself making justifications for your favorite?

the only thing
we have to fear

(or, mighty mountains)

11 The Supreme Fear

The fear of the Lord is a fountain of life,
  turning a person from the snares of death. [Proverbs 14:17]

Learning to Fear

President Franklin D. Roosevelt once famously said to a nation mired in the depths of a Depression: "The only thing we have to fear is fear itself."

Nonsense. There are many real dangers out there. We are not making them up. There is a lot more to fear than just fear. Such as:

- **Dangers of personal violence:** terrorist bombs; school shootings; burglary and theft; assault; rape; domestic abuse
- **Physical dangers:** car accidents; plane crashes; house fires; hurricanes; environmental pollution
- **Dangers of destitution:** losing a job or not being able to find a job; low wages; investments crashing; struggling with debt
- **Moral dangers to our children:** internet porn; materialistic media messages; prevalent drug and alcohol use
- **Health dangers:** carcinogens in household products; adverse drug reactions; cancer; crippling arthritis; Alzheimer's
- **Emotional dangers from hurtful people:** difficult bosses and co-workers; nasty neighbors; critical parents or spouse

The educator Angelo Patri once said: "Education consists in being afraid of the right things at the right time..." We teach our children that stoves are hot, that bottles under the sink contain poison, that running in the road can get you killed. Being afraid of the right thing at the right time is wise.

When I first started researching the topic of fear in Scripture, I assumed that most of what I would find would be injunctions not to be afraid. I assumed I would find much instruction on how to conquer fear. I assumed that I would be assured, as the President said, that we have nothing to fear but fear itself.

I was wrong. Over two thirds of the Scriptural references to fear turned out to **recommend** it, and to commend those who have it. As I studied, I was being educated in being afraid of the right thing at the right time. Here are a few of these fear recommendations, from the Psalms:

- Let all the earth **fear** the Lord; let all the people of the world revere him. [33:8]
- Serve the Lord with **fear** and celebrate his rule with trembling. [2:11]
- The **fear** of the Lord is the beginning of wisdom; all who follow his precepts have good understanding. [111:10]

It turns out that most of the times the word "fear" is mentioned in Scripture, the subject is the fear of God. And this last verse helps us see that, as Mr. Patri tells us, this fear is where our education in wisdom begins. This is the fear that is to possess and control us all our days.

"The Fear" is even given as one of the names of God by Jacob in Genesis 31: "*If the God of my father, the God of Abraham and **the Fear of Isaac**, had not been with me...*" [v.42]. "*The fear of the Lord*" is the common description of true religion throughout the Old Testament; "*God-fearing*" is the term for righteous people in the New Testament.[1]

Trembling Before God

We tend to dumb down this idea of fearing God. Perhaps we think of it as a strictly Old Testament concept, left behind in this New Covenant era of love and grace. Or we reduce it to something like thinking of God as "awesome." However, in a culture where we say things like, "This cheesecake is awesome," we may have lost a sense of how akin awe is to terror.

In reality, both Testaments speak of the fear of God, with Jesus himself saying, "*I will show you whom you should fear: Fear him who, after your body has been killed, has authority to throw you into hell. Yes, I tell you, fear him*" [Luke 12:5]. The main Hebrew word for fear is *yarē*, which comes from a root meaning "to tremble." The chief Greek word for fear is *phobos,* from which we get our English word "phobia." This is not a flippant response to something mildly impressive, but a visceral reaction to something truly frightening.

And God is the scariest thing in our whole universe.

The first time I skied in the Alps, I experienced unnerving visceral fear. Standing at the top of what I had been assured was an easy red slope, I looked up at the icy Eiger and Jungfrau peaks towering over me. Then I looked down at the pristine ski piste sloping steeply away from me, and I felt very, very small. In fact, I was so frightened that I sat down on the snow and began to cry. These mountains were a lot bigger than me—and I had better respect them, for they could surely break me into many fractured bits.

Just as I would have been silly as a novice skier to feel that I was superior to the mountains, we as creatures make a big mistake when we do not recognize that there is a Creator who is far, far greater than we are. Isaiah 40:12 says: *Who has measured the waters in the hollow of his hand, or with the breadth of his hand marked off the heavens? Who has held the dust of the earth in a basket, or weighed the mountains on the scales and the hills in a balance?* If the mountains are to be regarded with awe and respect, how much more the One who made them?

If God were to take his hand off me, not only would I cease breathing, my very molecules would fly apart and cease to be. My whole history would be unwritten; I would be erased as if I had never been. My being is entirely in his hands. He is not just my Creator; he is the Sustainer and Author of my life, the Source of all I have and need. Jeremiah rebukes the foolishness of those who fail to say, *"Let us fear the Lord our God, who gives autumn and spring rains in season, who assures us of the regular weeks of harvest"* [Jeremiah 5:24].

Not only this, but this God who rules the entire universe is also my Ruler and Judge. This is even more frightening, for as the universe is his stadium, we must play by his rules. As the Psalmist says, *"My flesh trembles in fear of you; I stand in awe of your laws"* [Psalm 119:120].

And woe to those who fail to fear him, who break his laws with insolence: *"**So I will come to put you on trial.** I will be quick to testify against sorcerers, adulterers and perjurers, against those who defraud laborers of their wages, who oppress the widows and the fatherless, and deprive the foreigners among you of justice, but **do not fear me**,"* says the Lord Almighty [Malachi 3:5]. No wonder Jesus reminds us to *"**fear him** who... has authority to throw you into hell."*

Fear and Perspective

As with my fear of the mountain, this fear is a matter of honest perspective, of truly seeing myself in comparison with the limitless, sovereign, holy God of the cosmos. As I gaze upward on this transcendent God who towers over me like infinite Everest, here are a few things I should begin to realize:

- I am tiny; He is great.
- My efforts are puny; His power is boundless.
- His ways are perfect; mine fall short.

Proverbs 22:4 reveals to us: **Humility is the fear of the Lord; its wages are riches and honor and life.** When I reach this point of humility and awe, of trembling before His greatness, it is the beginning of everything good in my life. Proverbs 9:10 affirms: **The fear of the Lord is the beginning of wisdom,** and knowledge of the Holy One is understanding. This perspective is the beginning of our life's education, as we discover what it is we are truly to fear.

It turns out that the only thing we have to fear is The Fear Himself.

For in putting myself in perspective, I discover that the other dangers I have feared are similarly small—even the catalogue of dangers we looked at earlier. It is like fearing a tiny kitten after facing a roaring, hungry lion. What is a house fire next to the One who ignited the sun?

And furthermore, as we discover the God who has revealed himself to us, we find our fear of him transformed by other equally infinite aspects of who He is. He is not just our Creator and Judge, but also Father and Provider, Redeemer and Restorer. Listen to the Psalms proclaim it:

- Fear the Lord, you his holy people, for **those who fear him lack nothing.** [Psalm 34:9]
- But **the eyes of the Lord are on those who fear him,** on those whose hope is in his unfailing love... [Psalm 33:18]
- How abundant are **the good things that you have stored up for those who fear you,** that you bestow in the sight of all, on those who take refuge in you. [Psalm 31:19]

No wonder Moses exhorts the people of God: And now, Israel, **what does the Lord your God ask of you but to fear the Lord your God,** to walk in obedience to him, to love him, to serve the Lord your God with all your heart and with all your soul, and to observe the Lord's commands and decrees that I am giving you today for your own good? [Deuteronomy 10:12-13]

We are to tremble before the great God of the universe, majestic and holy—and love him with all our hearts. Because the transcendent Sovereign of all is good to those who fear Him, and fear Him only.

Reflections:

The only thing we have to fear is The Fear Himself.

"The remarkable thing about God is that when you fear God, you fear nothing else, whereas if you do not fear God, you fear everything else." — Oswald Chambers

Look back at your own Reflections from Chapter One ("On Becoming a Lion"). What did you record as your greatest fears?

Now think about this concept of **"the fear of God."**
- Do you like or dislike this concept? Why or why not?
- How does it impact your view of this fear to think of it as something like "a perspective of humility before infinity"? How might this resemble knee-trembling, skin-draining terror?
- **Why do you think Scripture tells us that this kind of fear is *the beginning of wisdom*?**
- How does a fear of God put the fear you noted above into perspective? What metaphor would you use to compare the greatness of God next to your greatest fear? ("It is like… ")
- Look back at the Psalms and Proverbs quote on the previous page. Which of these speaks most to you today? Which might you like to note/memorize as you go through this section?

Look again at Deuteronomy 10:12-13 (at the end of the chapter), and list all the requirements of God for his people.
- How does this list present a balanced picture of the kind of fear we are to have?
- How does obedience relate to fear of God? How is this different than obedience out of fear of punishment?
- How does love relate to fear of God? How might we able to fear and love him at the same time?
- How does serving God relate to fearing him? What does this indicate about our perspective concerning the relative position of ourselves to God?
- Why would God's commands and decrees be given *for our own good*? How does this relate to fear?

If you have not been regularly praying the prayer of loving fear called St. Teresa's Bookmark (on page 19), start now!

12 Demolishing the Idol of Security

This is what the Lord says to me with his strong hand upon me,
   warning me not to follow the way of this people:
"Do not call conspiracy everything this people calls a conspiracy;
   do not fear what they fear, and do not dread it." [Is. 8:11-12]

Though No One Pursues...

Everyone remembers just where he was when those planes ran into those towers. For Americans, who had never before been attacked on their own soil, beliefs about their own invulnerability were rewritten. It seemed a new and more dangerous world, where there could be a bomb in any subway and a terrorist on any transport. Security procedures changed at airports all over the world, resulting in long lines and agents intently peering at x-ray machines.

Already preoccupied with our own safety and security in so many ways, our paranoia began to explore new boundaries. Security became our idol.

There are real dangers out there, as we have already seen. But at the same time, we in the 21st century West live in one of the safest times and places in history. Our infant mortality is low. Relatively few of us are victims of war, either as soldiers or civilians. Most of us have secured homes, and have never truly known hunger. We can stroll down the street in most neighborhoods without fearing imminent attack. Many diseases that slew thousands only a generation ago have been overcome.

There are still places in our world where none of these statements would be true. In our family's travels, we have visited places where people eat baked dirt to stave off hunger. Where girls hesitate to get up and go outside to relieve themselves at night because someone might rape them. Where corruption in the system means people have to bribe doctors to get medical help. Where the only drinking water available is a source of deadly disease. Where kidnapping for ransom is a commonplace occurrence. We in the West cannot comprehend this daily level of danger.

However, the level of **fear** that one encounters in Western countries regarding the dangers that threaten is as much or more than is often found in countries far worse off.

Perhaps this is partly because fear is the currency our media trades in. After a plane wreck, a school shooting, a child murder, a terrorist threat, an epidemic scare, or any other disaster you could name, facts and innuendos are trumpeted loud on our televisions, over and over. Not only this, but also the various possibilities that the monster could be outside your door, soon, ready to attack you as well, are examined in detail. Intense fear equals good ratings.

Idolatrous Fear

The truth is, **that which we fear most automatically becomes our god:**

- We will allow it to occupy the premier place in our minds.
- We will allow it to control our thoughts and actions.
- We will direct all of our energies toward prevention.

We tend to think that an idol is anything we **love** more than God. In reality, it is anything that occupies the place in our hearts and minds that God is supposed to occupy. Therefore, **anything we are more afraid of than God—the Creator and Judge of the universe, the most worthy of fear—is an idol to us.** We have allowed it to be bigger than God is.

As some of the safest people in the world, we worship security. Any small threat of danger, and we immediately build systems to make the tiny chance of it happening to us as miniscule as possible.

We issue warnings for everything. Styrofoam cups warn that the coffee in them is hot. Road signs remind us that paving becomes slippery when wet. My hairdryer has a large tag that tells me it should not be used in the bathtub. Before you go skiing, or participate in just about any sort of sport, you have to sign a waiver saying that you understand such activity is dangerous, and that you might possibly be injured or worse.

The reason for this is that, in America especially, danger is pretty much illegal. Those who do not reduce danger to an infinitesimally negligible factor may be held liable by law. In order to protect oneself from these liabilities, warnings and waivers are issued to reduce the danger of lawsuit. Meanwhile, a tort system originally designed to prevent true negligence and abuse now must deal with frivolous lawsuits inflated by greed and the belief that **any** threat to my safety, however miniscule, must be punished.

When I come back to the U.S., I am always a little shocked by TV advertisements for prescription medication. This is not only because it seems strange to me that a person with no medical training should be telling a doctor what they want to take for the worrying symptoms they looked up on the Internet. It is also because the legally required warnings, rapidly gabbled at the end of the ads, almost always caution the consumer that taking this prescription could result in death. Death!

In reality, this is the fear that enslaves us. Hebrews 2:15 describes humanity as *"those who all their lives were held in slavery by **their fear of death**."* Every fear comes down in the end to our inevitable death. This may be a small "death"—of our reputation, or our fortune, or our comfort and well-being—or it may be the real thing, kicking the actual bucket. Either way it enslaves us, and holds us captive to keeping the beast at bay for as long as possible.

Toppling the Impotent Idol

In ancient times, idols were revered and feared and appeased because they were thought to have power in averting the deaths people feared. Jeremiah brings the word of the Lord to his people regarding those idols [10:2-5]:

> **"Do not learn the ways of the nations or be terrified by signs in the heavens,**
> **though the nations are terrified by them.**
> *For the practices of the peoples are worthless;*
> *they cut a tree out of the forest, and a craftsman shapes it with his chisel.*
> *They adorn it with silver and gold;*
> *they fasten it with hammer and nails so it will not totter.*
> *Like a scarecrow in a cucumber field, their idols cannot speak;*
> *they must be carried because they cannot walk.*
> **Do not fear them; they can do no harm nor can they do any good."**

The idols feared by pagans were powerless in averting the disasters they feared, the portents they saw heralded in the heavens. Jeremiah warns Israel not to follow in their ways: they are to fear neither the portents nor the impotent idols. Isaiah relays a similar warning from God in the verse quoted at the beginning of this chapter. Only this time, when he tells Isaiah *not to follow the way of **this people**,* he is talking about the people of Israel, the people of God, who have themselves become victims of *fear* and dread, in spite of the very real God they serve. They whisper to each other rumors of conspiracies, the things that might happen. Just so may we allow the fear of death to enslave us, even as God's people.

We need to heed this word of the Lord regarding the idol of security in our dangerous world. The dangers that are real are in the hands of the Almighty. Many other potential dangers turn out to be nothing more than conspiracy theories and scaremongering not worthy of a people who fear God. And the idol of security, that illusion that we can create own safety, turns out to be an impotent scarecrow in a cucumber field. Helen Keller wisely said:

> "**Security is mostly a superstition.** It does not exist in nature, nor do the children of men as a whole experience it. Avoiding danger is no safer in the long run than outright exposure. The fearful are caught as often as the bold. **Life is either a daring adventure, or nothing."**[2]

The idols of security we cling to—warnings and waivers, walls and wealth, plans and procedures—turn out to be inadequate. They cannot prevent all danger. They cannot even control our fear of death, which grows even as we put new measures into place. No matter how we adorn our idols, no matter how many nails we use to keep them from tottering, they cannot save us.

God promises that he alone can *free those who all their lives were held in slavery by their fear of death* [Hebrews 12:15]. And as God, he alone is worthy of our fear. After dismissing portents of danger and impotent idols as unworthy, Jeremiah goes on to say [10:6-7]:

> No one is like you, Lord;
>   you are great, and your name is mighty in power.
> Who should not fear you, King of the nations?
>   This is your due.

Reflections:

"You all know," said the Guide,
"that **security is mortals' greatest enemy.**"
— C.S. Lewis[3]

- What do you think Lewis meant by this? Why might this be true?
- What priority do you believe security holds in your society? In your city? In your church? Among your friends? In your family?

That which we fear most automatically becomes our god.

Consider the above statement. If this is true, what is **your** god?
- What fear tends to often occupy your mind?
- What fear often ends up controlling your thoughts and actions?
- What fear do you struggle most strenuously to prevent?

Reflect on this quote about terrorism by a security expert:
"Terrorism isn't a crime against people or property. It's **a crime against our minds,** using the death of innocents and destruction of property to make us fearful... And **when we react out of fear,** when we change our policy to make our country less open, **the terrorists succeed—even if their attacks fail.** But when we refuse to be terrorized, when we're indomitable in the face of terror, the terrorists fail—even if their attacks succeed." —Bruce Schneier[4]
- How is the *fear of death* exploited by terrorists?
- How is the *fear of death* exploited and expanded by the media?
- How do we adopt a *fear of death* as a kind of idol as a result?
- How are we complicit in spreading this *fear of death* in the hearts and minds of those around us?

"A false sense of security is the only kind there is." —Michael Meade[5]
- What does this quote say about the idols of security we create?
- How do the Isaiah and Jeremiah passages we read affirm this?
- What difference would it make if we affirmed the powerlessness of our idols of security to protect us from anything that we fear?

Has security has been an idol to you? Spend some time now in repentance, acknowledging it as an illusion, and demolishing this scarecrow. Ask God to begin to replace your unholy fear with fear of the One True God who made the universe—and, in love, you.

13 The Fear that Drives Out Fear

*Moses said to the people, **"Do not be afraid.** God has come to test you, so that **the fear of God** will be with you to keep you from sinning."* [Exodus 20:20]

Don't Be Afraid—Fear God

One of my favorite comedy clips features Bob Newhart as a psychiatrist interviewing a patient. The patient confesses her overwhelming fear of being buried alive, and relates how this has crippled her life by making her afraid of any enclosed spaces. Bob Newhart calmly tells her he has two words that will help her overcome her fear and change her life. She asks if she should write them down, but he assures her that she can probably remember them. Then he leans across the table and yells at her, "STOP IT!"[6]

When we look at the dangers we listed earlier, along with many others that are present in our world, it is hard to conquer our fear of all of them. Does God really just say to us, "Stop it"? Somehow, we have to find a definitive answer to the real risks that surround us every day if fear of those dangers is not to cripple our lives.

As we have hinted already, that answer is found in a fear of God.

The verse above is an interesting illustration of this. Imagine with me the scene that presented itself to the Israelites at the foot of Mt. Sinai. It was truly awesome—and not in the "awesome cheesecake" sense. They had already roped off the mountain so that no human or animal would accidentally touch it and be struck dead. Then God himself makes his appearance, in the most overwhelming way imaginable:

*On the morning of the third day there was **thunder and lightning**, with a thick cloud over the mountain, and **a very loud trumpet blast**. Everyone in the camp trembled... Mount Sinai was **covered with smoke**, because the Lord **descended on it in fire**. The smoke billowed up from it like smoke from a furnace, and **the whole mountain trembled violently**. As the sound of the trumpet grew louder and louder, Moses spoke and the voice of God answered him* [Exodus 19:16-19].

Vicious lightning storms. Volcanic eruptions. Violent earthquakes. And an otherworldly trumpet blast growing louder and louder, like celestial feedback. An assault on the senses, as the smoke filled their nostrils and sound their ears. All this is before God even speaks, in *such a voice... that those who heard it begged that no further word be spoken to them* [Hebrews 12:19]. Hebrews goes on to tell us: *The sight was so terrifying that Moses said,* **"I am trembling with fear"** [v. 21]. And this from a man with whom God regularly communicated!

And yet, Moses tells the people, **"Do not be afraid,"** while paradoxically announcing, *"God has come to test you, so that the* **fear of God will be with you** *to keep you from sinning."* How can this be? How are they supposed to not be afraid, and yet fear God? When I studied this passage, I assumed that these must be two different Hebrew words, one meaning "afraid" and the other meaning something like "reverence." But it turned out that this verb and noun are actually from the same root, both capturing the idea of uncontrollable trembling. So the people are meant to be afraid and not afraid simultaneously. How does this work?

A lot of people are afraid of thunder, and fire, and earthquakes. But Moses is telling the people that these manifestations are nothing compared to the God who is revealing his Law to them. This is only a test: will they be more impressed with the fireworks, or the One to whom these terrors are nothing more than squibs and sparklers? They should not be afraid—because they fear God more than his special effects.

Fearing the God Who Controls Everything

If we fear God, we need fear nothing else. He is the God of the universe, in sovereign control of every danger we could possibly dream up. When Israel was about to be overrun by the Assyrian invader, God spoke to the prophet Isaiah and, as we saw in the last chapter, told him:

> *"Do not call conspiracy everything this people calls a conspiracy;*
> **do not fear** *what they fear, and do not dread it.*
> *The Lord Almighty is the one you are to regard as holy,*
> **he is the one you are to fear,** *he is the one you are to dread."*
> [8:12-13]

Even when our worst fears look set to happen, God is the one who is in charge. Nothing happens to us without his say-so, and for his purposes. When we have this awed perspective on an infinite, transcendent God who is looking after us, when we see him as greater than everything that scares us, we can be fearless in the face of danger, even in the face of disaster.

This means he has the ability to protect and save us in the midst of the greatest danger as we fear him, trusting in his great might and his great love for us. David testifies to this in Psalm 34, which he wrote after God delivered him from the Philistine king:

I sought the Lord, and he answered me; **he delivered me from all my fears...** This poor man called, and the Lord heard him; he saved him out of all his troubles. **The angel of the Lord encamps around those who fear him,** and he delivers them... **Fear the Lord,** you his holy people, for **those who fear him lack nothing.** [v. 4,6-7,9]

And what if the worst **does** arrive, and we are not spared? What if, like Job, we can say: "What I feared has come upon me; what I dreaded has happened to me" [Job 3:25]? Throughout the book of Job, he asks God the question "Why?" and demands an answer. And when God finally comes, his response can be boiled down to: I am the Answer. I am God, and I hold all in my hands.

Where were you when I laid the earth's foundation? Tell me, if you understand. Who marked off its dimensions? Surely you know! Who stretched a measuring line across it? On what were its footings set, or who laid its cornerstone—while the morning stars sang together and all the angels shouted for joy? [38:4-7]

This is followed by an incredibly beautiful picture of God's intricate workings in the natural world: sea, sun, and snow; wind, lightning and rain; birds and beasts of all kinds. (Highly recommended reading for those seeking to fear the Lord...)

Many people have been offended by God's answer to Job. How dare He pull rank on a hurting man? How hard-hearted is it just to cite his sovereign schemes, and never address exactly why Job has lost so much, why God has allowed all his fears to be fulfilled? What kind of petulant bully is he?

But this criticism fails to take into account Job's own response to God's answer: it satisfies him. He says: "I know that you can do all things; no purpose of yours can be thwarted... Surely I spoke of things I did not understand, things too wonderful for me to know" [42:2-3]. God's descriptions of how he cares for even the smallest of his creatures, how he brings the wicked to justice, how he rules over every force of nature, bring this man who feared God in the best of times to the recognition that God is still in control, that he still cares for him, in the worst of times. Job realizes God is truly worthy of his fear, and that even the disasters that had come on him were mediated by the gracious hand of God, his creator, who was watching over him. We, too, must allow God himself to be the Answer to our questions in all our danger and disaster.

Cast Your Anxieties on Your Caring Creator

Jesus, too, helps us understand that if we fear God, we need fear nothing else, not hunger nor loss, not mistreatment nor persecution—not even death:

> "I tell you, my friends, **do not be afraid** of those who kill the body and after that can do no more. But I will show you **whom you should fear: Fear him** who, after your body has been killed, has authority to throw you into hell. Yes, I tell you, **fear him.** Are not five sparrows sold for two pennies? Yet not one of them is forgotten by God. Indeed, the very hairs of your head are all numbered. **Don't be afraid**; you are worth more than many sparrows." [Luke 12:4-7]

We can trust that God's plans for those who fear him are for their good. We are not just pawns in his great master game, fulfilling his purposes in the wide world. Rather, we can have faith in his intentions for each individual man and woman who is known and loved by him. Romans 8:28 has reassured many a God-fearer struggling with being afraid: *And we know **that in all things God works for the good of those who love him,** who have been called according to his purpose.*

Verse 31 caps this triumphantly: *What, then, shall we say in response to these things?* **If God is for us, who can be against us?**

Once, when I was telling the story of the Ten Commandments in Sunday School, I dramatically described the fear and trembling of the Israelites at the foot of Mt. Sinai to a rapt group of children. One little blonde girl, remembering a previous memory verse, asked in a puzzled voice, "But don't they know that they should *cast all their anxieties on him, because he cares for them?*"

So we should fear God, and not be afraid. We should tremble before him as the one who flung the galaxies across space—and trust him as the one who holds every circumstance of our lives, present and future, in his loving hands.

Reflections:

Don't be afraid; fear God.

In the previous chapter, we identified an idol as something you fear more than God: that preoccupies your mind, that controls your thoughts and actions, and that drives you to self-protection.

"**Where does your security lie?** Is God your refuge, your hiding place, your stronghold, your shepherd, your counselor, your friend, your redeemer, your savior, your guide? **If He is, you don't need to search any further for security**." — Elisabeth Elliott

What difference would it make to your greatest fears if:

God were primarily to occupy your mind?

- *My spirit grows faint within me; my heart within me is dismayed. I remember the days of long ago; I meditate on all your works and consider what your hands have done. I spread out my hands to you; I thirst for you like a parched land.* [Psalm 143:4-5]

God were allowed to control your thoughts and actions?

- *Those who live according to the flesh have their minds set on what the flesh desires; but those who live in accordance with the Spirit have their minds set on what the Spirit desires. The mind governed by the flesh is death, but the mind governed by the Spirit is life and peace.* [Romans 8:5-6]
- *Do not conform to the pattern of this world, but be transformed by the renewing of your mind. Then you will be able to test and approve what God's will is—his good, pleasing and perfect will.* [Romans 12:2]

God enabled you to risk rather than self-protect?

- *We are hard pressed on every side, but not crushed; perplexed, but not in despair; persecuted, but not abandoned; struck down, but not destroyed… For we who are alive are always being given over to death for Jesus' sake, so that his life may also be revealed in our mortal body.* [2 Cor. 4:8,11]
- *I can do all things through Christ who strengthens me.* [Philippians 4:13, NKJV]

What difference could this fear of God make even **when our greatest fears seem to have come true,** as with Job?[7]

14 Two Mountains

Therefore, since we are receiving a kingdom that cannot be shaken, let us be thankful, and so **worship God acceptably with reverence and awe,** *for our "God is a consuming fire."*
[Hebrews 12:28-29]

Fearing the Forbearing Judge

Jonathan Edwards was not a particularly inspiring orator. He always read his sermons in an even voice, without shouting or the rhetorical gimmicks used by many Colonial preachers of his day. And yet when in July 1741 he delivered his sermon, "Sinners in the Hands of an Angry God," in the village of Enfield, Connecticut, the audience began weeping and moaning before he was even finished, with people crying out, "What must I do to be saved?" Here is a sample of the sermon that so moved Edwards' hearers:

> Your wickedness makes you as it were heavy as lead... and if God should let you go, you would immediately sink and swiftly descend and plunge into the bottomless gulf, and your healthy constitution, and your own care and prudence, and best contrivance, and all your righteousness, would have no more influence to uphold you and keep you out of hell, than a spider's web would have to stop a falling rock... The sovereign pleasure of God, for the present, stays his rough wind; otherwise it would come with fury... and you would be like the chaff on the summer threshing floor.[8]

Edwards' audience acknowledged the truth of what Moses had told the Israelites as God thundered his Ten Commandments: *God has come to test you, so that* **the fear of God will be with you to keep you from sinning** (Exodus 20:20). Nothing we fear in this world can equal the Creator's judgment against those who fail to acknowledge his authority. Moses reminds us in Psalm 90:

> *We are consumed by your anger and terrified by your indignation.*
> *You have set our iniquities before you,*
>   *our secret sins in the light of your presence.*
> *All our days pass away under your wrath;*
>   *we finish our years with a moan...*
> *If only we knew the power of your anger!*
> **Your wrath is as great as the fear that is your due.** *[v. 7-9,11]*

Even the threat of death in itself is not as terrifying as God's judgment. Consider once more Jesus' words: *"Do not be afraid of those **who kill the body and after that can do no more**... Fear him who, **after your body has been killed, has authority to throw you into hell.** Yes, I tell you, fear him"* [Luke 12:4-5].

For all our society's scaremongering, this is one fear that is definitely unfashionable. The traditional picture of hell as a place of eternal fiery torment, populated by grinning demons with pitchforks, is regarded as positively medieval, to be scorned by thinking people. And perhaps, indeed, our theological pictures of hell have been too simplistic and childish, not taking into account that judgment is not just flames and forks. Rather, eternal death is to have the Creator completely remove his present gracious and forbearing hand from us—and with it any hope of *entering our Master's happiness.*

Many times, Scripture tells us that fear of God should motivate us toward righteousness:

- *Blessed are all who fear the Lord, who **walk in obedience to him*** [Psalm 128:1].
- *Do not be wise in your own eyes; fear the Lord and **shun evil*** [Proverbs 3:7].
- *Whoever fears the Lord **walks uprightly,** but those who despise him are devious in their ways* [Proverbs 14:2].

Afraid of the Hard Man

This may raise a question. We saw already that the third servant in the Parable of the Talents acknowledges his fear of the Master, and its impact on his choices. So if we are supposed to fear God as Judge, why was **his** fear not acknowledged and accepted?

Look once more at the servant's reason for his fear as he approaches the Master: *"I knew that you are a hard man, **harvesting where you have not sown** and gathering where you have not scattered seed. **So I was afraid...**"* [Matthew 25:24-25]. The servant's fear is based on his image of the Master as tricky, capricious and unfair. He acknowledges the Master's **power** to rule over him, but not his **right.** Inside he rebels against the commission he is given, and conforms only so far as he thinks he must to avoid punishment. He is, as in the Proverb above, *devious in his ways.* His fear of the Master is not born of any kind of love, but rather a kind of hate and rejection, even as it trembles before his resented rule.

In just such a way, James 2:19 says, *"You say you have faith, for you believe that there is one God. Good for you!* **Even the demons believe this, and they tremble in terror"** [NLT].

Some may live lives that outwardly appear to be righteous, but inwardly are motivated by this unholy terror that secretly hates their Creator. Jan van Ruysbroeck, the 14th century Flemish mystic, comments on such people:

All that they do, they do, not out of love, but from sheer necessity, lest they shall be damned. And, because they are inwardly unfaithful, they dare not trust in God; but their whole inward life is doubt and fear, travail and misery... But all their prayers, all their labor and all the good works, whatsoever they do, to cast out this fear, help them not; for the more inordinately they love themselves, the more they fear hell. And from this you may learn **that their fear of hell springs from self-love,** which seeks its own.[9]

Moses sets before God's people his requirements: **To fear the Lord your God,** *to walk in obedience to him,* **to love him,** *to serve the Lord your God with all your heart and with all your soul, and* **to observe the Lord's commands and decrees that I am giving you today for your own good...** [Deuteronomy 10:12-13]. Fearing God means acknowledging that he, and he only, has the right to judge your actions, your words, your thoughts, and your attitudes. It means also that fear pairs not with self-love, and thus with self-protection by means of self-justification, but with love of God, as we walk in the ways he gives us for our *own good.*

Perfect Love Drives Out Fear

This puts us in a predicament. For how may we possibly love a God whom we constantly disobey? How can we trust a God who, as we saw, has *set our iniquities before Him, our secret sins in the light of his presence* [Ps. 90:8]? How can we feel anything but terror when his judgment may fall at any time?

It is true that God has the right to judge his creatures. But he also has provided a way for that judgment to be taken by One who did not deserve it, by One who lived a sinless life. Jesus, the Lamb of God, sacrificed himself on our behalf, so that we, with growing awe, could throw ourselves trembling at the feet of a just God and find not only forgiveness, but righteousness. God's great love fulfills his great justice, and grants us great grace.

And as we cast ourselves on this grace and mercy, we find that the sinner's trembling, that unholy terror that consumes us and drives us to self-justification, is replaced by peace and love. The trembling ceases, to be overcome by immense awe at the foot of infinite Everest. Hebrews 12:18-24 describes it by comparing two Biblical mountains, in this way:

> **You have not come to a mountain that can be touched and that is burning with fire;** to darkness, gloom and storm; to a trumpet blast or to such a voice speaking words that those who heard it begged that no further word be spoken to them...
> **But you have come to Mount Zion,** to the city of the living God, the heavenly Jerusalem. You have come to thousands upon thousands of angels in joyful assembly, to the church of the firstborn, whose names are written in heaven. **You have come to God, the Judge of all, to the spirits of the righteous made perfect, to Jesus the mediator of a new covenant,** and to the sprinkled blood that speaks a better word than the blood of Abel.

We have come perfect circle, to the point where fear of God drives out **all** fear, even terror of Him as Judge. As I John 1:19 says: *There is no fear in love. But perfect love drives out fear, because fear has to do with punishment. The one who fears is not made perfect in love.* If Jesus took our judgment, we have no condemnation left to fear; we can be not only the *righteous made perfect,* but also *made perfect in love.*

John Newton captured this idea perfectly in the second verse of his famous "Amazing Grace":

> 'Twas grace that taught my heart to fear,
> and grace my fears relieved...

Nothing in all creation can reverse Jesus' judgment. Nothing in all creation can separate us from his perfect love. Meditate now on these triumphant words:

> **If God is for us, who can be against us?** ... *Who will bring any charge against those whom God has chosen? It is God who justifies. Who then is the one who condemns?* **No one.** [Romans 8:31, 33-34]

Reflections:

Jesus is the Judge who takes away our fear of judgment.

In this chapter, we have considered one aspect of the fear of God being the **acknowledgement of his right to Judge us,** as the Ruler of All. As we have seen: *Humility is the fear of the Lord* [Prov. 22:4a].

- How would you express, in your own words, the difference between this kind of fear of God and the fear expressed by the servant who was afraid of the Master as a *hard man*?
- How would you express the difference between this kind of fear of God and the fear described by Ruysbroeck on p. 90?

Many struggle with the idea of God sending people to hell. For some of us, it seems vindictive—an example of God as a *hard man.* One writer who helped me come to terms with the justice of hell is C.S. Lewis, who points out that human **self-love** which repudiates God's right to rule and resists his love is what determines the destination of the damned: "There are only two kinds of people in the end: those who say to God, 'Thy will be done,' and those to whom God says, in the end, 'Thy will be done.'"[10]

- Does this help you to come to terms with God's right to judge those who refuse to acknowledge and fear him as Sovereign Lord? That God does not impose on the free will of his creatures, but allows them the consequences of their choices?

Meditate again on I John 1:19: *There is no fear in love.* **But perfect love drives out fear, because fear has to do with punishment.** *The one who fears is not made perfect in love.*

- Have you ever lived your life in fear of God's punishment? (Do you now?) How did/does this impact the way you relate to Him?
- What difference does it make to know that Jesus has not only taken your punishment, but has given you his righteousness? What does it change to know that because of this God sees you as perfect in his sight, and is eternally pleased with you?
- Look again at the descriptions of the two mountains from Hebrews 12 at the end of the chapter. Which mountain do you see yourself dwelling on in your daily life? If it is the first, what is the truth about God you need to make a part of yourself so that *perfect love drives out your fear*?

15 Roped In To The Rock

*"**Do not tremble, do not be afraid.***
Did I not proclaim this and foretell it long ago?
You are my witnesses. Is there any God besides me?
*No, **there is no other Rock**; I know not one." [Isaiah 44:8]*

School of Rock

Did you know that rock music started with the Bible? This may be a shocking revelation, I know. But here is a little history of Rock songs in Scripture. First, let's listen to Moses rock out in an early Rock song:

I will proclaim the name of the Lord.
Oh, praise the greatness of our God!
***He is the Rock,** his works are perfect, and all his ways are just.*
A faithful God who does no wrong, upright and just is he...
How could one man chase a thousand,
or two put ten thousand to flight,
unless their Rock had sold them,
unless the Lord had given them up?
*For **their rock is not like our Rock**, as even our enemies concede.*
[Deuteronomy 32:3-4,30-31]

Then there's David, that sweet, sweet singer-songwriter of Rock songs:

***The Lord is my rock**, my fortress and my deliverer;*
***my God is my rock**, in whom I take refuge,*
my shield and the horn of my salvation.
He is my stronghold, my refuge and my savior... [2 Samuel 22:2-3]

The ladies aren't left out either. Here's Hannah, riffing on the Rock:

My heart rejoices in the Lord; in the Lord my horn is lifted high.
My mouth boasts over my enemies,
for I delight in your deliverance.
There is no one holy like the Lord; there is no one besides you;
there is no Rock like our God. [I Samuel 2:1-2]

And as we can see at the beginning of this chapter, the prophet Isaiah had his own Rock act, with the catchy chorus, *"Do not tremble, do not be afraid..."*

So what do all of these Rock songs have in common? That they celebrate the one Rock—the transcendent God who created the mountain strongholds, and who is a stronger protection against life's enemies and dangers than any fortress we could fabricate. Not only is He the **best** safety and security that we could imagine—he is the **only** one. As Isaiah says, there is no other Rock.

Safely Roped In

From my earlier story about bawling at the top of the ski slope, you may have gathered that I have a healthy respect for heights, and for the gravity that they tend to engender. However, when my husband and I were doing youth ministry, I learned to love climbing around the treetops in various high ropes courses. One might be surprised to observe this weeping skier blithely daring to walk on swinging log steps suspended many meters above the earth.

But there is one simple reason why I am (relatively) unafraid in this situation. It is because I trust the climbing harness that ropes me in to the strong cable above. I know that if I fall, the worst hurt I am likely to suffer is pinching, scratching or bruising—as opposed to being shattered on the ground below. Were I not securely fastened to this cable, I would never step off the first platform.

This is what it is like to be roped in to the Rock. Instead of the mountain breaking you, the mountain becomes your support and safety. The mountain is a stronghold where you are high above the dangers that attack. The mountain is your fortress, your refuge, as the Rock songs sing.

But you are not meant just to hide on the mountaintop. Because you are roped in securely to the Rock, you can venture out on cliffs and ledges that would otherwise scare you silly. You can run risks that alone, without the rope, would be foolish and impossible. You can even dangle in the void for a time, knowing that the Rock will not give way.

One high ropes course I ventured on required me to jump from a high tree into a much lower net. (Not a big net, either.) I had to hook my carabiner into a long rope—shorter than the distance to the ground, but longer than the distance to the net—and free-fall. In the split second it took to drop, it felt like there was nothing holding me up, no sensation of the rope's support. And yet I was able to step off the ledge because I knew that, if I somehow missed the net or bounced out of it, I was still roped in.

This is what it is to trust the transcendent, eternal Creator and Judge who holds all the world in his hands—and yet knows every hair on your head. Right after Jesus tells us to *"Fear him who...has authority to throw you into hell,"* he goes on to say, *"Are not five sparrows sold for two pennies? Yet not one of them is forgotten by God. **Indeed, the very hairs of your head are all numbered. Don't be afraid;** you are worth more than many sparrows."*

Risking at the Rope's End

God calls us to step out in faith and trust, risking while roped in to the Rock. Where is this faith built? It seems we should learn to depend upon him through his constant grace and provision for us. But more often, we become complacent in dependable provision, developing a sense of entitlement as though God feared us and not the other way around.

Thus God chooses to build our faith, as Andrée Seu Petersen puts it, through "creative and judicious deprivation." She further says: "Faith is always in the stretching. In fact, psychologically speaking... faith is always only exercised in the not having. Once a person receives, the faith, in a sense, ends, at least in that particular exercise."[11] When the net caught me after my split-second tumble, I was still grateful to be roped in—but I did not depend on it the same way as I had a moment earlier.

He does not withhold from us every good thing; in fact, what he withholds is always a tiny fraction of what he generously gives every day. That is where the "creative and judicious" part comes in: he chooses challenges that are just the right stretch for us, where we must trust that we are roped in even when we cannot feel the tautness of the support. Sometimes, as we saw earlier, these challenges are presented as a calling and choice to dare the heights, to step out in faith towards places and people previously considered too dangerous. Other times, the challenges are presented as an abyss that must be crossed opens up before you, when God brings circumstances requiring the choice to cower and complain—or to affirm your confidence in Him.

When you do step out, many times you will find the deliverance that Moses and Isaiah, David and Hannah, all sang about. Dangers miraculously deflected, as with Daniel in the den of lions. Enemies defeated, even at the odds of one man to a thousand. Victories that cause you to sing, "I delight in your deliverance."

Singing Rock Songs in Death's Face

Being roped into the Rock does not mean you will not fall. It means that the hurt you suffer when you do is not ultimate death. On the other hand, if we try to save our own life—to attach our rope back to ourselves, so to speak—we will discover that no person can be their own support. This is how life is lost. (As Proverbs 28:26 says: *Those who trust in themselves are fools...*) But, roped into the Rock, we can even lose our physical lives, and our very selves will be kept safe.

This is how Saint Patrick could return as a missionary to pagan country that had enslaved him to confront bloodthirsty people with Gospel truth.

This is how Mother Teresa could lovingly hold thousands of sick, dying children with no thought for her own health.

This is how Corrie and Betsie Ten Boom could hide persecuted Jews in their house, risking deportation and death.[12]

Jesus said, "*Whoever wants to be my disciple must deny themselves and take up their cross daily and follow me. For whoever wants to save their life will lose it, but **whoever loses their life for me will save it**. What good is it for someone to gain the whole world, and yet lose or forfeit their very self?*" [Luke 9:23-25]

What do we do with Jesus' words of calling and challenge? Do we moan about the crevasses at our feet and try to run the other way? Or do we trust the Rock we are roped into and cross them? And do we even begin to challenge the great rock faces of faith, knowing that true safety is found on His heights?

Jesus has his own Rock song that he would like us to learn:

*"Therefore everyone who hears these words of mine and puts them into practice is like **a wise man who built his house on the rock**. The rain came down, the streams rose, and the winds blew and beat against that house; yet it did not fall, because it had its foundation on the rock. But everyone who hears these words of mine and does not put them into practice is like a foolish man who built his house on sand. The rain came down, the streams rose, and the winds blew and beat against that house, and it fell with a great crash."* [Matthew 7:24-27]

I hope that you will be getting together with some like-minded singers, and forming your own Rock band very soon...

Reflections:

Our ultimate safety comes from being roped into the Rock.

Look back at the four "Rock Songs" at the beginning of the chapter.

- Read through each of them aloud.
- Which one speaks most to you? Why? (You might want to look up its context in Scripture and meditate on it further.)
- Consider making up your own little tune to this Rock Song (or part of it) so that you can remember it and sing it to yourself when you need to encourage yourself to stay roped in.
- Alternatively, take the time to write your own Rock song, calling to mind the ways God has been faithful to you in the past, as well as his great attributes that make him worthy of your trust.
- Who are some others that you could get together with to form a "Rock band," encouraging each other to greater adventure while roped in to a Sovereign God?

Look back at your Reflections on Chapter 2 ("Designed for Good Works"):

- What did you identify as a **Practical Catalyst** in your life: a risk God might be calling you to step into? Have any others come up since then?
- What about a **Providential Catalyst**: a risk that has entered your life not through your own choice? Have there been any new ones since you recorded this?
- How, in each of these, might you have been attaching your rope to yourself, in thoughts, plans, attitudes or actions? (The "Five Habits" might help you identify these.)
- How, in each of these, can you recognize a "creative and judicious deprivation" that challenges your faith, and requires you to trust the Rock you are roped into?
- How might you lean into this void with confidence? What does it look like practically? How will you dare the rock faces with faith, securely roped in—not even fearing death?

exchanging castles for tents

(or, flimsy fortresses)

16 There's No Place Like Home

My people will live in peaceful dwelling places,
  in secure homes,
  in undisturbed places of rest. [Isaiah 32:18]

Hiding in the Castle

For five years, we lived in quite a remarkable house in Brussels: a 19th century neo-Gothic *maison de maître* (city mansion). It belonged to friends who wanted to rent it out to people they knew while stationed elsewhere in Europe, and asked us. With its paneled and elaborately painted walls, colorful tiles and sumptuous stained glass windows, it resembled someone's fantasy of a medieval castle—or the Addams Family house. Indeed, the rumor circulated among our friends and family in the U.S. that we in fact did live in a castle.

The castle illusion was furthered by the fact that our neighborhood of Schaerbeek, very fashionable at the time the house was built, had become rather down-at-heel. Most of our neighbors came from either Turkey or Morocco, and I regularly found myself the palest face in the crowd. I often said that inside the house, I did not know what century I was in; and outside, I did not know what country I was in. The two huge old churches on our street were virtually empty, but the two mosques buzzed with activity. As a male-dominated community, groups of men, young and old, congregated on every corner when the weather was fine, while women remained practically invisible. Alienated from the community outside my door— so foreign to the young Europeans we had come to minister to—I at first mostly stayed in my safe castle, venturing outside only when absolutely necessary.

Consider the following quotes:

- "The home to everyone is to him his castle and fortress, as well for his defense against injury and violence, as for his repose." (Edward Coke)
- "A man's house is his castle." (James Otis)
- "A man's home is his wife's castle." (Alexander Chase)[1]

We are, both men and women, deeply involved in creating a comfortable, secure home for ourselves and our families, a fortress where we and they can feel safe, a place where evil cannot enter. We guard our privacy and embellish our security. The yard around the house, for suburban American families, is a kind of moat surrounding the inner keep, off limits to any outside the approved circle. We don't have to have a bad neighborhood outside the door to justify immuring ourselves in our castles.

I would like to challenge you (along with myself) to begin to think of your home, the place where you live, a bit differently. That is, I would like you to imagine your home as a tent, rather than a castle.

Dwelling in a Tent

Tents are just about as different a place to live from a castle as they can be. Castles are hard and strong; tents are soft and flimsy. Castles are walls within walls; tents are permeable, with gaps in their sides. Castles immure one from the outside world; tents, close to nature, keep out only the rain. Castles are static and immovable, and may be piled with hoards of wealth or junk; tents are transience embodied, requiring the camper to travel light as he depends on the resources he can carry or gather. Castles might be defended by a tiny army until siege starves them out; tents depend for their defense on being clustered together.

The vulnerability of living in a tent first struck me when I was six years old in Australia. My family was camping on the holiday island of Rottnest off the western coast, an island famous for its population of a rare marsupial known as a quokka. As you can see in the picture, these look a little like knee-high hopping teddy bears with long tails. We spotted three of them during our first day and thought they were unbearably cute. What we didn't yet know, however, was that they are nocturnal—and that evening they turned out in the hundreds. They found the fabric walls of our little tent no obstacle at all, and lost no time raiding our Styrofoam cooler full of camping food. I clearly remember my indignant mother and a quokka playing tug-of-war with a loaf of bread. (I don't remember who actually won.)

God called Abraham to leave one of the first cities in the world, and set out on a journey with his whole family in vulnerable tents. He never, for the rest of his life, lived in any other kind of home, until he was laid to rest in a cave, the only plot of promised land he ever owned. Hebrews 11:9 tells us: *By faith he made his home in the promised land like a stranger in a foreign country;* **he lived in tents,** *as did Isaac and Jacob, who were heirs with him of the same promise.*

This is also the kind of dwelling that the ancient Hebrews were inhabiting at the time they came to Mount Sinai. In fact, one of the main Hebrew words generally translated as "dwelling" in the Bible (*mishkan*) literally means "tent." However, they were not too happy about living as nomads like their father Abraham, as for several generations they had lived the settled lives of slaves. Often in Exodus and Numbers we find them complaining about how much they missed their little veggie gardens back in Egypt, reminiscing dolefully about their cucumbers, leeks and onions.

But God had called them, like their forefathers before them, to live *la vida loca* in a community of tents. They had to travel light, finding water and food for their families and flocks as they went. To defend themselves against enemies, they camped all together. And after a time, they would pull up the stakes to move on to the next place.

Remembering the Tents

Of course, they were on a journey to the Promised Land, and on a journey tents are the most versatile of dwellings. But once they got to the land God had promised them, and conquered it, and parceled it out among the twelve tribes so that each family received their own, they must have thought they were done with tents.

Not so. Each year God required them to return to Jerusalem for a fall harvest festival when all the crops had been gathered in for the year. During this time, God commanded them: *"Live in temporary shelters for seven days: All native-born Israelites are to live in such shelters…"* [Leviticus 23:42]. These shelters, known as *sukkot*, were not even well-sewn tents, but created from materials gathered from the environment. To this day during the Jewish Feast of Sukkot (or Booths), each *sukkah* is required by rabbinic law to be roofed with natural materials such as palm branches.

God made his purpose for such a camping experience clear to them: *"… so your descendants will know that I had the Israelites live in temporary shelters when I brought them out of Egypt. I am the Lord your God"* [Leviticus 23:43]. This was no mere trip down memory lane. The juxtaposition of harvest with living in a tent was meant to strongly remind the Israelites that every provision they had—including their home and the land on which their harvest grew—came from the hand of Yahweh. He had provided for them when they had nothing, when they were mere slaves wandering in the desert, dependent on him for the water they drank and the daily manna they ate. Yet as God reminds them in Deuteronomy 29:5-6, *"During the forty years that I led you through the wilderness, your clothes did not wear out, nor did the sandals on your feet... I did this so that you might know that I am the Lord your God."*

Dependence on God was not just for the time of the journey, until they could reach the Promised Land and settle down into self-reliance once more. Rather, God reminds Israel that life is a continuous journey, and that dependence is our natural state no matter how stable our life may look. If it took a week in a *sukkah* hut once a year to remind them of this, the time was worth it.

Building Your Own Sukkah

Perhaps we, too, would benefit from spending seven days in a *sukkah.* Perhaps it would remind us that all the castle walls we erect for our own security are as flimsy as tent curtains, were we not protected by Almighty God. Perhaps it would help us consider that our stockpiles might be weighing us down on the journey, and that we could rely on the His faithful provision for our daily need—and even some over to share with others. Perhaps when the rain dripped through the leafy roof, we could ponder how circumstances that cause us discomfort often paradoxically provide the nourishment that God grants us to grow. Perhaps we could meditate on the transitory nature of our temporary structures, and on the joy of the journey for those who keep faith with their Father throughout the pilgrimage.

And perhaps we could return home again to our castles to see them with a new eye, transformed into tents.

Read once more the verse at the beginning of this chapter. It sounds like a promise you might cross-stitch and hang on your living room wall, something you might claim for your castle. But the promises of peace and security that are given to God's people here are for **open places, places of apparently vulnerable sojourn:**

- The Hebrew word for *dwelling places,* "naveh," refers to the sheepfold, the abode of sheep and shepherds out in the open meadows. It is qualified by the word "shalom," the peace that arises only from the blessing and favor of God himself.
- "Mishkan," translated as *homes,* is the Hebrew word we have already noted literally means "tents." But the adjective that describes it—translated in the NIV as *secure*—has as its

primary meaning "trust" or "confidence." This indicates that the security experienced in this tent comes from confidence in an outside source of protection.

- The final phrase, *undisturbed resting places*, uses two words that describe a sense of ease and a place where one can find repose. The second word, *"menuchah,"* is familiar to us from Psalm 23, where it describes the *"still" waters* where the Shepherd leads his sheep.

So perhaps we could loosely paraphrase this verse in this way:

> *My people will live in God-blessed sheepfolds,*
>   *in trusting tents full of confidence in Him,*
>   *in restful stillness.*

This peace in an exposed position is all the more remarkable considering **the context** of these verses: a great calamity that Isaiah prophesies will fall on God's people, removing all that might previously have made them feel secure.

> **The fortress will be abandoned,**
>   **the noisy city deserted;**
>   **citadel and watchtower will become a wasteland forever,**
>   *the delight of donkeys, a pasture for flocks,*
> *till the Spirit is poured on us from on high,*
>   *and the desert becomes a fertile field,*
>   *and the fertile field seems like a forest.*
> *The Lord's justice will dwell in the desert,*
>   *his righteousness live in the fertile field.*
> **The fruit of that righteousness will be peace;**
> **its effect will be quietness and confidence forever.**
>   *My people will live in peaceful dwelling places,*
>   *in secure homes,*
>   *in undisturbed places of rest.*
> **Though hail flattens the forest**
>   **and the city is leveled completely,**
> **how blessed you will be,**
>   *sowing your seed by every stream,*
>   *and letting your cattle and donkeys range free.* [Is. 32:14-20]

We live in an age when the Spirit **has** been *poured on us from on high*. Why not recognize that the castles you build are no more secure than a *sukkah*? Why not let the Spirit transform your own fearful fortress into a tent filled with trust?

Reflections:

God wants us to abandon fearful fortresses for trustful tents.

Imagine yourself actually having to permanently live in a tent.

- How would it impact your priorities?
- What would be the hardest things to get rid of, if you couldn't take them camping with you?
- What would be the biggest inconvenience?
- How would the members of your family react if you told them this was what you were going to do from now on?
- How would it affect your reputation in society?
- What would be your biggest fear about living this way?
- What could be freeing about living this lifestyle?
- In what ways (real or metaphorical) is it more like the lifestyle Jesus is calling us to, than living in a real/metaphorical castle?

God called his chosen people to live this way for some time: Abraham and his descendants, right down to the time when they gained property in the promised land. Later, after the exile prophesied by Isaiah, they found themselves living once more as displaced persons.

- What do you think God was trying to teach his people through these times?
- What do you think was the point of making them live in a *sukkah* for a week once a year?
- What do you think **you** might get out of this exercise? What truths would it help you remember?

As you read this section, **consider memorizing Isaiah 32:18,** keeping in mind the precarious situation of its context. You might even try creating an artistic reminder of this verse for your own home, through paint, photography, embroidery, calligraphy, or whatever inspires you.

> *My people will live in peaceful dwelling places,*
> *in secure homes,*
> *in undisturbed places of rest.*

17 From the Mountain to the Plain

Who is like the Lord our God,
  the One who sits enthroned on high,
who stoops down to look
  on the heavens and the earth? [Psalm 113:5-6]

God on the Mountain

In ancient cultures, the high places have often been considered the abode of the gods. Think of the Greek pantheon gathered on Mount Olympus, or the Norse divinities in Asgard, reached from our realm by a rainbow bridge. And when the Israelites reached Canaan, God instructed them: *"Destroy completely all **the places on the high mountains,** on the hills and under every spreading tree, where the nations you are dispossessing worship their gods"* [Deuteronomy 12:2]. There is something, it seems, about a mountain that symbolizes divine power, and the means to climb a little bit closer to a transcendent being that can never really be reached.

The true God also chose a mountain as the place to manifest himself to Israel, in fire and thunder, as the One they alone must fear. This was the same mountain upon which the I AM had disclosed his name to Moses in a burning bush, and to the top of which he again calls Moses after speaking the law to his terrified people, to unveil more of his holy will.

Throughout Scripture, God is commonly depicted as living on high, on a holy mountain, sanctifying it as his home:

> *Mount Bashan, majestic mountain,*
>   *Mount Bashan, rugged mountain,*
> *why gaze in envy, you rugged mountain,*
>   *at **the mountain where God chooses to reign, where the Lord himself will dwell forever**?* [Psalm 68:15-16]

We pondered in the last section how God is the Transcendent Sovereign, higher and holier than anything we might imagine, the object of our fear. He sits on high as the One who holds all that he has made in the palm of his hand: in the famous picture of Julian of Norwich, like a tiny hazelnut. He dwells outside us, beyond us, as a Being wholly other than we are, unknowable by any means we ourselves might devise.

He himself declares:

"For my thoughts are not your thoughts,
  neither are your ways my ways," declares the Lord.
"As the heavens are higher than the earth,
  so are my ways higher than your ways
  and my thoughts than your thoughts." [Isaiah 55:8-9]

In Scripture, this depiction of God on the mountain is especially used when speaking of him as Israel's Fear, the Creator and Judge of all. As he thundered from Mt. Sinai, so he is depicted as dispensing justice and righteousness to the nations from his holy dwelling on high:

The Lord will roar **from on high;**
  he will thunder **from his holy dwelling**
  and roar mightily against his land.
He will shout like those who tread the grapes,
  shout against all who live on the earth…
for the Lord will bring charges against the nations;
  he will bring judgment on all mankind… [Jeremiah 25:30-31]

How must we respond to such a transcendent God? First, as we have seen already, we must fear him. We, and our whole world, are nothing in comparison. As Julian contemplates the hazelnut in God's hand, she says, "I marveled how it might last, for I thought it might suddenly have fallen to naught for littleness."[2] Second, this fear must cause us to bow down in worship before him as the only Ruler and Maker, to acknowledge that his will must be done. Third, we must seek to obey all he commands as our Sovereign and Judge, knowing that his laws prevail over us, and fall on his mercy when we fail.

So far, this sounds pretty overwhelming—till we begin to recognize that this Creator is also our Provider who gives us all we need and our Protector who is greater than all we fear. Then we may add to our responses gratitude, and as we observe the consistency of the provision and protection, a measure of trust. This trust and gratitude can then color our worship, fear, and obedience with a kind of warmth approaching love. But it is difficult to truly love a Being that is so high, holy, and wholly other; one that we can never reach or know through our own efforts; one that we fail to obey perfectly; one that is so far away on the distant mountaintop.

And so God calls Moses up to spend time with him on the mountain—to reveal his plans for moving down to the plain.

God on the Plain

For forty days and nights, God unveils his plans to pitch a Tent among the tents of his people. (It takes up seven whole chapters of description in the Bible: Exodus 24-31.) This Tent will be in the middle of the camp, and the glory of the Lord will hover over it in a pillar of cloud by day, and fire by night, so that all will know that the Almighty God, the Transcendent One, has come down to be among them. God calls it "the Tent of Meeting."

He tells Moses: "*For the generations to come this burnt offering is to be made regularly at the entrance to* **the Tent of Meeting** *before the Lord.* **There I will meet you and speak to you; there also I will meet with the Israelites,** *and the place will be consecrated by my glory...* **Then I will dwell among the Israelites** *and be their God. They will know that I am the Lord their God, who brought them out of Egypt* **so that I might dwell among them**" [Exodus 29:42-46].

Not only is this Tent a place where Moses, the leader, could encounter God—the people themselves would be able to meet with him there. And God reveals the amazing reason he brought them out of Egypt in the first place: not to overwhelm them with his thunder, but to dwell among them.

There are plenty of aspects of this dwelling that would remind them that he is the same God who revealed himself on the mountain: gold to represent his majesty; an ever-burning lampstand to symbolize his holy purity; a table with constantly renewed bread to remind of his provision as Creator; and most of all, the ark which would be the seat for the manifestation of his glory. But there would also be furnishings designed to enable feeble, sinful people to come near to this holy God.

For along with the blueprint for this dwelling-place, he unveils the beginning of a whole system of worship that would enable his people to approach him with confidence, their trespasses forgiven and atoned for. His mercy and grace—previously only hoped for—became accessible as he showed them the path to repentance and restoration, and even joy in the presence of their God. There is an altar where sacrifices may be offered not only for sin, but in gratitude and worship. Another smaller altar burns incense, symbolic of the prayers of the people rising to heaven to be heard. A huge basin for washing speaks of the purification that God has made possible, so that people may stand clean before their God. And a high priest mediates the people's approach so that their worship will be accepted by a holy God, so that He will smile on them.

In contrast to God on the mountain, we see that:

- The Tent on the plain was a place of meeting between God and man, instead of God being far off
- The Tent on the plain was a place of forgiveness, not judgment, where sins could be atoned for
- The Tent on the plain was a place where God lived with and among his people, as part of them

Heaven now became a place on earth. God pitches his tent among the tents of his people. He reveals to them that he is not only the Transcendent Sovereign; he is also Immanent Love and Grace. He has come near to them, and has made a way that they can dwell together in love and joy.

Later, God would institute this daily blessing that the priests were to speak over the people who visited his Tent [Numbers 6:24-26]:

> "The Lord bless you and keep you;
> the Lord make his face shine on you and be gracious to you;
> the Lord turn his face toward you and give you peace."

The "you" in this blessing is singular: meant to awaken in each person receiving it the sense of God's smiling face turned toward them personally. It is a picture of a parent beaming down with love on their tiny child, evoking a smile in return. God's presence and blessing in their midst was based on his love for them, and his compassion for them in weakness. God does not stop being high and holy for having descended to the plain, but additionally reveals to them the Love central to his character.

> For this is what the high and exalted One says—
> he who lives forever, whose name is holy:
> **"I live in a high and holy place,**
> **but also with the one who is contrite and lowly in spirit,**
> to revive the spirit of the lowly
> and to revive the heart of the contrite." [Isaiah 57:15]

Dame Julian, after perceiving all of creation as a fragile hazelnut that might "fall to naught for littleness" in God's hand, further realizes: "And I was answered in my understanding: It lasteth, and ever shall [last] for that God loveth it... In this Little Thing, I saw three properties. The first is that God made it, the second is that God loveth it, the third, that God keepeth it."[3]

Love Pitches a Tent Among Us

In the fullness of time, through his people the Jews, God revealed his immanent love among humanity in its ultimate expression:

> **The Word became flesh and made his dwelling among us.** *We have seen his glory, the glory of the one and only Son, who came from the Father, full of grace and truth.* [John 1:14]

Look again at that expression, *"made his dwelling."* Do you know what that phrase is, literally, in the Greek?

"Pitched his tent."

That's right. Once more, God *"pitched his tent among us."* As The Message version puts it, he *"moved into the neighborhood."*

This time, his immanence extended to the point of becoming one of us. He was born to a human mother, lived among a family, shared life with his friends, confronted enemies. He took on our weaknesses, faced our temptations, suffered as we do—even died. As Philippians 2:6-7 tells us, he *being in very nature God, did not consider equality with God something to be used to his own advantage; rather, he made himself nothing by* **taking the very nature of a servant, being made in human likeness.**

Heaven came down to earth, in a way no one could have imagined.

For in becoming one of us, Jesus also became our mediator, our high priest, so that we could be permanently reconciled to a holy God and forever see his smile. Jesus dwelt with us so we could dwell with his Father. Read Hebrews 8 and 9 to explore extensively how the Tent of Meeting in Exodus was just *"a copy and shadow of what is in heaven"* [8:5], and how Jesus acted as our high priest to make reconciliation possible: *But when Christ came as high priest of the good things that are now already here, he went through the greater and more perfect tabernacle that is not made with human hands, that is to say, is not a part of this creation* [9:11].

And how do we respond to the results of God's immanence through Jesus, this revelation of love and grace?

Hebrews 4:15-16 gives us a hint:

> For **we do not have a high priest who is unable to empathize with our weaknesses,** *but we have one who has been tempted in every way, just as we are—yet he did not sin.* **Let us then approach God's throne of grace with confidence,** *so that we may receive mercy and find grace to help us in our time of need.*

Reflections:

The Most High God pitched his tent among us.

One of the most important theological tensions we must grapple with is the equal reality of God's **transcendence** and **immanence**: that He is high, holy, and wholly other, but at the same time near to us.

- When you think of God, which of these aspects is the first to come to your mind? Which is the most natural way for you to think of God? Why do you think this is? (Something in your background, or personality, or your experience with God...)
- To what degree is the other aspect more difficult for you to contemplate? Is it a close second, or more removed than that? Is it almost hard to believe at all? Why do you think this is?
- What do you think is the danger of thinking of God only as transcendent and not as immanent? What would be lost in your relationship with God? What errors of thought, emotion, or action might result?
- What might be the danger of thinking of God only as loving and near, but not as high and holy (the infinite Everest we talked about in the last section)? What would be lost in your relationship with God? What errors of thought, emotion, or action might result?
- How might this picture of God moving down to the plain from Mt. Sinai to camp with his people begin to help you hold these two thoughts in tension? What are some other pictures that help you? (Dame Julian's hazelnut analogy helps me.)

The Incarnation is the ultimate expression of God's immanence. God has always been everywhere, including near us, but in becoming human he became our fellow camper in every way, experiencing all the same rigors and vulnerabilities of living in a tent as we do. (We will explore the implications of this more in the fifth section, "Willing to be Wounded.")

- Take time to read through Hebrews 8 & 9 and contemplate the parallels between God's revelation of himself as he comes close to his people in the Tabernacle, and his new revelation of himself in Jesus. What strikes you in these chapters?
- How would you like to respond to any new thoughts you have had about God's coming near to you, who has pitched his tent with yours? Write an expression of your thoughts to Him.

18 Dwelling in God's Protective Presence

*"Be strong and courageous. Do not be afraid or terrified because of them, for **the Lord your God goes with you;** he will never leave you nor forsake you."* [Deuteronomy 31: 6]

Protected from the Center

Tents are vulnerable to invaders. As we saw before, even knee-high hopping marsupials can invade their floppy sides. The only way that tent-dwellers have a hope of defense is to gather together for protection. Early American settlers, journeying in their own flimsy travel-dwellings, called this "circling the wagons." They gathered together in the middle of the circle, their covered wagons forming a barrier on the outside, the better to defend themselves in a threat.

But for the Israelites, their protection came from the Tent in the middle of the camp, rather than any barrier around them. The Lord commanded that three of each of the twelve tribes would camp together on the east, south, west, and north of the tabernacle [Num. 2]. All the Israelites had to do, if they doubted their protection, was to look at the pillar of cloud or fire as it rested over the Tent of Meeting, and remember how that same pillar had separated them from the pursuing Egyptians and kept them safe. They could recall the words Moses spoke to them on that day: *"Do not be afraid. Stand firm and you will see the deliverance the Lord will bring you today... The Lord will fight for you; you need only to be still"* [Ex. 14:13-14].

When the time comes for Moses to hand off the leadership of his people to Joshua, he reminds them of this Presence in the verses at the beginning of this chapter. Why should they be afraid of their enemies, he says, when the great God they saw on the mountain goes with them? When he promises never to leave or forsake them?

Then Moses blesses them, saying:

> The eternal God is your refuge,
>   and underneath are the everlasting arms.
> He will drive out your enemies before you...
> **So Israel will live in safety, Jacob will dwell secure**
>   in a land of grain and new wine, where the heavens drop dew.
> Blessed are you, Israel!
>   Who is like you, **a people saved by the Lord?**
> He is your shield and helper and your glorious sword.
> [Deuteronomy 33:27-29]

Even though they dwelt in puny tents, inadequate protection from the dangers of the world, they could feel as safe as if in a fortress—for he **was** their fortress. He was both the Almighty God who ruled the universe, and the One who loved and lived among them, guarding and keeping them. Moses saw clearly that this had always been so for the people of God, even before the Tabernacle had been fabricated to make it plain. As he states in Psalm 90:1-2:

> **Lord, you have been our dwelling place**
> *throughout all generations.*
> *Before the mountains were born*
> *or you brought forth the whole world,*
> *from everlasting to everlasting, you are God.*

Throughout All Generations

Later, Solomon built the Temple in Jerusalem to replace the Tabernacle. Its grand site on Mount Zion brought to mind God's awesome and terrible appearance on Sinai, while its architectural beauty and glory reminded those who saw it of the holiness and majesty of God. But its layout of grace, providing means of mercy to imperfect people, remained the same as in the Tabernacle. It was the very center of the nation, the place to which the people journeyed three times a year to rejoice in the festivals.

Solomon prays an eloquent prayer over the Temple, recognizing both God's transcendence and his presence with his people: *"**Will God really dwell on earth with humans?** The heavens, even the highest heavens, cannot contain you. How much less this temple I have built! Yet, Lord my God, give attention to your servant's prayer and his plea for mercy... **May your eyes be open toward this temple day and night, this place of which you said you would put your Name there...** Hear the supplications of your servant and of your people Israel when they pray toward this place. **Hear from heaven, your dwelling place; and when you hear, forgive"** [2 Chronicles 6:18-21].*

In this amazing prayer (well worth studying), he goes on to specify many situations in which God's anxious people would petition him here for his protection, his provision, and his mercy, and to ask for his hearing ear and gracious response:

- When people are wronged and in need of justice
- When, because of sin, Israel is defeated by enemies
- When God withholds rain because the people are faithless
- When plague or famine, or any other disaster, comes

- When foreigners recognize God and petition him
- When the people must contend against their enemies
- When they have sinned (here he adds, *"for there is no one who does not sin"*) and are in need of forgiveness

The Psalms show us many examples of such prayers. One such is the short Psalm 4, which starts with the distraught cry: *Answer me when I call to you, my righteous God. Give me relief from my distress; have mercy on me and hear my prayer.* It continues with a call to repentance and faithfulness, and the admonition: *Know that the Lord has set apart his faithful servant for himself; the Lord hears when I call to him.* Finally, it ends with this amazing verse—only eight verses after the first call for help:

> *In peace I will lie down and sleep,*
> *for you alone, Lord,*
> *make me dwell in safety.*

As much as the faithful people of God loved the Temple as the place where God's presence was manifest in their midst, they knew he was not bound by it, as heathen idols were. They could pray from where they were, and know that God in heaven would hear them. His presence at the center meant that he dwelt with them wherever they were, protecting and providing for them in the farthest-flung town or farm of the kingdom. And even when the people as a whole were wandering off in search of other gods, one faithful person could be sure that the one true God, who would *never leave or forsake* the man or woman who cried to him, would hear his prayers.

Such was the case with the prophet Elisha, living in the idolatrous northern kingdom of Israel after it broke off from Judah [see 2 Kings 6]. The Syrian king, enraged because Elisha kept informing the king of Israel how to avoid his ambushes, sent an army to capture the prophet in the city of Dothan. When Elisha and his servant came out in the morning and saw all the horses and chariots surrounding the city, the servant became more than a little anxious. But Elisha answered, *"Don't be afraid. Those who are with us are more than those who are with them."* Then he prayed that God would open the eyes of his servant to see. And when the servant looked, he saw the hills all around filled with a multitude of horses and chariots of fire! (Guess who prevailed?)

Never underestimate the armies of God that encircle his faithful follower. Take heart from Psalm 91:9-11, which tells us: *If you say,*

"The Lord is my refuge," and **you make the Most High your dwelling**, *no harm will overtake you, no disaster will come near your tent. For he will command his angels concerning you to guard you in all your ways...*

New Testament Temples

With the Temple as the nation's center for faith and worship, you can imagine how shocking it was for the Jews when Jesus said, *"Destroy this temple, and I will raise it again in three days."* They replied, *"It has taken forty-six years to build this temple, and you are going to raise it in three days?"* Then John tells us: *But the temple he had spoken of was his body* [John 2:19-21]. He could say this because, as Paul tells us in Colossians 1:19-20: *God was pleased to have* **all his fullness dwell in him,** *and through him* **to reconcile to himself all things,** *whether things on earth or things in heaven, by making peace through his blood, shed on the cross.* Jesus combined both the presence and the purpose of the temple in himself as he *"pitched his tent"* among us, and became one of us.[4]

But this body of Jesus, raised in power after his death, is not **only** his perfect incarnate resurrection body. His Body is also the Church, founded by him through his glorious resurrection power. He is building this Body to be a new Temple of God, to show his glory to the nations:

> *You are no longer foreigners and strangers, but fellow citizens with God's people and also members of his household, built on the foundation of the apostles and prophets, with Christ Jesus himself as the chief cornerstone.* **In him the whole building is joined together and rises to become a holy temple in the Lord.** *And in him you too are being* **built together to become a dwelling in which God lives by his Spirit** [Eph. 2:19-22].

The old Temple, where foreigners and felons could be heard and answered by God, is replaced by a spiritual building, made up of these same unworthy people. They are transformed into *living stones* who also form a *holy priesthood,* able to approach God and lead others into his presence [2 Peter 2:5]. In this Temple, as in the Temple of old, we should find mercy and grace from God mediated through each other as we act as priests to one another. Here are just a few of the ways we experience God's grace and glory as *God's Spirit dwells in our midst,* in the center of our camp [1 Corinthians 3:16]:

- *Therefore confess your sins to each other and pray for each other so that you may be healed. The prayer of a righteous person is powerful and effective.* [James 5:16]
- *Let the message of Christ **dwell among you richly** as you teach and admonish one another with all wisdom through psalms, hymns, and songs from the Spirit, singing to God with gratitude in your hearts.* [Colossians 3:16]

There is a great deal of protection and provision that comes from being part of this Temple, when its *living stones* are encouraging one another, caring for each other's needs, lifting one another up. And God promises too that this Temple is under his protection: *If anyone destroys God's temple, God will destroy that person; for God's temple is sacred, and **you together are that temple*** [1 Corinthians 3:17].

Not only are we God's temple together as Christ's body, but each of us individually has become a temple in which God dwells: *Do you not know that **your bodies are temples of the Holy Spirit, who is in you,** whom you have received from God?* [1 Corinthians 6:19]

This is beyond incredible; it is mind-blowing! God dwells with us: not just among, but within us, in the center of our beings. And this is why, in the first section, we talked about **this treasure in jars of clay,** showing that **this all-surpassing power is from God and not from us.** (Like the Genie's Lamp in *Aladdin*: "Phenomenal Cosmic Power! Itty bitty living space!")

If the living God dwells within us, we can say with the apostles:

*We are hard pressed on every side, but not crushed; perplexed, but not in despair; persecuted, but not abandoned; struck down, but not destroyed. We always carry around in our body the death of Jesus, so that **the life of Jesus may also be revealed in our body**... Therefore we do not lose heart. Though outwardly we are wasting away, yet inwardly we are being renewed day by day. For our light and momentary troubles are achieving for us an eternal glory that far outweighs them all."* [2 Corinthians 4:7-10, 16-17]

We are not alone. We may look undefended, but the Presence dwelling at our very center, between us and within us, is also our protection. And as he builds his Temple in us, his glory can shine to the world through every window.

Reflections:

Our protection is not from walls without, but from Who dwells within.

Jesus came as the New Temple in his Incarnation, declaring: God is in charge, and he has come to live with us! As he came, he established two other New Testament Temples by which God not only lives with us, but among us and within us: **the Body of Jesus Christ, his Church,** and the **individual bodies of believers indwelt by the Spirit.**

- How does this transform your view of the sacredness of both the Church Body and your own body? (Both are things we can easily take for granted and disdain.)
- How does it increase your sense of security even in the midst of danger and suffering, especially in light of the Scripture discussed in the last section of the chapter? Which passage struck you most and why?

Because God dwells in the midst of us, **he hears every prayer and petition we bring to him in our distress and danger,** and he promises to answer. **Pick one** of the following scriptural outlines to pray through the difficult and dangerous situations in your own life, and those of people around you:

- Use **Psalm 4** as a template to pray through **one specific difficulty** that you, or someone you want to intercede for, are facing. Go slowly, and allow the words of the psalm to search your heart and transform it. Take your time with each verse until you are able to truly act on the last verse: *In peace I will lie down and sleep...*
- Use Solomon's prayer in **2 Chronicles 6** to pray through **various situations** in your life and in the world around you. Perhaps, for instance, you will think about "defeat and drought" in your own life in a spiritual way, or perhaps you will pray for literal instances of defeat or drought in a particular situation God has brought to your attention. Be open to confessing not only your own sin, but also that of the groups you belong to. Use Solomon's categories to intercede for yourself and others in a deeper way than you usually do, knowing that his *eyes are open and ears attentive to the prayers offered* [v.40].

19 A Tent on a Rock

> One thing I ask from the Lord,
>   this only do I seek:
> that I may dwell in the house of the Lord
>   all the days of my life,
> to gaze on the beauty of the Lord
>   and to seek him in his temple.
> For in the day of trouble
>   he will keep me safe in his dwelling;
> **he will hide me in the shelter of his sacred tent**
>   **and set me high upon a rock.** [Psalm 27:4-5]
> **Read all of Psalm 27.**

Have you ever felt attacked? Like people were slamming you behind your back, or perhaps even to your face? Like they would oppose your plans and suggestions, simply because you made them? Like all you said or did was twisted and re-interpreted in an evil way?

Have you ever felt rejected? Like you were the odd person out in every room you entered? Like nothing you ever did or said could make a particular person or group accept or like you? Like you were abandoned, left by the wayside, uncared for and forgotten?

Then you and the psalmist David have something in common.

Self-Talk in Strife-filled Situations

Psalm 27 doesn't tell us the exact situation that David was facing—but it gives us a lot of hints. He talks about *the wicked* and *my foes;* he refers to *the enemies that surround me.* He mentions *false witnesses... spouting malicious accusations.* He uses a Hebrew metaphor of these people *advancing against me to devour me*—a graphically cannibalistic depiction of slandering someone.

What do **you** say to yourself in these situations? I can tell you what my tendencies are. Fear rises. I immediately feel abandoned, and tell myself I am all alone. I defend myself (at least in my own mind) against the criticisms of my accusers, recounting all the ways I have been right and all the good things I have done, and why this slander is unjust. (But at the same time, I take it to heart, listening to the little voice that whispers, "Maybe you are no good, after all...") I worry about the impact that the *malicious accusations* will have on my friends—maybe they will believe the lies and reject me as well. Or maybe they, too, already see me this way, and are saying the same things behind my back. I am dejected, and discouraged, and defensive, and above all—alone.

I need to take a tip from David's self-talk in this Psalm.

The whole tenor of the psalm is the opposite of fear; rather it shows assurance, confidence. Notice that almost the entire psalm is written in a future tense: *I will... I shall... he will...* He is telling himself that God is worthy of his trust, that God is his Defender and Deliverer. Even in the thick of the situation, David looks forward to God's deliverance, and assures himself that it **will** come:

> *I remain confident of this:*
> *I will see the goodness of the Lord in the land of the living.*
> *Wait for the Lord;*
> *be strong and take heart, and wait for the Lord.* [v.13-14]

He does not justify himself, or defend himself. His self-talk is not mostly about himself, or even the situation, but about God. And since his self-talk is about God, it quickly turns **towards** God in prayer: *Hear my voice when I call, Lord; be merciful to me and answer me* [v. 7].

But is this just "positive thinking," a visualization technique that makes it easier to deal with the difficulties he faces?

No. Because the foundation for this self-talk is Rock-solid.

The Stronghold of My Life

The Psalm opens this way:

> *The Lord is my light and my salvation—whom shall I fear?*
> *The Lord is the stronghold of my life—of whom shall I be afraid?*

The foundation of David's confidence—his reason not to fear in a dangerous and depressing situation—is that he is sure of who God is:

- **My light:** God is the Sovereign Guide, giving clarity, order and understanding even in the chaos of conflict. As we saw in Proverbs, his purposes will prevail both in the big scheme of things, and as he orders my individual steps. As David prays: *Teach me your way, Lord; lead me in a straight path...* [v.11]
- **My salvation:** God is the One who alone can redeem any and all situations; he is my source of rescue. As David remembers in prayer: *You have been my helper* [v.9].
- **The stronghold of my life:** God is my Rock, my protection, and my fortress. If I am defended by his walls, no one can truly harm me. As David tells himself: *Though an army besiege me, my heart will not fear...* [v. 3].

These are all very strong metaphors, rooted in Gods omnipotence and transcendence. If God is in charge, if he is my defense, David asks—*of whom shall I be afraid?* No wonder he pronounces himself confident, even in his precarious situation. David very deliberately ropes himself into the Rock that is the Eternal God, banishing fear.

But David recognizes the immanence of God as well, the individual care God has for him. He looks for God in a personal way, for his smiling face, in the way encouraged by the Priestly Blessing each time he sacrificed at the Tabernacle:

> My heart says of you, "Seek his face!"
>   Your face, Lord, I will seek.
> Do not hide your face from me...
> Do not reject me or forsake me, God my Savior. [v. 8-9]

Apparently he receives reassurance that God will accept him, for in the very next verse he makes one of the most powerful assertions of God's personal care and affirmation one can find in the whole of Scripture: *Though my father and mother forsake me, the Lord will receive me* [v.10]. For those of us whose father and mother would be the last people to reject us, we can take heart that God's constant, unconditional love goes infinitely further. And for those of us who have experienced rejection and abandonment from our parents, this verse can be healing balm to a wounded soul.

The One Thing: Dwelling in God's House

I don't know about you, but when I am facing opposition and rejection, and I **do** remember to pray, my prayers are usually for the situation to end. I ask that God would convict my persecutors, and show them how wrong they are. I ask him to arrest the situation, and minimize its fallout. But that is not what David asks here.

Rather, he makes the remarkable request you can see in the verses quoted at the beginning of the chapter: that he would be able to dwell with God. He does not simply want to know God is among his people; he wants, personally, to live in his house, with him. This *one thing* David asks of God is far deeper than simply being removed from trouble and kept safe; it is a request to draw close to him, for intimacy with him. And yet at the same time, it is an admission that close to God is the only safe place to be. In this lovely passage, David paints five pictures of dwelling with God:

1. The house of the Lord. The Hebrew word "house" here is *beth,* often used with a descriptor, as in *Beth-El,* "house of God." In this way it is similar to the French word *chez,* meaning the home of someone; it is redolent of family. Here David longs to be part of God's household, wishing that God himself would be his home. He identifies himself with God's family, and with the sense of love, comfort and security that come with being a part of that family—even if his own mother and father would reject him. To *dwell in the house of the Lord all the days of my life* means that he is always **accepted.**

2. His temple. *Heykal,* the Hebrew word for "temple," also means "palace," and comes from a root word meaning "spacious." You might remember that at the time of David the Temple had not yet been built. In fact, David felt uncomfortable about the situation, saying, *"Here I am, living in a house of cedar, while the ark of the covenant of the Lord is under a tent"* [1 Chronicles 17:1]. Though God did not allow him to build this temple himself, David knew that as Sovereign of the universe, God deserved a palace far more than he himself did. Here he imagines a spacious place where one could go to *gaze on the beauty of the Lord,* to contemplate his majesty, power, riches and might, to worship him as Ruler over all. And here, in the palace, as the vassal of the almighty King, he always **knows who is in control.**

3. His dwelling. This word, *sok,* meaning a "hut" or "thicket," probably refers primarily to the hiding place of a wild animal, where it would remain safe as the hunter passed it by. It is a word also related to the *sukkah,* the booths that the Israelites would dwell in once a year during the Festival of Sukkot. It is this flimsy dwelling—not the palace—in which he states that God *will keep me safe.* Perhaps he is remembering harvest festivals, gazing up at the woven roof of his *sukkah* and thinking how God had protected and provided for his people in the desert. Here, in God's *sukkah,* he knew himself to always be **secure.**

4. His tent. This is the Hebrew word, *ohel,* simply meaning a "tent." (The descriptor "sacred" is an interpretation not in the Hebrew.) Here David talks about being *hidden in the shelter* (or *secret*) of this tent. In that time, a host that took someone into his tent was obligated to give him sanctuary against his enemies; so that even though the tent was a flimsy structure, it became a protection against attack, as the inhabitants would also fight for him.[5] Being hidden in God's tent means he is always **protected.**

5. A rock. The Hebrew word, *tsuwr,* or "rock," indicates a fortified place high above danger where enemies could not come. David would have had experience with this, hiding out in the hill country on high ground that gave him the advantage against his enemy. Here, however, he does not have to fight to gain this high ground and hold it. God simply sets him on the rock, on high, out of reach. As David, like Moses, many times refers to God as "The Rock," we must suspect this stronghold is identified with God himself. Being set up on the high Rock by God means he is always **rescued.**

A Tent on a Rock

A tent on a Rock: it is **a picture of our strength even in vulnerability.** As we live in God's presence, without self-defense, we can trust his sovereign power and his loving protection to keep our eternal selves safe, no matter what.

David's confidence comes from his knowledge of God's smiling face, his assurance that he will be heard and answered. He is sure God will accept him, not reject or forsake him, or turn away from him in anger. He can rely on God to teach him his way, and not to turn him over to his enemies' desires. He had taken to heart the blessing spoken each time the sacrifice was made, so that he could draw near to God: *The Lord turn his face toward you, and give you peace.* This *shalom* he could take even into this situation, with trust.

> Then my head will be exalted
>   above the enemies who surround me;
> at his sacred tent I will sacrifice with shouts of joy;
>   I will sing and make music to the Lord. [v.6]

How much more should we preach to ourselves with confidence in the face of opposition, we who have the sacrifice of Jesus and all the riches of his righteousness? How much more should we sing and make music, who have the opportunity not just to dwell **with** God, but to have him dwell **within** us?

> I pray that out of his glorious riches he may strengthen you with power through his Spirit in your inner being, so **that Christ may dwell in your hearts through faith.** [Ephesians 3:16-17]

As you face opposition from sinful men—attack and rejection—do not be afraid. What do you have to fear if you live by faith in God's presence? One man or woman plus God is a match for any army. Pitch your tent on the Rock.

Reflections:

When you pitch your tent on the Rock, you need never fear.

Later in section 5 ("Willing to be Wounded"), we will discuss the vulnerabilities we face as God calls us to relationship with other people. For now, let us ponder God's word as it calls us to renounce our fear of other people:

❖ *Fear of man will prove to be a snare,*
   but whoever trusts in the Lord is kept safe. [Proverbs 29:25]
❖ *Let those who fear the Lord say: "His love endures forever."*
   When hard pressed, I cried to the Lord;
      he brought me into a spacious place.
   The Lord is with me; I will not be afraid.
      What can mere mortals do to me?
   The Lord is with me; he is my helper.
      I look in triumph on my enemies.
   It is better to take refuge in the Lord than to trust in humans.
   [Psalm 118:4-8]
❖ *Who is going to harm you if you are eager to do good? But even if*
   you should suffer for what is right, you are blessed. "Do not fear
   their threats; do not be frightened." [I Peter 3:13-14]
❖ You might also want to look up Psalm 3:3-6 and Isaiah 51:7-8.
   • **What situation(s) are you experiencing right now** that might
     cause you to be fearful of other people's attitudes toward
     you and treatment of you?
   • **Which of these verses speaks most to you** in this situation, as
     you consider the Rock on which you dwell? (Remember also
     the text from Psalm 27 in this chapter.)

In Psalm 27, David describes **five "dwelling-places"** where he pictures himself living in the security of God's presence.
   • Which of these pictures of dwelling with God are most
     meaningful to you at this time? Why?
   • Think about the last combination of pictures: **a tent on a**
     Rock. How does this describe both the vulnerability and
     security that we experience as dwellers with God?

Look back over the whole Psalm. Which future faith statement of David's would you like most to take to heart today?

20 The Journey Home

*By faith [Abraham] made his home in the promised land like a stranger in a foreign country; he lived in tents, as did Isaac and Jacob, who were heirs with him of the same promise. For **he was looking forward to the city with foundations**, whose architect and builder is God.* [Hebrews 11:9-10]

In 2015, Carlton and I took an eight-month sabbatical from our ministry in Brussels. Our suitcases circled a lot of airport baggage claims, and we calculated at the end that we had slept in 39 different beds in seven countries since moving out of our apartment the previous December. Although it was a transformational time of learning and growing, of meeting new people and building important relationships, I found myself in that final month looking forward to settling down in the new apartment we had arranged to rent, in the difficult neighborhood in Brussels to which we are called.

I thought: *It will be nice to be home.*

Like a Stranger in a Foreign Country

Abraham must have felt a little like this. After all, he was a city dweller, from Ur, one of the first urban centers in the world. He was used to having the stability and safety of a house built of permanent materials, known neighbors, secure city walls with high gates, goods brought in for sale and trade, a proud metropolitan identity. But God called him to leave all this to live the life of a nomad, to *"Go from your country, your people and your father's household to the land I will show you"* [Gen. 12:1]. So Abraham went, a pioneer in the land of promise.

But I suspect he expected that, eventually, God would show him where to settle down. A place to put down roots, to build a city of his own. Gradually, he must have realized that even though he had come to the land of promise, claiming a secure home there lay far in the future. He had to haggle and pay an inflated price just to have a plot of earth to bury his beloved wife, where he could be laid to rest beside her one day. As the text at the top of the page says, *he made his home in the promised land like a stranger in a foreign country.*

And as we saw earlier, Abraham's descendants, the *heirs of the promise,* continued the journey: wandering in the promised land, migrating to Egypt, wandering back again. And God continued to remind them of their nomad status even when they seemed settled and safe, saying, *"The land is mine and you reside in my land as* foreigners and strangers" [Leviticus 25:23]. The Psalmist admits this as he says, "I dwell with you as a foreigner, a stranger, as all my ancestors were" [Psalm 39:12]. Later, when the people of God went into exile, they struggled with a very real sense of being strangers sent from home: How can we sing the songs of the Lord while in a foreign land? [Psalm 137:4]

For Jesus and the apostles, the itinerant life without any home for the sake of the Gospel was a physical as well as a spiritual reality:

- Then a teacher of the law came to him and said, "Teacher, I will follow you wherever you go," Jesus replied, "Foxes have dens and birds have nests, but **the Son of Man has no place to lay his head.**" [Matthew 8:19-20]
- For it seems to me that God has put us apostles on display... To this very hour we go hungry and thirsty, we are in rags, we are brutally treated, **we are homeless.** [1 Corinthians 4:9,11]

In truth, we are all citizens of a foreign country, a kingdom that Jesus told Pilate was not of this world [John 18:36]. We are not meant to "fit in" here. We are meant to live our lives like the faith-filled saints cited in Hebrews 11, of whom the writer tells us: All these people were still living by faith when they died. They did not receive the things promised; they only saw them and welcomed them from a distance, admitting that **they were foreigners and strangers on earth** [v.13]. Even those of us from stable homes, who have lived in one house or one town all our lives, are meant to perceive ourselves as campers on a journey, only stopping here for a time, traveling light because we don't know when we will have to pull up stakes and move on.

So why, if the journey is our normal state as people of faith, does it go against the grain? Why is the desire for home so deep in our souls?

Looking Forward to Getting Home

We all long for home—a settled place, a place where we belong. This might be a house, a neighborhood, a city, a country. Various writers have tried to capture this longing:

- "There is nothing like staying at home for real comfort." (Jane Austen)
- "Home is the nicest word there is." (Laura Ingalls Wilder)
- "The ache for home lives in all of us, the safe place where we can go as we are and not be questioned." (Maya Angelou)

All of these quotes tend to look back to home as a place where we are from, where our identity is rooted. But we must turn this on its head: **home is not the place we are from, but the place we are going.** That is why even those of us who have the best experience of home still find ourselves vaguely wishing for more. It is precisely this future home that is the goal of our journey, and the one for which we are truly homesick.

Jesus reveals this to his confused and grieving disciples: **My Father's house has many rooms**; *if that were not so, would I have told you that I am going there to prepare a place for you? And if I go and prepare a place for you,* **I will come back and take you to be with me that you also may be where I am** [John 14:2-3].

In the old King James Version of the Bible, the word "rooms" was translated as *"mansions."* Sounds like they are pretty big and fancy rooms! In fact, the whole scale of the home our Father is preparing for us is more vast and beautiful than we might imagine. Here is John's vision of it in Revelation 21:

> Then I saw a new heaven and a new earth, for the first heaven and the first earth had passed away... **I saw the Holy City,** the new Jerusalem, coming down out of heaven from God... It shone with the glory of God, and its brilliance was like that of a very precious jewel, like a jasper, clear as crystal. [v.1-2,11]

One peculiarity of John's picture of this new City is that it is a giant cube, stretching 1400 miles (2200 km) in its length, height and depth. This is about 1/6 of Earth's diameter, but unlike Earth, it is the volume rather than the surface of this cube that is inhabited. *Many rooms, indeed!* In this symbolic representation, there is abundant room for all of God's people to live together in this perfect cube, in perfect harmony.

All of us would recognize that in the end, home has much less to do with the actual building we inhabit than who is there with us. Our parents and siblings. Our spouse. Our kids, our grandkids. Best friends. Familiar neighbors. When we look back with nostalgia on the homes of our childhood, no favorite climbing tree or swimming pool or cozy bedroom can compare to being warmed by the affections of those around us. It is this sense of warmth that usually imparts to physical manifestations of home their power and their comfort. As C.S. Lewis reminds us, "Affection is responsible for nine-tenths of whatever solid and durable happiness there is in our natural lives."[6]

The love we have received from our families, friends, and neighbors is only a dim shadow of the love that waits for us in the home that Jesus prepares for those who love and follow him on their journey. And reunion with dearly loved companions from our earthly journey is not even the half of it. As Jesus tells his disciples, *"My Father will love them, and **we will come to them and make our home with them**"* [John 14:23].

Revelation 21:3 restates that God is making his home with us: *And I heard a loud voice from the throne saying, "Look! **God's dwelling place is now among the people,** and he will **dwell with them**. They will be his people, and God himself will be with them and be their God."*

Can you guess the literal meaning of the Greek phrase here translated *"dwell with them"*?

*"He will **pitch his tent** with them."*

This time, the Tent of Meeting, rather than having rooms only accessible to priests at special times, will have rooms for all the Father's children. Such is the City of God that we anticipate! This is the city that Abraham looked forward to, *the city with foundations, whose architect and builder is God.* It is also the city the faithful of Hebrews 11 anticipated while they lived as *foreigners and strangers on earth:*

> *If they had been thinking of the country they had left, they would have had opportunity to return. Instead, **they were longing for a better country**—a heavenly one. Therefore God is not ashamed to be called their God, for he has **prepared a city for them**.* [v. 15-16]

Making Home Like a Stranger

So what do we do in the meantime? How do we live our lives as *foreigners and strangers* here on earth? Do we sell all our possessions and camp on a mountaintop to wait for God's city to come down? If we are *not of this world*, do we therefore separate ourselves from it and not engage with it?

I think a key is found in the fact that Abraham **made his home** *like a stranger in a foreign country*. He may have lived in a tent, but he made that tent a prophetic reflection of the home that he anticipated in the future. He knew it would not be the perfect city for which his heart longed, but in the meantime, he filled it with things that would foreshadow that city: welcome and hospitality, grace and generosity, prayer and protection, love and family, gratitude and worship.

This is also how the Israelites in exile, mourning their lost homes, were encouraged to engage with the foreign city in which they found themselves: **"Build houses and settle down**; *plant gardens and eat what they produce. Marry and have sons and daughters... Also, seek the peace and prosperity of the city to which I have carried you into exile. Pray to the Lord for it, because if it prospers, you too will prosper"* [Jer. 29:5-7].

Charles Henry Parkhurst, a 19th century clergyman, wisely said:

"Home interprets heaven. Home is heaven for beginners."

The trick is not to start believing that the tents we have pitched here are our ultimate homes. Perhaps the most famous quote on home is from the Roman historian Pliny: "Home is where the heart is." And maybe that is why Jesus tells us: *Store up for yourselves treasures in heaven... For where your treasure is, there your heart will be also* [Matthew 6:20-21]. As we have seen, we can be great stockpilers of earthly stuff, intended to enhance our own security as well as our home's beauty and value. But some of the greatest treasures that we can store up are the eternal relationships that we make with our future roommates in our Father's home.

Jesus promises that if we live lightly, traveling as tent-dwellers, we will receive treasures that we can store up or use for future gain even in this life: **"No one who has left home** or brothers or sisters or mother or father or children or fields for me and the gospel **will fail to receive a hundred times as much in this present age: homes,** brothers, sisters, mothers, children and fields—along with persecutions—**and in the age to come eternal life"** [Mark 10:29-30].

In the next section, we will explore some practical ways we can make our earthly homes prophetic reflections of the home we long for, a "heaven for beginners." We can do this because we have found our fortress in our true dwelling, the God who lives among us, and inside us, and who will *pitch his tent* directly with us one day.

In the meantime, if we have happy memories of a childhood home, let us regard them with gratitude as dim pictures of what we are looking forward to. If our past recollections are painful, let us rejoice that our true home is yet to come. And when we feel displaced, or foreign, or weary of travel, or just plain homesick, let us remember Hebrews 13:14:

For here we do not have an enduring city, but we are looking for the city that is to come.

Reflections:

Home is not where we are from, but where we are going.

Paul and Peter both refer to our earthly bodies as "tents." They contrast them both with the *eternal kingdom* to come, and with the incorruptible bodies given us when Jesus makes all things new:

❖ *Therefore, my brothers and sisters... you will receive **a rich welcome into the eternal kingdom** of our Lord and Savior Jesus Christ... I think it is right to refresh your memory as long as I live in **the tent of this body,** because I know that I will soon put it aside...* [2 Peter 1:10-14]

❖ *For we know that if the **earthly tent we live in** is destroyed, we have a building from God, **an eternal house in heaven,** not built by human hands. Meanwhile we groan, longing to be clothed instead with our heavenly dwelling... For while we are in this tent, we groan... to be clothed instead with our heavenly dwelling, so that what is mortal may be swallowed up by life.* [2 Corinthians 5:1-4]

- How do these passages encourage you to regard not only your earthly home, but also your present (aging and unreliable) body, as you look forward to a permanent home?
- How does it encourage you to know this is not "all there is"? What are some things in your eternal home that you find yourself homesick for?
- How does this help you put your treasure in the right place?

Our earthly homes should be "heaven for beginners."

As we saw in Abraham's example, just because we are looking forward to a heavenly home does not mean that we should not *make our homes* here—even if it is *like a stranger.*

- What is your response to Parkhurst's idea of home interpreting heaven—as "heaven for beginners"?
- Here are some things I mentioned Abraham filling his home with: welcome and hospitality, grace and generosity, prayer and protection, love and family, gratitude and worship.
  - How do these reflect heaven to you?
  - Which are reflected in your home already? How?
  - Which ones would you like to see growing in your home?

traveling light

(or, tranquil tents)

21 Camp in Community

"Build houses and settle down; plant gardens and eat what they produce. Marry and have sons and daughters... Also, **seek the peace and prosperity of the city to which I have carried you into exile.** *Pray to the Lord for it, because if it prospers, you too will prosper."* [Jeremiah 29:5-7]

I felt isolated, alienated from the place where I lived.

Several chapters ago, I described to you our castle-like house in the middle of a difficult immigrant neighborhood, and my sense of truly being a foreigner there. Why, I spoke French better than a lot of my neighbors did! Hadn't we come to reach out to young Europeans in Brussels, the smart French or Finnish functionaries who worked in and around the EU institutions? Why on earth did God send us to the neighborhood of Schaerbeek, where most of the people in the surrounding streets came from one town in rural Turkey?

Camping in Christian Community

We knew we had been sent to camp in community with others. That was why we started an international church focusing on the global nomads that fill Brussels. One of the advantages of being uprooted from your country and your culture: you feel the need to truly tent together with those of like faith. Perhaps back at home, church attendance was a perfunctory, once-a-week ritual where you sat in a pew and faced the front with everyone else, leaving with hurried and shallow greetings to those around. Or maybe it was a chance to fill yourself up with some solid Bible teaching or exciting worship time—a chance to personally consume spiritual nourishment, but not to connect.

But for those who gather with us at The Well, who had literally *made their home like a stranger in a foreign country,* the truth has been brought home of Jesus' statement: *"Here are my mother and my brothers!"* [Mark 3:34]. Having left behind our own families, we find new family among *those who do God's will.* Throughout the New Testament, we hear the members of Jesus' body address one another as *brothers and sisters;* we read the apostles calling followers *my dear children.* We all know church is supposed to be this kind of family. But we received the grace in this place to experience it in a new and different way, as fellow sojourners in a foreign land.

Abraham, our father in faith, did not set out on his journey alone, like a hermit in the desert. Genesis 12:5 tells us: *He took his wife Sarai, his nephew Lot, all the possessions they had accumulated and the people they had acquired in Harran, and they set out for the land of Canaan, and they arrived there.* This was not just a small family group; we can see by the fact that among *the people* mentioned here were *318 trained [fighting] men born in his household* that Abraham led a large community indeed [Genesis 14:14]. Abraham as the patriarch naturally assumes care for the physical well-being of his encampment, as he searches for good grazing and digs wells for their sustenance. But he also assumes spiritual leadership, as when he extends circumcision, the sign of his covenant with God, to *every male in Abraham's household, including those born in his household or bought from a foreigner* [Genesis 17:27].

We see this same sense of solidarity, of care for spiritual growth and practical needs, among the newborn church of Acts 242-46: *They devoted themselves to the apostles' teaching and to fellowship, to the breaking of bread and to prayer... **All the believers were together** and had everything in common. They sold property and possessions to give to anyone who had need. Every day **they continued to meet together** in the temple courts. They broke bread in their homes and ate together with glad and sincere hearts...*

The "One Another" commands of the New Testament encourage members of the Body of Christ to continue camping together in just such a way. Here is just a very small sampling of the dozens of these:

- Be devoted to one another [Romans 12:10]
- Encourage one another [1 Thessalonians 5:11]
- Forgive one another [Ephesians 4:32]
- Be hospitable to one another [1 Peter 4:9]
- Serve one another [Galatians 5:13]

You can see that the kind of committed relationship pictured here is not a perfunctory "How was your week?" over a cup of coffee in the fellowship hall. Rather, it is a life of involvement that deeply cares for each other's spiritual and practical needs, sometimes resulting in friction and forgiveness.

What about you? Does your church involvement feel more like disconnected urban apartment dwellers passing in the hallway, or a caring caravan of community? And what could **you** do to draw together with fellow sojourners?

Planting Community Gardens

The phrase "circling the wagons" has come to have a pejorative connotation—that of defensiveness toward outsiders. Here is one definition: "to stop communicating with people not in your group; to avoid their ideas and beliefs."[1] We may have great connection and care with our fellow Christians, spending all of our time in Bible studies and fellowship groups and church softball leagues, but fearfully avoid the world outside our wagons. Indeed, some Christians would firmly believe that this is what we are **meant** to do.

But Abraham, camping among the pagans of Canaan, interacts with them. In Genesis 21 we see Abimelek, a Philistine king, approaching him with recognition that *"God is with you in everything you do"* [v. 22]. They make a treaty of peace together, naming the place "Beersheba" or "well of the oath." Then: *Abraham planted a tamarisk tree in Beersheba, and there he called on the name of the Lord, the Eternal God. And Abraham stayed in the land of the Philistines for a long time* [v.33-34].

As postmodern people, the significance of this incident is likely to pass us by. But this is how Abraham honors Abimelek's request to show kindness to him and *"the country where you now reside as a foreigner"* [v. 23]. He plants a tree—a symbol of God's favor and grace—and prays in that place. Aramaic paraphrases of the Torah read into this action additional significance:

> And Abraham planted a garden in Beersheba, and put in it food for those who passed by. Now it happened, when they were eating and drinking, they would seek to give him the price of what they had eaten and drunk. And he would say to them: You are eating from the bounty of the One who said, and the world came into being... He taught them to give praise to the Lord of the universe. And he worshiped and prayed in the Name of the Word of the Lord, the God of the universe.[2]

This is the same kind of instruction that we see in the text quoted in the beginning of this chapter, in which the Lord says through Jeremiah to the Jews in exile: *"Build houses and settle down;* **plant gardens... Pray to the Lord for [the city],** *because if it prospers, you too will prosper."* [Jeremiah 29:5-7]

Walking around the streets of our own troubled neighborhood, my husband Carlton noticed that colorful tiled mosaics had replaced some of the Belgian blocks that pave our sidewalks. As he looked at these little spots of beauty made out of brokenness, the Spirit prompted him to pray for a community of beauty, justice and compassion in that place. Not long afterwards, a small group of people—some of whom were just discovering Jesus—began meeting weekly in our home to pray for our neighborhood. And the first thing to change was not the graffiti on the walls or the homelessness in the streets: it was our own hearts to truly see our neighbors around us. We began to see how we, too, could *plant gardens* in that place, for God's glory and our neighbors' good.

Early in our neighborhood adventure, we visited friends in Minneapolis who inspired us. The first thing we noticed when we drove up to the yard of their suburban house was a large-size chess set, right on the curb, with two benches on either side of it. Our hosts explained that, rather than privacy in a back yard, they wanted to have a place where neighbors could gather in their front yard—even if they weren't home. Once a month, they would host a dinner for all of the neighbors in their subdivision, where one of the guests presented to the rest an answer to the question "What is something you are passionate about?" All of the residents grew closer to each other, and the Jesus-following hosts naturally expressed their deepest passion as well. Building on this foundation, all the neighbors had worked together the previous summer to clear a space in our hosts' yard to plant a community garden, growing vegetables for the whole street as well as to share.

We read described in Revelation 22:2 a city garden in which *the tree of life, bearing twelve crops of fruit, yields its fruit every month,* where *the leaves of the tree are for the healing of the nations.* Abraham—and our friends—demonstrated in their temporary homes the City of God that we anticipate. Their homes were "heaven for beginners."

The One Who Showed Mercy

When the teacher of the law asked Jesus, *"Who is my neighbor?"* he likely hoped for an outline restricting whom he should consider part of his caravan. He certainly didn't expect the answer to include kindness to Samaritans. Even less would he have expected that Jesus would tell a story in which a Jew **receives** the kindness of his Samaritan neighbor! But when Jesus asks, *"Which of these... do you think was a neighbor to the [robbed] man?"* he is duty bound to say: *"The one who had mercy on him"* [Luke 10:36-37].

We find that one of the best ways to camp in community is to show kindness in practical ways to our neighbors. And best of all is when neighbors join hands to show mercy to the people around them who need it most. In our neighborhood, our small prayer group was first led to help one disabled lady who needed to move out of a bad rental situation. Later, some of our group started serving coffee, cake, and conversation to geriatric patients in the local hospital. Still others started bringing food to homeless guys at the train station and getting to know them. More kindnesses were initiated as we ran across people in our area who were, metaphorically or literally, lying in our path.

We did not go *en masse* to do these things, like a Christian commando team. Rather, different ones of us joined hands with other neighbors **outside** the group who, like the Good Samaritan, *took pity* on the needs of others. Some of these were believers in other churches. Others, not knowing our Creator, still cared for those made in his image. We believe that such as these may not be far from the kingdom of heaven. Perhaps Abraham might have termed them *righteous people,* for whom he pleaded with God in the doomed city of Sodom [Genesis 19].

Abraham could have felt smug about God's revelation of impending judgment on Sodom when he himself was under God's blessing. Instead, he boldly asks God for mercy for the city, if only fifty righteous people were found there. God says he will withhold judgment if those people are found.[3] Abraham continues to bargain with God till he agrees that he will suspend judgment for only ten people. He models for us God's later command to his people in exile: *Seek the peace and prosperity of the city... pray to the Lord for it.* Perhaps as we discover the *righteous people* around us and join hands with them, to pray and to serve, we too avert God's judgment that gives our cities over to their own selfish impulses.

One of the habits of self-protective people we have considered is to look the other way and ignore those outside, especially those we deem "wicked." We would rather "circle our wagons," criticizing and keeping separate from them. We would rather hide ourselves in our house-castles. We become alienated from the place where we are planted.

But when we begin to form community with those in the same campground, when we pray for its peace and prosperity, we may find that we begin to build a model on earth of the city we are looking for.

In this place, *there will be no more death or mourning or crying or pain, and he will wipe every tear from their eyes* [Revelation 21:4]. As we link arms with those around us to do this in a small way, we **make our home** *like a stranger in a foreign country*—a taste of our real home.

And we might even find in those glimpses that we begin—as I have—to feel connected, less alienated, more at home.

Reflections:

Making home like heaven means connecting in community.

How are you connecting to **Christian community,** the Body of Christ?

- Are you connected to one? If not, why not? If so, how committed is your connection (in standard measures like attendance and ministry involvement)?
- Do you have real relationships within your Christian community? How do you maintain these? Do you see each other outside regular church meetings? Eat together? Contact each other? Babysit for each other? Play together? Serve each other?
- What could you do to build stronger bonds with other Christians in your community—to practice for the eternal city to come?

Sometimes we fail to connect (or connect meaningfully) to any church because we see flaws wherever we go. If this is true for you, I would like to challenge you to change your perspective. Paul says: *Now you are the body of Christ, and each one of you is a part of it* [1 Corinthians 12:27]. We **are** already part of Christ's body, and to behave as though we were too good for any local expression of it is to amputate ourselves and insult Jesus himself. (We will consider this a little further in the next section, in the chapter "Faithful and True.")

How are you **being a neighbor** to those who live around you?

- One evaluative exercise we use is something called **"Tic-Tac-Go."**[4] Draw a large tic-tac-toe board on a piece of paper. Put your name in the center square. Now think about all the neighbors that surround you in nearest proximity and fill in squares.
  - Which of them do you know by name? What do each of them do for a living? What is something else interesting that you know about them—a hobby or interest?
- **Now come up with ideas for filling up the empty squares.**
  - How could you **get to know your neighbors better**? What would be the equivalent of a community dinner for you?
  - How could you **work/play together**? (A community garden?)
  - How could you **serve those in need together** where you are? (Local schools? The disabled/elderly? Single moms? Hospitals?)
  - How do you think being a neighbor **with** neighbors—showing mercy—could be a way to make a "heaven for beginners"?

22 Open the Tent Flaps

Do not forget to show hospitality to strangers, for by so doing some people have shown hospitality to angels without knowing it. [Hebrews 13:2]

You never knew whom you would be sitting next to at the dinner table, in the house I grew up in. It might be an erudite professor, holding the chair of economics at a prominent university. It might be a Vietnamese refugee struggling to speak English. It might be an elderly couple who had been planning to go to KFC for Christmas dinner, not knowing it was closed. It might even be a paroled convict, looking for help to get back home.

My parents took the above verse rather seriously. And it wasn't just limited to dinner. In Australia, Aboriginal friends from the country often stayed with us when they were in town. We hosted US Navy guys who were spending a few days in port, a seminary student doing an internship, an unwed mother who had been kicked out by her parents, a newly-arrived missionary couple who needed a place to stay. I don't know if any of them were angels, but just in case...

Waiting to Welcome the Strangers

Abraham, of course, is the prototype of hospitality to whom the text refers. Genesis 18 opens with him sitting in the doorway of his tent in the heat of the day when he sees travelers approaching. There are many reasons he should not have gone out of his way to welcome them. After all, it was very hot. And he was around a hundred years old—what better excuse to take an afternoon nap? It is also very likely that he was still recovering from his circumcision, reported in the previous chapter. But yet, when he sees strangers coming from far off, he actually gets up and **runs** to meet them and invite them in.

There is no reason that Abraham would have identified his three visitors as the angels they turned out to be. As far as he knew, they were just strangers—likely idol-worshipers, like the rest of his neighbors. And yet he treats them with the utmost of honor and generosity: washing their feet, offering them cool yogurt to drink in the heat, having a tender young animal roasted and serving it to them himself. If all this was without knowing anything about who they were, we can assume this was how he treated **any** strangers who would cross his path. In fact, the Talmud comments that the reason he sat in the doorway instead of the cool of his tent was that he was actively looking for people to welcome.

In this way, we can see how Abraham, *making his home like a stranger,* uses that home to interpret heaven, his real home, to other strangers. For this is exactly how God behaves in his own home:

> A father to the fatherless, a defender of widows,
> **is God in his holy dwelling.** [Psalm 68:5]

We see this hospitality of God extended further in the teaching of Jesus, in the parables he tells about the Great Banquet. In the Matthew 22 version, the Master tells his servants, *"Go to the street corners and **invite to the banquet anyone you find."** And they gathered all the people they could find, the bad as well as the good...* [v.9-10]. In Luke 14, the Master is even more specific, instructing his servants to *"bring in the poor, the crippled, the blind and the lame... **compel them to come in, so that my house will be full"*** [v.21,23]. Not only is God pictured as inviting strangers into his house—he is painted as **filling** his house with the kind of strangers that would not normally be invited anywhere.

Guess what? Those strangers? The poor, blind cripples? That's us.

He not only welcomes us—he turns us from strangers to friends, as he makes us members of his household, citizens of his kingdom.

> *Remember that at that time you were separate from Christ, **excluded from citizenship** in Israel and **foreigners to the covenants** of the promise, without hope and without God in the world. But now in Christ Jesus, **you who once were far away have been brought near** by the blood of Christ... Consequently, you are **no longer foreigners and strangers, but fellow citizens** with God's people and also **members of his household...*** [Eph. 2:12-13,19].

Since we have been invited as strangers, as beggars even, into God's house, he asks us to show that hospitality to others. We can spiritualize this to a generalized "love" of mankind that speaks pious words and does nothing practical. Or we can actually exchange the drawbridge for tent flaps and invite people into our physical homes.

You Invited Me In

So, then, what are the practical implications of following Jesus' instructions in Luke 14:12-14? *"When you give a luncheon or dinner, do not invite your friends, your brothers or sisters, your relatives, or your rich neighbors; if you do, they may invite you back and so you will be* *repaid. But **when you give a banquet, invite the poor, the crippled, the lame, the blind, and you will be blessed.** Although they cannot repay you, you will be repaid at the resurrection of the righteous."*

We would like to spiritualize this to say: "Don't just do something so you will profit from it." But as Bonhoeffer warns us, "The paradoxical [metaphorical] understanding of the commandments has its Christian justification, but it must never lead to the abandoning of the single-minded [literal] understanding of the commandments."[5] What if Jesus seriously would like us to consider inviting **real people** into our homes that we would not normally invite? People that are different? Even a little dangerous?

Inviting these people in is not without irritation or risk. One of our regular Aboriginal visitors frequently borrowed items of clothing and other articles from my father and conveniently forgot to return them. The unwed mother talked unendingly about aspects of her pregnancy we would rather not have heard described at the dinner table. The missionaries filled our kitchen with their special health food and took over my bedroom with their Bible teaching materials. And the former convict threatened to rob a grocery store to get the money he needed to travel. (Dad had to take some steps to prevent this.)

It is not simple; this is not a wholesale directive to take in every stranger you see. Nor is it acting out of duty or self-righteousness that wants to look good through ostentatious serving. Rather it is to offer hospitality those whom is God sending to you, and to whom he sends you. You have to keep in step with the Spirit to discern this, to listen to his voice, always ready to obey his call.

But perhaps there is more long-term risk in quickly striking people off our hospitality list than having a generally open policy that takes considered risks and shoulders inconvenience. Consider another parable of Jesus in Matthew 25, where the King says to a whole group of people: *"Depart from me, you who are cursed, into the eternal fire prepared for the devil and his angels. For I was hungry and you gave me nothing to eat, I was thirsty and you gave me nothing to drink, **I was a stranger and you did not invite me in**... Truly I tell you, **whatever you did not do for one of the least of these, you did not do for me**"* [v.41-43,45].

What if, in failing to extend hospitality, we not only turn away angels, but Jesus himself? The very one who shed his blood to make us part of his Family?

Setting the Lonely in Families

If we are members of God's household, then it should be taken as obvious that we will show hospitality to our brothers and sisters. It is one of the "One Anothers" we talked about earlier: *Offer hospitality to one another without grumbling* [1 Peter 4:9]. And this also includes distant cousins that we have not met yet.

Did you know the whole little book of 3 John is about such hospitality? It commends John's friend Gaius for welcoming some itinerant missionaries who had passed through: *Dear friend, you are faithful in what you are doing for the brothers and sisters,* **even though they are strangers to you...** *It was for the sake of the Name that they went out, receiving no help from the pagans.* **We ought therefore to show hospitality to such people so that we may work together for the truth** [v.5,7-8].

Jesus especially commended hospitality to Gospel-bearers like these: **"Anyone who welcomes you welcomes me,** *and anyone who welcomes me welcomes the one who sent me... And if anyone gives even a cup of cold water to one of these little ones who is my disciple, truly I tell you, that person will certainly not lose their reward"* [Matthew 10: 40-42]. As with the *least of these* in Matthew 25, he equates hospitality offered to these family members as being offered to him, and also to his Father.

Sometimes, we try to protect our own physical families by keeping the home closed, by not inviting others into it. We think it will take away from our "family time," or that if an outsider does something different or expresses an opinion we disagree with, that it will have a bad impact. It is part of the practice of self-protective people to put up defenses against potential danger, and to guard their gates.

But Psalm 68:6, after describing how God behaves *in his holy dwelling,* tells us this: *God sets the lonely in families...* If we are going to make our homes "heaven for beginners," maybe we should begin to keep our eyes open for the lonely people he intends to set in our families, in order that they might truly become part of his family.

If you have an open family, you might find that sometimes your children teach you things. My son was always bringing home somebody lonely, from his youngest years up. When he was in second grade, it was a hyperactive boy who just about bounced off the ceiling and talked constantly in a loud, high-pitched voice. Another year, it was a child who had skipped two grades in school—highly intelligent, but struggling socially. Later, in high school, a good friend with family problems spent many of his weekends at our house. As a parent, I likely would have picked friends for my son from the popular, cool kids. But God gifted him from a young age to see the lonely ones that needed for a time to be part of our family.

Sometimes the lonely are that way because they are foreigners, true strangers in a land where they are trying to make a home. When my friend Jere in Virginia Beach began teaching English as a Second Language after her retirement, she naturally invited home some of the individuals and families she connected with. For one Chinese couple, who had been in the US twelve years, it was the first time they had ever entered an American person's house. Now, they call Jere "Grandmother," seeing her as part of their family as God sets them in hers. In our mobile global society, there are probably foreigners near you who would love to share a meal in your home.

Sometimes we fail to invite lonely people because their beliefs or lifestyle may conflict with ours. We vaguely feel that such defects might be catching if we let them into our houses. But why do we think that our values are so weak that caring for someone would compromise them? Larry Dixon, in a chapel message at a conservative Christian university, told students that he was going to outline for them ten Biblical principles for relating to their gay friends. His first principle? "Have gay friends."[6] Jesus was constantly criticized for accepting the hospitality of tax collectors and "sinners"—but he knew who he was and what he had to offer these people. Perhaps we also, knowing who we are as children of God, should seek to befriend those who are in need of adoption.

My parents come from a strongly conservative theological background. But that did not stop them from befriending a transgender person who began attending their small church in England. Other people in the church felt uncomfortable with this: were we condoning this lifestyle by welcoming him? But my mother invited him over for afternoon tea, and began to get to know the painful story behind the choices that had been made. It did not change her theology. But it did help her to be Jesus to a lonely person—and perhaps to see Jesus in him.

We are the crippled, the blind, and the lame. But we are also the ones of whom it is said: *Blessed are those who are invited to the wedding supper of the Lamb!* [Revelation 19:9]. If God welcomes into his home people like us, how can we be justify being such snobs?

Reflections:

Making home like heaven means opening it up to those God sends you.

What keeps you from extending hospitality to others?

- Lack of resources? (Time, money, space, dining furniture...)
- Feeling pressure to entertain perfectly? (Gourmet cooking, fine china, perfect housekeeping...)
- Kids at home? (Chaos of preschoolers, activities of school-age kids, wanting to protect 'family time' from outsiders...)
- Only wanting to invite those who are close to you? (No strangers allowed.) Or something else...?

After considering this chapter, how do you think God might want you to rethink these barriers to hospitality? How are they evidence of the self-protective behaviors we looked at in Section 2?

Who are some **lonely people** that you know already that you think God might be prompting you to invite into your home/family— whether for a meal, a weekend, or just a cup of coffee?

- **Here are some ideas**: a single parent with kids; an elderly person at church; a disabled friend; particular friends of your kids; someone who has just gone through a divorce; a single student living away from home; a missionary couple needing a place to stay... What other people come to mind?

Pray for God to open your eyes to **the strangers that he might want you to invite into your home**. Remember that Jesus said you are blessed when you do this, whereas inviting your friends and relatives is only normal (Luke 14)!

- **Here are some opportunities**—many of which are offered by local ministries and charities—that you could keep your eyes open for: international students at local universities; summer temporary workers coming from other countries; new people at your church; neighbors you don't know; disabled/elderly people in group homes or senior homes...

Who are you worried about/prejudiced against inviting into your home? How could you pray that God would make you ready if he sent a person like this to your tent? How could you see them as Abraham did the angels—or as Jesus himself in disguise?

23 Lighten Your Loaded Backpack

And God is able to bless you abundantly, so that in all things at all times, having all that you need, you will abound in every good work... **You will be enriched in every way so that you can be generous on every occasion,** *and through us your generosity will result in thanksgiving to God.* [2 Corinthians 9:8,11]

Consider the following proverbs from various countries:

- "God gives nothing to those who keep their arms crossed." (Mali)
- "What you keep rots; what you give flourishes." (France)
- "Every man goes down to his death bearing in his hands only that which he has given away." (Persia)

In the wide world, wise people acknowledge the paradox that somehow, generosity benefits the giver. A recent sociological study, published under the title *The Paradox of Generosity,* demonstrated that Americans who regularly behaved in a generous manner with their money, resources, time, and attention live a qualitatively better life. The authors also state:

> The generosity paradox can also be stated in the negative. By grasping on to what we currently have, we lose out on better goods that we might have gained... By always protecting ourselves against future uncertainties and misfortunes, we are affected in ways that make us more anxious about uncertainties and vulnerable to future misfortunes... It is no coincidence that the word "miser" is etymologically related to the word "miserable."[7]

The Sowing Principle

Remember the servant who buried what he had in the ground? He saved the gold, but he missed out on sharing his Master's happiness. He saw the Master as a *hard man,* who *harvested where he had not sown, and gathered where he had not scattered seed.* He missed seeing **he** was the one had failed to sow, and yet hoped to receive a reward.

Our opening text frames this nugget of wisdom: *Now he who supplies seed to the sower and bread for food will also supply and increase your store of seed and will enlarge the harvest of your righteousness* [v. 10]. You cannot harvest a lot of seed if you do not sow at least a little. And those who sow a lot will reap even more.

Here's another Proverb:

> One person gives freely, yet gains even more;
>   another withholds unduly, but comes to poverty. [Prov. 11:24]

Look back at the bountiful language of verse 8: **Abundantly. All things. All times. All that you need. Abound in every good work.**

This is what God has **already** provided so that we can give. No matter how little we think we have, it is everything we need to be generous—the "talents" our Master has entrusted to us to invest. That is how a widow giving two small copper coins can earn the praise of Jesus: *"Truly I tell you, this poor widow has put more into the treasury than all the others. They all gave out of their wealth; but **she, out of her poverty, put in everything**—all she had to live on"* [Mark 12:43-44]. She trusted that God could provide for her even if she sacrificed her means of living.

Why was she doing this? Was it like a coin-operated vending machine, where you give in order to make sure you get? Did she hope that somehow, by giving her all to the temple, she could bargain with God to become wealthy?

Probably not. The returns gathered on generosity only come when the focus is on the giving and not on the reward. *The Paradox of Generosity* notes, "Generosity must be authentic. It must be believed and practiced as a real part of one's life… For generosity to enhance well-being, it must be the generosity, not the well-being, that we are after. The enhanced well-being then comes indirectly and secondarily."[8]

This also is what Paul is saying when he tells the Corinthians: *Whoever sows sparingly will also reap sparingly, and whoever sows generously will also reap generously. Each of you should give what you have decided in your heart to give,* **not reluctantly or under compulsion, for God loves a cheerful giver** [2 Corinthians 9:6-7]. It is the *harvest of your righteousness* that is in view—in blessing others, in *thanksgiving to God,* in your deepening faith in the One who cares for you—more than guaranteed prosperity in physical terms. Of course, if God chooses, he may grant you that as well, in order that you may further invest it in his purposes, as he does with the two faithful servants.

Investing in Futures

We can see this dramatically displayed in the life of our father in faith. Abraham, we are told, *had become very wealthy in livestock and in silver and gold* [Genesis 13:2]. In fact, there were no longer enough local resources to support both his livestock and that of his nephew and foster son, Lot. When they decide to separate, Abraham, as the patriarch, has the right to first dibs on rich pasture land. But he offers the younger man the choice instead. Lot looks around, sees the well-watered land on the plain of the Jordan and chooses it for himself: a seemingly wise investment. Abraham, meanwhile, moves off toward dusty Canaan, promised by God to the descendants he still lacks.

But in the next few chapters, we see that Lot's grasping does not turn out so well. He moves into a city where greed is the main good: *Now this was the sin of... Sodom: She and her daughters were arrogant, overfed and unconcerned; they did not help the poor and needy* [Ezekiel 16:49]. Lot's goods are seized in a regional war between kings, and he is carried off captive; it is Abraham who comes to his rescue. Later, Sodom itself is destroyed, and Lot loses everything: his flocks, his possessions, even the rich vegetation he had been so attracted to [Genesis 19:25]. His wife escapes with him, but longing for her lost riches, she turns back and becomes *a pillar of salt.*

Abraham, on the other hand, continues to prosper, but he does so with an ongoing attitude of generosity. We have already noted his generous hospitality to strangers. And when he meets Melchizedek, a priest of the Most High God, he gives him ten percent of all he owns—surely a princely sum—as a way of giving back to God out of all he had been entrusted. On the other hand, when the king of Sodom offers him spoils of war, he refuses: *"I will accept nothing belonging to you, not even a thread or the strap of a sandal, so that you will never be able to say, 'I made Abram rich'"* [Genesis 14:23]. Later, in Genesis 24:35, Abraham's servant testifies: **The Lord has blessed my master abundantly,** *and he has become wealthy. He has given him sheep and cattle, silver and gold, servants, and camels and donkeys.*

Yet Abraham never really receives the land that God had promised to give him, even though he lives in it half his life. Unlike Lot and his wife, who claimed Sodom as home, Abraham *looked forward to the city with foundations, whose architect and builder is God.* So his treasure was not really in this place, no matter how much he had. He was free to give it away, to invest it in his future home.

This is what Jesus is talking about when he says: *"Do not store up for yourselves treasures on earth, where moths and vermin destroy, and where thieves break in and steal. But* **store up for yourselves treasures in heaven,** *where moths and vermin do not destroy, and where thieves do not break in and steal.* **For where your treasure is, there your heart will be also"** [Matthew 6:19-21]. Once again, there is a completely practical aspect to this. It does not only mean to pray, do good, and wish for heaven; it also indicates that we should spend the earthly resources we have on more permanent treasure.

The first way we might think of doing this is by investing in the work of the kingdom, both in your local church and in other local or foreign ministry. From the beginning of the Church, the generosity of Jesus followers has made the spread of the Gospel possible. The book of Philippians is, in fact, an expanded thank-you letter from Paul for this church's faithful support of him: *When I set out from Macedonia, not one church shared with me in the matter of giving and receiving, except you only; for even when I was in Thessalonica, you sent me aid more than once when I was in need* [4:15-16]. (My husband and I, as missionaries, are more grateful than we can express for the many people who have given faithfully and sacrificially to enable us follow and focus on our call.)

Another way we might invest in the future is suggested by the rather odd Parable of the Shrewd Manager in Luke 16. In this story, a manager is threatened with being fired for mismanagement uses his last few days on the job to reduce the amounts owed by his employer's debtors (possibly by forgoing his own commission on the transactions), so as to find favor with his neighbors later when he is out of a job. His master commends him for his ingenuity, and Jesus further comments: *For the people of this world are more shrewd in dealing with their own kind than are the people of the light. I tell you,* **use worldly wealth to gain friends for yourselves, so that when it is gone, you will be welcomed into eternal dwellings** [v.8-9].

I assume that one welcome anticipated in this text is from the Father who has prepared a place for us. But I wonder if it is also from the people whom we befriended through our generosity, and who as a result have found a future home as well. Certainly the one thing we can take from this world into the next are the eternal friendships made in Christ, and it is worth spending our physical resources on those who could be new neighbors in the coming City.

A Loan to God

This parable is followed by another which, in contrast, assesses the results of **not** investing in the future: The Rich Man and Lazarus. Jesus sketches the picture quickly: *There was a rich man who was dressed in purple and fine linen and lived in luxury every day. At his gate was laid a beggar named Lazarus, covered with sores and longing to eat what fell from the rich man's table. Even the dogs came and licked his sores* [Luke 16:19-21]. Jesus makes it obvious that the rich man uses his wealth primarily for his own comfort, and does not even bother to give his discarded food to the miserable man outside his gate. But when both die, it is Lazarus who is *welcomed into eternal dwellings*, while the rich man languishes in torment.

The scene is highly reminiscent of another parable we have considered: *"Depart from me, you who are cursed, into the eternal fire prepared for the devil and his angels. **For I was hungry and you gave me nothing to eat**, I was thirsty and you gave me nothing to drink..."* [Matthew 25:41-43].

Some people, justifying their own lack of generosity to the poor, will glibly quote Jesus: *"The poor you will always have with you..."* [Mark 14:7]. But they fail to notice the context. First, Jesus is paraphrasing a command in Deuteronomy 15:11: *There will always be poor people in the land. **Therefore I command you to be openhanded** toward your fellow Israelites who are poor and needy in your land.* Second, it ignores the end of the Mark version of the quote: *"... and you can help them any time you want."* Far from deprecating alms to the poor, he is calling out Judas' false show of piety in response to a woman's generous gift to Jesus: *"Why wasn't this perfume sold and the money given to the poor? It was worth a year's wages"* [John 12:5].

John goes on to tell us that Judas *did not say this because he cared about the poor but because he was a thief; as keeper of the money bag, he used to help himself to what was put into it* [v.6]. When we use Jesus' rebuke to Judas to avoid our own acts of compassion, and keep our possessions for ourselves, we are thieving from Jesus, and behaving no better than Judas.

If you happen to visit our Serve the City office in Brussels, look up toward our windows before you enter our building. Just under them, you will see inscribed:

Donner aux pauvres, c'est prêter à Dieu.

This leftover from the time our building belonged to a convent is taken from Proverbs 19:17: **Whoever is kind to the poor lends to the Lord,** *and he will reward them for what they have done.* If you can rely on anyone to repay a loan—surely it is our faithful Lord. And you can expect it will be repaid with interest!

Do you really need all the stuff you carry around with you? Could you use it for a better purpose? Could you use it to love Jesus by serving the poor? Could you throw parties, sponsor scholarships, and meet practical needs, investing in people to make eternal friends? Could you support the Body-building work of the kingdom, in your local community and elsewhere? Start lightening your load, and see what God grants you in exchange.

Reflections:

Making home like heaven means joyfully sharing God's resources.

Do you really believe that in *all things at all times,* you have *all that you need* in order to *abound in every good work* [2 Corinthians 9:8]?

- *All things:* Do you believe that the resources God has already given you are enough to share with others, and could be multiplied to do all of *the good works he has prepared for you to do* [Ephesians 2:10]?

- *All times:* Even after a market crash? Even when you've lost a job? Even when you're trying to put a kid through college? Two kids?

- *All that you need:* That the resources God has are enough for your daily needs (not necessarily for a big stockpile) as well as for the daily needs of those with whom he has called you to share?

- *Abound in every good work:* That you can do big, extravagant deeds, even with small resources, because God has given you the means to be generous in the works he made for you?

- **What difference would it make to your life to believe this and act on it?** What difference would it make to your attitude? To your family? To your own sense of scarcity or abundance? To your joy?

Remember, the point is not to give **so that** you get. The point is to give with enthusiasm, with extravagant joy.

- Why does this make a difference? What changes when we give while keeping our eyes on the bottom line instead of on God?

Think of the servants with the talents again. The third guy was afraid to gamble on an investment he might lose and make the Master mad. But the others saw it as an investment in the future, and found out that by taking the risk, they shared in the Master's happiness.

- How is giving toward the work of the church and of missions an investment in the future? How are you involved in this?

- How is *using worldly wealth to gain friends for yourselves* [Luke 16:8] an investment in the future? How are you doing this now? What are some new ideas you have for doing this more?

- Do you think that *a loan to God* is a good investment? How can you begin to think of giving to the poor in this light? In what ways would you like to be openhanded to the poor? What means do you have for sharing your resources with them?

24 Help Your Kids be Happy Campers

Whoever fears the Lord has a secure fortress,
and for their children it will be a refuge. [Proverbs 14:26]

The deans call them "teacups." They are beautiful, but fragile. They come into their first year of university for the first time separated from the all-powerful beings who have smoothed all the obstacles that stood in their way: obstacles such as the teacher who docked their grade for handing in a late paper, the coach that cut them from the basketball team, even the classmate who didn't invite them to the birthday party.

Now they are on their own, with only a mobile phone as umbilical cord linking them to the people who usually intervene to protect them from any failure or danger. As a result, some, let off the leash for the first time, engage in extremely risky—even life-threatening— behavior. Others, facing alone the load of expectations and a threat of perceived failure, exhibit serious anxiety and depression. In one much-publicized case, this pressure, combined with having earned a B+ grade average instead of the expected A in her first semester, influenced a college freshman to jump to her death from the roof of a building.[9]

What has happened to remove the resilience from our children? And how could we, as parents, equip them to face life with boldness instead of fear?

Parenting to Eliminate Pain

Multiple articles have begun to crop up in the psychological and popular press to recognize and address this problem, with titles like "A Nation of Wimps"[10] and "The Overprotected Kid."[11] In such publications, you will hear quotes like this one, from Julie Lythcott-Haims, a dean at Stanford University:

> I think some time ago ... parents started to be more involved with ensuring outcomes for their children. Parents began to change, and for good reasons, trying to be more helpful, useful, leverage their own expertise, connections, life experience to help place their children in better outcomes. But a line was crossed and parents started to do things for kids that kids should do for themselves... The implicit message is 'I don't think you can do this without me... You're that fragile, or you're that

incapable, or you're that unfamiliar with the workings of life ... [that you can't] do for yourself."[12]

Of course, as parents we are responsible for the protection of our children, and to be sensitive to their needs, as well as to demand certain standards of behavior from them. Psychological research has strongly established the link between high responsiveness and high demandingness from parents, and the behavioral and emotional well-being of the child.[13] In Scripture, also, we see these two facets of behavior taken for granted as being part of good parenting:

- **Responsiveness**: *"Which of you, if your son asks for bread, will give him a stone? Or if he asks for a fish, will give him a snake?* [Matthew 7:9-10]
- **Demandingness**: *Moreover, we have all had human fathers who disciplined us and we respected them for it.* [Hebrews 12:9]

In fact, these two aspects are used as evidence that God is a good and gracious Father to us:

- *If you, then, though you are evil, know how to give good gifts to your children, how much more will your Father in heaven give good gifts to those who ask him!* [Matthew 7:11]
- *[Our fathers] disciplined us for a little while as they thought best; but God disciplines us for our good, in order that we may share in his holiness.* [Hebrews 12:10]

But we can take even a good thing too far, or in the wrong direction:

- **Overly high responsiveness** may interfere in every negative emotional reaction of the child to remove the source of distress; to change the circumstances; to step in to "help" by solving the problem for them, to relieve them from struggling. It may involve an inappropriate focus on "the bright side," or offer distractions or pleasures in order to divert their attention and eliminate sadness.[14] It may also grant any of the child's wishes with as little delay as possible, in order that they might not suffer the pain of waiting for fulfillment.
- **Overly high demandingness** may expect from children a kind of performance based primarily on external measures, such as academic or athletic achievement, or a standard of conduct

beyond their developmental capabilities, or a moral perfection of behavior that is shocked, angered and/or personally wounded by any shortfall. In some cases, the parent may end up acting for the child to make sure the performance is reached: by hanging over their shoulder to correct their homework as they do it; by constant "coaching," checklists, or reminders; or by never leaving them unsupervised in case they make the wrong choices.

Both of these responses find their roots in fear. Fear motivates "snowplow parents," who clear out of the way any obstacles in their children's path so that their road is always smooth and clear. Fear turns us into "helicopter parents," hovering over our children to make sure that every decision they make is the right one, that every misstep is caught before it becomes a fall, that proper caution about possible dangers is instilled in them. Out of fear, we build little fortresses for our children to live in, protected from everything.

But if God is calling us to live in a tent, our parental fears must be re-placed.

Whose Children Are They?

Earlier, we looked at Psalm 127:1: *Unless the Lord builds the house, the builders labor in vain. Unless the Lord watches over the city, the guards stand watch in vain.* We noted that our security is in God's hands, not our own, no matter how many systems we put in place to feel safe. The second verse of the Psalm warns us against anxiously working to make sure we have "enough."

The rest of that short Psalm (v.3-5) goes like this:

Children are a heritage from the Lord,
   offspring a reward from him.
Like arrows in the hands of a warrior
   are children born in one's youth.
Blessed is the man whose quiver is full of them...

The implication here is that like our possessions, our security, and our peace of mind, our children also come from God. In fact, not only are they His to begin with: we can't keep them. Arrows that are kept in a quiver have no purpose – they are supposed to be shot out ahead, to hit a mark. In the context of the Psalm, these verses imply that our children have a flight path away from us that is directed by God. We receive them from him, and we send them out with as much skill as we are able. Our whole purpose in having children is not to keep them, but to give them the best start possible as they fly into God's future.

So this means parenting with a view to letting go, right from the beginning.

Abraham had to learn this in a very painful way. After waiting twenty-five years for Isaac, the child promised him by God, one can only imagine how protective and doting he might have been. But God asks him to take this child— *"your son, your only son, whom you love"*—and to sacrifice him as a burnt offering [Genesis 22:2]. This must have been not only painful for Abraham, but confusing. Hadn't God said that he would give him many descendants through Isaac? But he obeyed God, setting out on a three-day journey to the stipulated place. What a long three days those must have been! To give up his child to death—at his own hand! Even as he *"reasoned that God could even raise the dead"* [Hebrews 11:19], he still must have shrunk back at inflicting such a blow on his sheltered and protected boy. And when he, in manner of speaking, did receive him back from the dead, he must have seen Isaac with different eyes—as the child who was dedicated to God.

We are called to do this too, even if not so dramatically. My son was an extremely active toddler who at two years old liked to climb everything in sight. This scared me out of my wits. One day, anxiously watching my husband spotting him as he climbed, I heard a voice in my head that I believe was the Holy Spirit: *This boy is going to break some bones. You have to accept that.*

Two months later, my son fell from a jungle gym—not a high one—and ended up in hospital. He had twisted his leg on the way down, resulting in a spiral fracture. What a horrible night, sitting by his bedside in the wee hours, seeing him in such pain! But the memory of that voice kept me calm, and I reminded myself that my son was not my own. No use looking for someone or something to blame as though injury was the worst evil to be avoided. Though I would have done almost anything to spare him the pain, it was part of life, something allowed in God's gracious providence for him. (I had to remember this later, too, as other broken bones—not to mention the emotionally painful events that complicate childhood and adolescence—came along...)

Pain that leads to Peace

Pain, sadness, and failure, are a part of learning, part of life. We learn not to touch hot things when we burn ourselves. We learn compassion for others when we experience loss. We learn not to lie when we get caught and suffer the fallout.

Sometimes we as parents even have to create artificial pain in terms of disciplinary consequences for misbehavior. Proverbs reminds us that the pain of discipline is worth the learning, worth the larger and more serious consequences that might happen when a child is launched into adulthood: *Discipline your children, for in that there is hope; do not be a willing party to their death* [Proverbs 19:18]. Hebrews 12:11 agrees that the pain of discipline is worth its payoff: *No discipline seems pleasant at the time, but painful. Later on, however, **it produces a harvest of righteousness and peace for those who have been trained by it.*** Isn't it better to teach a tantrum-throwing toddler how to calm themselves in a timeout, than to launch a temper-prone adult who explodes with rage and hurts others?

But we tend to avoid inflicting this pain, in part because it is painful to us. It hurts to have your child whom you love angry at you, when it would be easier to soothe or distract or even deceive. It is time-consuming to continue to say "no" to repeated demands, or to administer consequences, when it is quicker to say yes or overlook behavior. Thus, we may only "discipline" when we have reached our limit and have become so angry that we find ourselves **wanting** to inflict pain, in return for the pain that the child has inflicted on us.

But anger must never, as far as we can help it, be part of discipline. The small pains we inflict—taking away privileges, firmly saying no and enforcing it, making them eat their vegetables—is not for our relief, but for their good. And why should we be surprised when they do wrong? Why should we be shocked and wounded? They are our children, after all—are we so perfect?

Padding the Room

An alternate strategy parents sometimes use to keep their children from pain is one I call "padding the room." It involves manipulating the environment so that children have no opportunity to be hurt or make wrong choices. I'm not talking about baby gates and electrical plug covers, which are smart protection for small people. It looks more like removing every single thing you might possibly have to prohibit a toddler from touching: breakable objects, books you don't want torn, candle holders, and so on. The child can then do whatever he/she wants in the environment, without having to learn any self-control or resist any kind of temptation.

This can cause some interesting situations when the child enters someone else's house that has not been "padded." It is far kinder to teach a small child that some behaviors are inappropriate and some objects are off-limits in their own home first, so that they can learn to respond appropriately to the different environments they might encounter elsewhere.

For older children and teenagers, "padding the room" might look more like reliance on electronic firewalls, parental filters, constant phone calls, and "spyware" that lets the kid know they are always being watched. Again, filters and firewalls are totally appropriate in an age where lewd and violent content can be accessed inadvertently. But they cannot be the sole means of protection. Learning how to make good choices and exercise self-control from an early age is a far better long-term plan.

Will they make wrong choices sometimes? Of course they will. We should expect this. Proverbs 22:15 tells us: **Folly is bound up in the heart of a child,** *but the rod of discipline will drive it far away.* Wouldn't you rather give some consequences to your toddler for having played with a prohibited decoration at home than deal with the fallout at Great-Aunt Agnes' house when he breaks Great-Uncle Ernie's urn? And wouldn't it be better to catch your twelve-year-old in a small lie now and deal with it than to have a habitual liar later? Rather than preventing them from the possibility of making those wrong choices, we have the far more powerful responsibility of helping them repent wrong choices made in the safety of the home context, and teaching them how to make better ones in the future.

Because the truth is: kids wiggle through fences, if they have not been helped toward the inner motivation not to do so. Tech-savvy kids learn how to hack firewalls, and plausible lies become a way of life for a lot of "protected" teenagers. A horrible story in the UK press told of a toddler whose mother, frustrated that he would not stay in his room, installed a stair gate on his door. When he stacked toys to climb over it, she installed a second gate on top of the first. Less than two days later, the boy was strangled when trying to squeeze between the two gates.[15] This is an extreme example, but it demonstrates how children who are simply blocked will demonstrate a great deal of persistence and ingenuity in breaking through barriers.

Saving Them From Your Pain

For some parents, a big motivation for protecting their child can be to save them from the pain of their own mistakes and poor choices. One woman I know recalled how her mother freaked out when she was thirteen because a boy gave her a gift. As her teenage years progressed, her mother seemed to be suspicious of every guy she dated, and constantly made arbitrary rules to put boundaries on her social life. Later, she discovered that her parents' marriage had resulted from a premarital pregnancy. Her mother's guilt and overwhelming fear of her daughter making the same mistake resulted in negative over-protection rather than positive teaching and encouragement in healthy relationships.

But don't we, as followers of Jesus, have the experience of his taking even our most sinful choices and painful experiences and transforming them into something that draws us closer to him? If we cannot identify times like this, maybe it is because we regard our Heavenly Father as a "hard man," and have not trusted Him to enter our pain. And if we **have** experienced this grace, how can we think he will fail to extend it to our children?

What if, instead of protecting them from pain and wrong, we worked to teach them to listen to God and obey him? What if, instead of ceaseless warnings to "be careful," we helped them dare to follow Jesus, trusting his leadership and protection? What if, instead of calling or texting Mom every five minutes, we encouraged them to learn to *pray without ceasing* to the God who dwells with them?

You are not responsible to control the outcomes of your children's lives. God is. Never forget: He cares more about them than you do. You are there to aim them as arrows into the future, to follow God's trajectory for them. Scripture urges us: *Start children off on the way they should go, and even when they are old they will not turn from it* [Proverbs 22:6]. And most of all, make the Lord your own Fear as you live in your vulnerable tent, trusting him with their protection, for *"whoever fears the Lord has a secure fortress, and for their children it will be a refuge"* [Proverbs 14:26].

Reflections:

**Making home like heaven means fearless parenting,
as you teach your children to fear God alone.**

What difference does it make to you to think of your children as **belonging to God rather than to you**?
- How does it redefine your ego boundaries regarding your children's behavior or performance?
- How might this help you deal with anxiety over their future?
- How might it help you let them make some of their own mistakes?
- How might it encourage you toward training over protection?

Look back at the verses on p. 154 on **responsiveness/demandingness**.
- What does a good level of responsiveness look like? How can we model our responsiveness to our kids on God's response to us?
- What does a good level of demand look? How can we model our discipline on how God works with us, his children?
- Which of these is more likely to get out of balance for you (too much or too little of either)? What does that look like in your parenting? How might God be convicting you to change?

In our society, **parenting sometimes is seen primarily as pain prevention**, by making things easier for them (ensuring success, refusing to use discipline) or by protecting them ("padding the room"). However, sometimes this is just as much about the parents' pain as the children's: not wanting their children to be angry with them when consequences are imposed, wishes are denied, or behavior is corrected. It may also be the result of the parent not having dealt with their own pain from poor choices or painful circumstances, and from anger with their heavenly Father over this.
- How much is this statement true for you as a parent?
- How could pain actually be beneficial to a child (whether through tough circumstances or imposed consequences to behavior)? How has pain been beneficial to you personally?
- Of course, one of the major responsibilities of parents is protecting their children from what they are not ready to handle. How could we balance this with the responsibilities of teaching them to make choices, helping them to deal well with their own pain, and guiding them toward God as their loving Father?

25 Sent on a Jesus Journey

Then I heard the voice of the Lord saying, "Whom shall I send? And who will go for us?" And I said, "Here am I. Send me!" [Isaiah 6:8]

On a Mission from God

I have had the incredible privilege to spend most of my life on the mission field: as a child in Australia; ministering in high schools in the United States; with international students in Geneva, Switzerland; and now as a church planter in Brussels, Belgium. On my first day of Bible college I met a remarkable man who, though he had never yet left the U.S., nevertheless felt a strong call of God to go to Western Europe—just as I had. That call became a strong tie between us, ending up in marriage and ministry together for the last 30 years.

So for most of my life, "missions" was something that you did when you got up and went to another place, another culture, or another language with the Gospel. I heard lots of missions conference sermons on the verse above, with stirring calls to go reach the heathen tribes or unreached people groups in far-flung lands. People at our Bible college, hearing this passage preached, would raise their hands and sign cards that said, "Any time, Any place, Any people."

It did not occur to me until very recently that Isaiah actually never moved anywhere. Certainly not to a foreign country.

His call was to his own people—a people that would be *"ever hearing, but never understanding... ever seeing, but never perceiving"* [Isaiah 6:9]. Talk about a tough assignment. (I wouldn't want to raise support for it.)

God sent Abraham, on the other hand, to *"Go from your country, your people and your father's household to the land I will show you"* [Genesis 12:1]. He was never specifically asked to convert the heathen that he found there—though, as we have already seen, he welcomed them and demonstrated his faith to them. Rather, God's purpose was to establish Abraham's faith and family in that place where God would reveal himself to the whole world.

All through the Scriptures, we find God sending. Lots of things: rain, hail, fire, angels, grass, his Word, panic, plagues, thunderstorms, lions, dreams, and on and on. We also see him constantly sending people: prophets, wise men, kings, armies, immigrants and exiles. Then, at the climax of history, he sends his Son to us, who in turn sends his Spirit on those who believe in this One the Father has sent.

The word for "send" in Latin is *missio,* from which we get the words "mission" and "missionary." When we look at the broad sweep of the Bible, we can see that God is a missionary God, the God who sends. Missions is not a personal career choice, a romantic notion of venturing out to convert heathen tribes, worthy of only the bravest and boldest among us. Rather, mission—a sense of being sent by God—is for everyone, for all of God's people.

This is why we must live in a tent. We never know where we might be sent next, when we might have to up stakes and go.

In the present-day church, the word "missional" has become kind of a buzzword, perhaps indicating that you sit at tables instead of pews in church, or that you are involved in social justice or serving the poor. Alan Hirsch, a "missional activist," sets the record straight:

> "Because we are the 'sent' people of God, the church is the instrument of God's mission in the world... [But] missional theology is not content with mission being a church-based work. Rather, it applies to the whole life of every believer. Every disciple is to be an agent of the kingdom of God, and every disciple is to carry the mission of God into every sphere of life. We are all missionaries sent into a non-Christian culture."[16]

You are a missionary as much as I am. God is sending you just as he sends me.

Sure, it is possible that God would send you across the world to another country. But he could send you with the military or with a diplomatic mission or with your spouse's job, just as much as with a mission agency. Wherever you are, however you get there—God has sent you on his mission. Even if He has sent you to stay put.

Go With God

The great thing about God sending you somewhere is that he does not send you alone, like a salesman sent out with a quota to sell and a commission to earn before he can return. Rather, he goes with you.

Jeremiah had a hard mission, similar to Isaiah's. He too was sent to speak God's words to a people that would not listen. And as we observe him, it seems obvious that he is constitutionally unfit for such a job: shy, depressive, anxious, a sensitive soul. Moreover, when God calls him, he is just a young man. How can he do what God is sending him to do—what God tells him he has been made for? Listen in:

"Alas, Sovereign Lord," I said, *"I do not know how to speak; I am too young."* But the Lord said to me, *"Do not say, 'I am too young.'* **You must go to everyone I send you to** *and say whatever I command you.* **Do not be afraid of them, for I am with you and will rescue you,"** *declares the Lord. Then the Lord reached out his hand and touched my mouth and said to me,* **"I have put my words in your mouth.** *See, today I appoint you over nations and kingdoms to uproot and tear down, to destroy and overthrow, to build and to plant."* [Jeremiah 1:6-10]

Whomever God calls, wherever he sends them, he also equips them, not least with his own Presence. And as we saw before, it is dwelling in God and having him dwell in you that is both your safety and your supply. We are not sent in our own power to "do a job for God." He goes with us as we are sent, giving us words, giving us resources, protecting and providing for us, enabling us to do greater things than we might feel capable of—even *uprooting kingdoms.*

No wonder as Abraham journeyed in the land where God had sent him, he constantly built altars to remind himself that wherever he went, the God who had told him "Go" had also come with him.

My Father's House <u>and</u> Business

Jesus, the Sent One of God, seems to have learned this principle of acting on God's mission in God's presence as a boy. When he was twelve years old, he traveled with his parents to Jerusalem for the Passover. On their return trip, his parents didn't realize for a day that Jesus was not with them. Mary and Joseph then returned to Jerusalem on a frantic search for their missing son, finding him three days later discussing Scripture with the teachers in the Temple.

Jesus' comment to them, after they have scolded him for worrying them so much, is: *"Why were you searching for me? Didn't you know I* **had to be in my Father's house***?"* [Luke 2:49]. Well—at least that is how it is in the NIV version. In the King James and many others, it is translated, *"And he said to them, How is it that you sought me? Knew you not that* **I must be about my Father's business***?"* So which is it? *In my Father's house* or *about my Father's business?*

The truth is: the text is inconclusive. It reads in Greek, *"I must be in the... of my Father."* Scholars argue for one interpretation, but footnote the other, because it is ambivalent. I believe that this is purposeful.

We so often draw a dichotomy between doing and being, between action and contemplation. Jesus does not, not even as a child. When he is in his Father's house, resting in his presence, he is also doing his work. As he explains later, on a Sabbath day, *"My Father is always at his work to this very day, and I too am working"* [John 5:17]. And when he carrying out his Father's mission, he is also aware of being in the presence of his Father, of always dwelling in his house as David prayed to do. Doing this work, the work he was sent to do, is deeply satisfying and restful to him, so much so that he describes it to his disciples in terms of a restorative meal: *"My food is to do the will of him who sent me and to finish his work"* [John 4:34].

Of course Jesus, being human and subject to tiredness, also made time for physical rest and for concentrated prayer. And as a good Jew who came to fulfill the law rather than abolish it, he observed the Sabbath in its original intended spirit (as opposed to obeying nit-picking add-on rules established by humans). These times of retreat and rest would have been concrete and regular reminders that mission is powered by **continual** resting in and dwelling with the Father, even in the midst of activity for his kingdom. [17]

Jesus encouraged seventy-two of his disciples to this same kind of missional dependence as he sent them out, two by two, into the countryside ahead of him: *"The harvest is plentiful, but the workers are few. **Ask the Lord of the harvest, therefore, to send out workers into his harvest field. Go! I am sending you out like lambs among wolves. Do not take a purse or bag or sandals…"*** [Luke 10:2-4]. They were to depend on God's provision for them on the way, through the "people of peace" who would invite them into their homes and give them food. And they were to announce the coming kingdom as they healed the sick and cast out evil spirits in Jesus' name.

We too, as Jesus' disciples, can only carry out the mission for which we are sent as the Spirit sends us provision and power. We are to rest in him, rely on him, rather than the resources we carry with us. This requires constantly *keeping in step* with him, knowing that he dwells within us and goes with us even as he sends us out [Gal. 5:25].

Here I Am, Send Me

But what is the mission that Jesus is sending **us** on? We are not prophets, are we? Or wise men? Or exiles?

Perhaps we are all three. In the days of the Old Testament, the prophets were the few who experienced the presence and power of the Spirit upon them. Now we have the Spirit dwelling within us, who can speak through us God's very words: *What we have received is not the spirit of the world, but the Spirit who is from God, so that we may understand what God has freely given us. This is what we speak,* **not in words taught us by human wisdom but in words taught by the Spirit,** *explaining spiritual realities with Spirit-taught words* [1 Cor. 2:12-13].

Thus we are sent out as wise men, explaining God's wisdom through the Spirit. We are also sent out as prophets, as we, like the seventy-two Jesus sent ahead of him, proclaim through our words and acts and lives that "The Kingdom of God is near." And we are sent out as exiles from our own country, the future City that we are all homesick for, so that we can recreate a reflection of it in our own houses and neighborhoods.

As we go where we are sent, we can get clues to our calling from the Great Commission (*"Go and make disciples"*) and the Great Commandment (*"Love God, and love your neighbor as yourself"*). These are the purpose of every journeyer with Jesus. All of us are sent to our families, to our Christian communities, and to the pre-believing "people of peace" God puts in our lives, to love them and point them toward following Jesus as we do the same. As we keep in step with the Spirit, the specifics of our sending will become clearer and clearer.

What exactly this looks like will be different for all of us. Some of us who never thought of leaving home will end up in the strangest places. And some of those dying to jump into foreign missions will end up staying put. (If you are in the second group, throw yourself into what he wants to teach you and how he wants to use you right **now** and right **here**. He will either use it to prepare you to go—or he will reveal to you a mission hand-crafted for you at home.)

We can try to refuse our mission. Like Gideon, we can say, "*I am the least in my family.*" Like Moses, we can say, "*What if they do not believe me?*" or "*I am slow of speech and tongue,*" or even, "*Lord, please send someone else*". Like Jonah, we can try to run away in another direction because we don't like the place or the people where he is sending us.[18]

But if you are truly on a journey with Jesus, he will not allow these excuses for long. He might even turn a rod into a snake, or send a great fish, to convince you. And if you really want to know where and to whom you are sent, roll up your tent, copy Isaiah, and say, "*Here am I, Lord. Send me!*" You will soon find out.

Reflections:

God is sending you on a Jesus journey.

Are you aware of God's mission for you?

- Why do you think God might have sent you to **the place where you live**? What evidence do you see that this is a place he has prepared for you to *make your home like a stranger*? Neighbors around you? The culture? Your background? The issues you are passionate about? Changes in the area? People in your church? In your family?
- Who are **the people God is calling you to** in the place where you live? Who are new people God is bringing to you right here: refugees and immigrants, international families, school friends of your kids...? (Think back over Chapters 21 & 22.)
- Are you **willing for God to move you** somewhere else? Why or why not? What difference might it make to your attitude, knowing that he will go with you if he sends you, and that he will provide all the resources that you need for the good works he has planned for you to do? (Think back over Chapter 23.)
- How does **your family** play in to this sending? Can you trust God to send you into mission (locally or elsewhere) and to take care of your children too? (Think back to the last chapter. I have worked with a lot of missionary parents who struggled with this because they wanted to protect their children from pain.)
- Do you feel like God **might be calling you to do go elsewhere**? What makes you think this? Are you willing to stay where you are, engaged with the Body of Christ and the neighborhood while you explore this call?

God does not send us into his calling alone. He also equips us with resources, and even accompanies us! We, like Jesus, are sent out on our Father's business while resting in his presence. Like the disciples, we can trust him for provision and power to carry out our mission.

- How does this knowledge help you to step into the risky missions on which God is sending you right now?

If you are ready to say to God, ***"Here am I, send me!"***—no matter the risk, no matter the resistance, knowing he will always be with you—sign your name on this page.

willing to be wounded

(or, righteous robes)

26 Sheep Among Wolves

Go! I am sending you out like lambs among wolves. [Luke 10:3]

Risky Relationships

I did not want to write this section, because it deals with my greatest fear.

I am not afraid of roller coasters, or of trying strange foods. I am not afraid of finding my way around new cities, or attempting to speak in a new language. I have a healthy respect for snakes and spiders and crocodiles (I grew up in Australia, after all), but they do not terrify me. I actually rather like speaking in front of a crowd, if I am convinced of my content. And even during the acts of terrorism that took place here recently in Brussels, I never felt like cowering in my house or running back to America.

But relationships scare me silly. I mean real ones, where you get close to people. I have some, and I value them. But that doesn't mean they don't make me terribly afraid.

For people can do worse damage than an attacking crocodile. They can wound you with angry words. They can talk about you behind your back, while behaving another way to your face. They can criticize and condescend and control. They can oppose or belittle your dream projects. They can tear down your reputation. They can form alliances against you. They can betray you, and desert you, and destroy you. People are dangerous.

As we saw earlier, we can set up self-protective methods to combat this danger. We can put up walls that never let people get close enough to us that they could hurt us, and call it "setting boundaries." We can behave as perfectly and responsibly as possible, working hard to please others so they will have nothing to complain of. We can defend ourselves and our reputations, pointing out all that we have done right (and they have done wrong). We can say, "I don't care what you think." We can try to manipulate and control them in various overt and subtle ways. We can attack them back, turn their own weapons against them.

I have tried all of these things. Let me tell you, they don't really protect you. You end up hurt and bleeding no matter which method of self-protection you use. Jesus calls us to renounce self-protection for the way that he himself walked: the way of vulnerability.

The Strength of Vulnerability

The word "vulnerable" comes from the Latin *vulnerare*, "to wound." It is the capability of being wounded. We use it to describe some part of our person that is open to being attacked, that is undefended.

We don't like this. As a teenager, having endured years of existence at the bottom of the social pecking order at my school, I adopted this poem as my motto of stalwart, stoic self-protection:

> Never admit the pain,
> Bury it deep,
> Only the weak complain,
> Complaint is cheap... [1]

Brené Brown's excellent book, *Daring Greatly*, explores the phenomenon of vulnerability from a well-researched sociological and psychological point of view. [2] One of the first myths that she debunks is this teenage misconception I possessed (and continue to fight), that vulnerability equals weakness:

> "Vulnerability is the core of all emotions and feelings... To believe vulnerability is weakness is to believe that feeling is weakness. To foreclose on our emotional life out of a fear that the costs will be too high is to walk away from the very thing that gives purpose and meaning to living... Vulnerability is the birthplace of love, belonging, joy, courage, empathy, accountability and authenticity." [3]

After presenting attitudes and actions that her research subjects had identified as "vulnerable"—things like admitting fear, asking for help, saying "I love you" first, laying off employees, displaying one's art, being accountable, or asking for forgiveness—she says:

> "Do these sound like weaknesses?... NO. Vulnerability sounds like truth and feels like courage. Truth and courage aren't always comfortable, but they're never weakness." [4]

This is what Jesus is talking about in the Beatitudes when he says, *"Blessed are the meek, for they will inherit the earth"* [Matthew 5:5]. *Meek* is just another word for vulnerable. It is not being a doormat. Rather, it means running the risk of standing for your principles, of doing the thing that might get you criticized, of loving others who may not love you back—of being willing to be wounded. Vulnerability is letting our hearts, too, live in tents, not fortresses.

Wounded Ministers

Whenever we renounce our castles for tents, in any area of our lives, we open ourselves up to vulnerabilities, to being wounded by other people. We are, like the disciples in Luke 10, *sent out like lambs among wolves.* I see it often, not only in my own life, but also in the lives of my friends and family, as they seek sincerely to follow the path on which God sends them:

- When Jerry and Elizabeth* got married, they felt like God had providentially placed them next door to an Egyptian couple. For two years, they befriended their Muslim neighbors, spending time in each other's houses, celebrating holidays together, even going on vacation with each other. Then one day, the FBI swooped in and arrested the man as a spy. Jerry, who worked a sensitive job with a defense contractor, had to submit to months of intense scrutiny and interrogation to prove that he was not a traitor.

- Corrie met a young homeless Belgian man while working alongside him as a volunteer with refugees in Brussels. She and her roommates were already providing temporary housing for an Iraqi refugee, but they made room for this guy too. They were pleased when he was finally able to find a job, and began to look for an apartment of his own. So it was a shock when only a week later Corrie returned home from work to find that he had left with her camera, her money, and many irreplaceable possessions.

- Adam and Caroline felt overjoyed when they brought home a baby boy from Ukraine to adopt—not because they couldn't have children of their own, but to give a home to one who needed it from a country they loved. As he grew, though, their son evidenced behavioral and learning difficulties that have made the job of parenting him exhausting and frustrating—not to mention time-consuming and expensive as they seek the help he needs.

- Tania and Rachel still feel the pain and bewilderment of their ministry partnership going wrong ten years ago. They had moved together to be part of a church-planting team in a major European city, but hurts mounted along with accusations, mistrust, and people taking sides.

---

* All the names on this page have been changed.

It's bad enough to experience the everyday betrayals that come from mean girls in the class, sarcastic or jealous co-workers, and power-hungry bosses. But when we step out deliberately in obedience to God's word and calling and in ministry to others, we often expect God, as his side of the bargain, to protect us from such wounds:

- That if I respect my husband the way God tells me to, then he will love me the way I want to be loved
- That if I parent my children according to God's Word, they will grow up perfect, godly, and well-adjusted
- That if I reach out to a person in need, they will be grateful and their life will be changed
- That if I make every effort to be the perfect pastor/team leader/team member in a ministry setting, then everyone I work with and lead will love and respect me

But it doesn't always work this way.

Look at poor Jeremiah. No one likes the things he is prophesying, reacting with hostility. Finally, he complains to God: *"You deceived me, Lord, and I was deceived; you overpowered me and prevailed. I am ridiculed all day long; everyone mocks me. Whenever I speak, I cry out proclaiming violence and destruction.* **So the word of the Lord has brought me insult and reproach all day long"** [Jeremiah 20:7-8].

Look at Paul. At the end of his life, in a dank prison, his biggest sense of pain comes from feeling left all alone: *"You know that everyone in the province of Asia has deserted me, including Phygelus and Hermogenes... Do your best to come to me quickly, for Demas, because he loved this world, has deserted me and has gone to Thessalonica. Crescens has gone to Galatia, and Titus to Dalmatia... At my first defense, no one came to my support, but* **everyone deserted me.** *May it not be held against them"* [2 Timothy 1:15, 4:9-10, 16].

Look at Jesus.

The Silent Sheep

It must have hurt Jesus to have his hometown reject him. To have a large number of disciples turn away from him when his teaching was not to their taste [John 6:66]. To have the opposition of the teachers of the law whom he had amazed with his wisdom as a child.

But nothing could have hurt like Judas' betraying kiss. Like the disappearance of the disciples at his darkest hour. Like hearing the blasphemous words of denial on Peter's lips—Peter, who swore he would die for him.

Jesus did not come as the strong and solitary hero. He did not say, "I am a rock—I am an island." He chose to surround himself with people, not as distant followers but as up-close family [Matt. 12:49].

Jesus feels his brothers' betrayal before they even carry it out. He says to Judas, *"What you are about to do, do quickly"* [John 13:27]. He beseeches his sleeping friends, *"Couldn't you men keep watch with me for one hour?"* [Matthew 26:40]. Even after rising, he asks Peter three times, *"Simon son of John, do you love me?"* [John 21:15-17].

Jesus lived the life of a vulnerable leader. Rather than coming with force, he came with gentleness. His openness to "sinners" opened him up also to criticism. He wept for his dead friend, and for the grief of his dead friend's sisters. He welcomed little children, held them in his arms, kissed them and blessed them. He did not rise to the rulers' sneering challenges to prove himself, to defend his reputation and authority, but remained silent in the face of unjust accusation. And when hanging on the cross, he prayed for his killers, *"Father, forgive them, for they do not know what they are doing"* [Luke 23:34].

Isaiah describes him in this way, this meek Lamb of God who came to us among the wolves:

> *He was despised and rejected by mankind,*
> *a man of suffering, and familiar with pain.*
> *Like one from whom people hide their faces*
> *he was despised, and we held him in low esteem...*
> *He was oppressed and afflicted, yet he did not open his mouth;*
> *he was led like a lamb to the slaughter, and as a sheep before its*
> *shearers is silent, so he did not open his mouth.* [Isaiah 53:3,7]

This is not weakness. It is ultimate courage and strength. And if Jesus, the *pioneer and perfecter of our faith,* set us the example of vulnerability before others, how can we turn from it? How can we fall back into selfish self-protection? How can we fail in our courage?

Indeed, the writer to the Hebrews tells his fearful readers, **"For the joy set before him** he endured the cross, scorning its shame, and sat down at the right hand of the throne of God. **Consider him who endured such opposition from sinners,** so that **you will not grow weary and lose heart"** [12:2-3].

Reflections:

Jesus calls us to the courage of vulnerability.

Consider this quote from C.S. Lewis: **"To love at all is to be vulnerable.** Love anything, and your heart will certainly be wrung and possibly be broken. If you want to make sure of keeping it intact, you must give your heart to no one, not even to an animal. Wrap it carefully round with hobbies and little luxuries; avoid all entanglements; lock it up safe in the casket or coffin of your selfishness. But in that casket—safe, dark, motionless, airless—it will change. It will not be broken; it will become unbreakable, impenetrable, irredeemable. The alternative to tragedy, or at least to the risk of tragedy, is damnation. **The only place outside Heaven where you can be perfectly safe from all the dangers and perturbations of love is Hell."**[5]

- What is Lewis expressing about the value of vulnerability in love? How does this relate to the self-protective behaviors we discussed in Section 2?

Earlier, in our "Mighty Mountains" section, we explored the concept of being roped in to the Rock—a metaphor for faith. We considered how even when we could not feel the rope holding us tautly, we could still trust it, even in the midst of "creative and judicious deprivations" designed to test that trust.

Now consider this verse: *"The only thing that counts is faith expressing itself through love."* [Galatians 5:6b]

- What is the object of faith here? And the object(s) of love?
- What is the connection here between risking in faith and being vulnerable in love? **How is love an expression of risky faith? How does faith motivate love, even when it is risky?**
- How do you see this attitude demonstrated in the life of Jesus? How does his unfailing love for you give you the strength and courage to be vulnerable?

Revisit the Scripture about our fear of people from our Reflections following the chapter, "A Tent on a Rock" (p.124).

- How are these true in the midst of vulnerability and wounding?
- What or whom are you afraid of right now? What steps can you take to express faith through love in courageously moving forward in spite of your fear?

27 Based in Belovedness

I will not leave you as orphans; I will come to you. [John 14:18]

Covering our Shame

We've all had it. That dream where you are presenting a speech, or singing a song, or defending your Master's thesis, and suddenly you realize: you are not wearing any clothes at all. People are giggling at you. It's awful.

This is what it feels like to be vulnerable: to be naked to everyone's gaze. No wonder Adam and Eve embarked on the world's first craft project in order to fabricate some cover-ups when they experienced this phenomenon: *Then the eyes of both of them were opened, and they realized they were naked; so they sewed fig leaves together and made coverings for themselves* [Genesis 3:7].

There is something deeper here than just vulnerability. A main reason we equate vulnerability with weakness is shame. Adam and Eve were not any more naked than they had been before they ate the forbidden fruit—they were just aware of a new fear about it. As Adam says to God, "I heard you in the garden, and **I was afraid because I was naked; so I hid**" [Genesis 3:10].

Dietrich Bonhoeffer, in his *Ethics*, equates shame with the grief that we feel over our disunity with God and with other people. To become like God, we have reached for a knowledge that belonged to Him alone—a knowledge of good and evil. Now, as we make ourselves judges through this knowledge, we become aware also of the judgment of others on us—and of how we are found wanting.[6] This is the source of both shame and blame.

Certainly we see both at work in Adam and Eve's relationship with each other, and also with God. Adam, having not succeeded in hiding from God in his shame, right away blames Eve for his failure, as well as God for having exposed him to such a pernicious influence as "that woman." He attempts to cover his shame with accusation and judgment when fig leaves won't do. And Eve follows where Adam leads.

Adam and Eve were amateurs at the shame-and-blame game. We are pros. We have had long millennia to perfect our techniques, and to craft the images, complete with fancy masks, that help us hide our shame from other people.

Here are some of the many masks that we wear in front of others:

- The Perfect Mom
- The Hard Worker
- The Innocent Victim
- The Talented Artist
- The Brilliant Intellectual
- The Health-Conscious Athlete
- The Longsuffering Spouse
- The Selfless Minister

We wear these masks because we can't let our true faces be seen. We Must-Be-Seen-As (fill in the blank).[7] We craft the image and then try to live up to it. When we can't live up to it (and we never can), we tie the Mask on tighter and try to pretend that it's really our face, sometimes even coming to believe it ourselves. If anyone sees anything different, it's someone else's fault.

The Mask also allows us to judge other people. We take our knowledge of good and evil and apply it like a sliding scale to reinforce our false image while simultaneously criticizing someone else's. We especially home in on other's faults related to our own shame—even more if they seem to be doing "worse" than we are.

Redeemed to be Worthy

There is only one antidote to shame. And that is to begin to feel ourselves as people worthy to be seen for who we are, even with our imperfections. Brené Brown again: "A sense of worthiness inspires us to be vulnerable, share openly, and persevere. Shame keeps us small, resentful and afraid."[8]

But how do we cultivate a sense of worthiness in the face of people or cultures that tell us otherwise? Especially when we are truly aware of the small, shabby, snide, and sinful things we are capable of?

In addition to shame, which focuses on how one is judged by others, we also bear a load of guilt, which has to do with how one is judged by God's Law. It is interesting that when we **say** we feel guilty, it is most often not guilt, but shame that we are feeling. We feel much worse about not having the house tidied up when someone comes over than we do about screaming at our spouse. We are far more ashamed of forgetting to return someone's book than about gossiping about them behind their back. We are more deeply embarrassed about our weight, and the way we look in a bathing suit, than we are about sneaking lustful looks at others in bathing suits.

We wallow in shame, but we have all kinds of excuses and justifications for guilt. (Remember that fifth habit of self-protection?)

Guilt is real and objective, because it is located in the law of God, in his perfect standards, and not in the perceptions of people. And therefore it needs a real solution if we are to even begin to address shame. This is possible because of Jesus.

Jesus righteous life, his death on our behalf, and his resurrection conquering death means that all of our sin is gone as we are remade, brand new: *But because of his great love for us, God, who is rich in mercy, made us alive with Christ even when we were dead in transgressions—it is by grace you have been saved* [Ephesians 2:4-5]. Our guilt has been dealt with in Jesus, and as we confess it and receive Jesus righteousness as our own, we can know ourselves worthy of presentation to the Master himself:

> *Let us draw near to God with a sincere heart and with **the full assurance** that faith brings, having **our hearts sprinkled to cleanse us from a guilty conscience** and having our bodies washed with pure water* [Hebrews 10:22].

And then—can you believe it? —it gets even better.

Beloved Children of the Father

Our new identity as righteous people restored through Christ's sacrifice, is not simply about a loss of guilt. No, it also removes our shame, reunifying us with God and others, as we are welcomed as beloved children of God, as Romans 8:15-16 tells us:

> *The Spirit you received **does not make you slaves, so that you live in fear again**; rather, the Spirit you received brought about your adoption to sonship. And by him we cry, "Abba, Father." The Spirit himself testifies with our spirit that **we are God's children.***

I think there are an awful lot of Christians who somehow feel their adoption in this text is kind of like how Cinderella was "adopted" by her stepmother. I know I did. I saw myself as having a place by the fireside, but as having to earn it by sweeping up the ashes. Jesus saved me from my sins—at least up to the point where I "accepted" him—but from then on, I had to be grateful and live up to the family that had taken me in by "being good." And so, shame followed me into the very house of the Father. I lived as a foster child in his house, an orphan like Cinderella, not much better than a slave. I lived under the misapprehension that if I came to his notice at all, it was probably because I had messed up.

It sounds a lot like what the Prodigal Son thought life would be like when he returned home: *"Father, I have sinned against heaven and against you. **I am no longer worthy** to be called your son; make me like one of your hired servants"* [Luke 15:18-20]. To be a hired servant in the Father's house still seemed better than being banished forever to the hungry world outside, even if he had to work for his keep. But Jesus in this parable reveals to us how the Father really saw him, how he really felt about him—and about us as well.

First, this son who is re-adopted into the Father's family is **really** his son, not some poor orphaned waif picked up along the way. It explains the Father's deep, primal love for this wayward boy. It is the Father that engendered him. Sometimes, in looking at the biblical concept of "adoption," we forget that our first origin in creation is from *Adam, the son of God* [Luke 3:38].

This is why the poorest, the most disabled, the weakest, and the most unlovely people in the world still have dignity, still have worth, simply as human beings. At the deepest level of our persons, we are created in God's image; we are sons as Adam was. This is the truest thing about us, deeper even than our sin. This image has been marred through turning away from the Father to our own ends, but when we go home, we will find that the waiting Father still recognizes us in spite of the unkempt beard, the matted hair, the filthy face.

Second, look at the gifts the Father gives as he re-adopts his estranged son back into the family. **Shoes:** for slaves went barefoot, but free men wore sandals. **A ring:** the symbol of the Father's authority over his property. Now, to this boy who had *"wasted his substance with riotous living"* (in the KJV's memorable parlance), he gives the privilege and responsibility of disbursing his Father's resources wisely.

And **a robe**, to cover his nakedness. Not just any robe, either: *the best robe.* It might remind us of Joseph, the favored son who was given a long-sleeved robe as a sign that he did not have to do any manual labor.[9] In the same way, this robe indicates the Father's intention that this young man will not have to earn his keep or his Father's favor by working for it. He has been declared **worthy** by his Father, simply because he returns as his Father's beloved son.

This is the thing about shame. We are not up to clothing ourselves, to making ourselves appear worthy with masks or any other flimsy image we can concoct. (Just try wearing an apron of fig leaves to the office.) When we rely on ourselves for such a thing, we will find that our new clothes are no better than the Emperor's suit in the famous fairy tale: *You say, 'I am rich; I have acquired wealth and do not need a thing.' But **you do not realize that you are wretched, pitiful, poor, blind and naked*** [Revelation 3:17].

Our shameful nakedness can be covered only by the Father. He tells us: *I counsel you to buy from me... white clothes to wear, **so you can cover your shameful nakedness*** [Revelation 3:18]. In such a way does the first death on earth take place, as God makes garments of skin from an innocent animal to clothe Adam and Eve [Genesis 3:21]. In such a way the Ultimate Death takes place, as the Lamb of God dies, in order that we be clothed with his righteousness.

And then the Father can say of us, as he does of the saints in Sardis, **"They will walk with me, dressed in white, for they are worthy"** [Revelation 3:4b]. This is the ultimate in worthiness: righteous, accepted, beloved by our Heavenly Father.

Bare-faced and Unashamed

To finally recognize this in my own life gave me a rock to stand on, the knowledge that **I was beloved** no matter what messages of shame seemed to be coming my way, from whatever source; that **I was worthy** because Christ had restored me to the Father's family, and because the Spirit was restoring me to the image the Father had created me in long ago.

When I look at myself in the mirror, naked, I still see the labels shame wants me to take to myself, but to hide from everyone else. And below these I see hiding my real guilt, the sins that I must confess daily before God and others. But when I wear my Father's robe, I know that paradoxically I can stand before the world with an authentic face. I can admit my flaws. I can confess my fears. I can ask for forgiveness for my failures. I can be vulnerable and love others, in spite of hurts they might cause, or have caused, to me. Having the security, the worthiness, of being beloved, can grant me all this.

And I can know that one day, in the resurrection, the flaws will be completely erased, and I will be remade in the image intended for me from always. And then the Father will give me a new gift: *I will also give that person a **white stone with a new name written on it**, known only to the one who receives it* [Revelation 2:17]. In this gift, I will discover my true worthiness.

Reflections:

As God's beloved child, you have no cause for shame.

Think of your relationships with others. Are there any in which you relate to a person or group in terms of an image you are trying to project? What is that image?

- What is the shame you are trying to mask here? What would happen if the other saw you as the opposite of your projection?
- Do you judge others using this mask? How does it affect your own image when they slip up? When they are doing better than you?

On the other hand, God sees us as we really are. And who are we? "Little teapots, short and stout…" As we saw in the first section, we are made in God's image, being re-formed in the image of Jesus, and created to do good works that God himself has prepared for us to do.

Think about how this is expressed in the story of the Lost Son:

- What difference does it make that boy really was **his Father's son**? What difference does it make to you to think of yourself as a legitimate child of the king, and not just a pitied foster-child?
- Think of the Father's **gift of the robe**: How is your guilt and shame covered by Jesus? How can you look at yourself as a person of worth from this point on, knowing yourself as a child of the King? As one who no longer has to work for your worth?
- Think of the **gift of shoes**: a sign of the boy's freedom. How much do you experience a sense of your own freedom? Or are you still relating to your Father as a slave who "must be seen as" a contributing member of the household?
- Think of the **gift of the ring**: all the riches of the house bestowed on the child. How might you lavishly spend the riches of Christ's righteousness on those around you?

Revelation 2:17 says that God will one day reveal to us our true names and natures in the gift of an engraved white stone. As George MacDonald describes beautifully: "It is only when the man has become his name that God gives him the stone with the name upon it… God's name for a man must be the expression of His own idea of the man, that being whom He had in His thought when He began to make the child, and whom He kept in His thought through the long process of creation that went to realize the idea. **To tell the name is to seal the success—to say, "In thee also I am well pleased."**"[10]

28 The Power of Humility

Brothers and sisters, think of what you were when you were called. Not many of you were wise by human standards; not many were influential; not many were of noble birth. But God chose the foolish things of the world to shame the wise; God chose the weak things of the world to shame the strong. [1 Corinthians 1:26-27]

The See-Saw of Status

"Hello." *"Hello."* "Been waiting long?" *"Ages."*

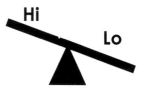

This was the complete dialogue for the first Theatre Games script Troy Cady used with our group as we looked at Status Transactions. He showed us how the essence of good drama lies in the juggling for status that is found in the simplest of daily interactions: as a person who considers their personal status high tries to keep it, or as a person who sees their status as low tries to raise themselves—at least to the level of the other person, if not above. We noticed how tone of voice changed, stance altered, facial expressions mirrored our perceptions. (Try reading the little script above with a friend; notice changes as you switch status around.)[11]

We began to realize that every interaction we enter begins with a perception of the social see-saw, and whether I am up or down on it in relation to the other person. It became clear how we always fight for the high side, either by raising ourselves or lowering the other person. We saw how we could "get high by playing low," through activating the other's pity or guilt. We even observed how we could play high or low status to objects, according to our perception of their value and desirability. And it was rather unnerving to keep noticing this see-saw in life, long after the games were over...

As humans who dislike vulnerability and equate it with shame, this status game is a daily matter for us in relationships. We look at others, then at ourselves, and decide if we are Better Than or Worse Than them. If we see ourselves as "superior, more important or right," and the other as "inferior, incapable or wrong," then we shut ourselves in a Better-Than box. But if we see ourselves as "powerless, deficient or ill-fated," and the other as "privileged, stronger, or luckier," then we seal ourselves in a Worse-Than box. A very insightful book called *The Anatomy of Peace* calls these "boxes of self-deception."[12]

A character in the book says, "When I'm in this [Better-Than] box... I feel superior to others because of these strengths or weaknesses. I use them to keep score of **my and others' relative worth**. So when I'm in this box, I'm doing more than simply noticing differences; I'm **making judgments about people's worth** based on these differences."[13]

And, lo and behold, we are back at the tree, eating that fruit that gives us the knowledge of good and evil. We become the judges of others and ourselves, sifting the evidence to discover who is worthy and who is not. In the end, our main aim is always to become worthy, to justify ourselves by whatever means. And this means that as we act in shame and in the struggle for status, we have to take away the worthiness of the other person by seeing them not as people made in God's image, but as objects.

Objectifying the Other

The Jewish philosopher Martin Buber observed that in every interaction with others we can have **two ways of being**: either seeing the other as a person, or seeing them as an object. He called the first way of being, "**I—Thou**" and the second way of being, "**I—It**."[14]

Think of how we treat objects. High status objects are utilized for personal gain and convenience, or prized by putting them on a pedestal. We covet them, and hope they will increase our own status by using or possessing them. If they are objects of low status—not valuable or useful to us at this time—we ignore them, avoid them as obstacles, or throw them out as trash. In each case, I am the arbiter of the worth of the object, and act accordingly.

In the same way, we ignore or avoid those we consider lower than ourselves, letting their calls go to voice mail and rolling our eyes at their efforts to impress or interact with us. We let them know their status through our criticism, sarcasm, and intimidating body language. With high status people, however—people who are useful or interesting to us—we seek their attention, draw their approval, look for their cooperation. If their distance above us seems too great for this, we might play the martyr or victim to tip the see-saw. Imagine an encounter where a beggar has successfully cornered and aroused the guilt of a rich man: who is now of higher status in the exchange?

Using, ignoring or discarding objects is appropriate. But is this how we are meant to treat beings made in God's image? As C.S. Lewis wrote, "There are no ordinary people. You have never talked to a mere mortal... it is immortals whom we joke with, work with, marry, snub and exploit—immortal horrors or everlasting splendors."[15]

And so Jesus shows us another way—the way of humility.

The Status of Jesus

This text is super-familiar, I know. For that reason, please resist the temptation to skim it, and instead read it with great care, prayerfully noticing Jesus' politics of status:

Do nothing out of selfish ambition or vain conceit. Rather, **in humility value others above yourselves,** *not looking to your own interests but each of you to the interests of the others. In your relationships with one another,* **have the same mindset as Christ Jesus:**
Who, being in very nature God,
  did not consider equality with God
  something to be used to his own advantage;
rather, he made himself nothing
  by taking **the very nature of a servant,** *being made in human likeness.*
And being found in appearance as a man,
  he humbled himself *by becoming obedient to death—*
  even death on a cross! [Philippians 2:3-8]

We tend to equate humility with being "Worse-Than," imagining everyone else is somehow worth more than we are, or acting in a groveling and obsequious manner like Dickens' Uriah Heep. But Paul here urges us to instead model ourselves on Christ's humility, which is completely different. Watch how the see-saw works here:

Christ starts out at the very highest position of status that can be imagined: *equality with God.* He is *in very nature God,* and therefore worthy of the worship of all. (The English word "worship" itself comes from "worth-ship": as part of the Godhead, Christ is the most worthy Being there is.)

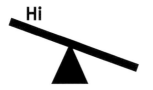

We also start out at a high position of status as children of God, as we saw in the last chapter. Each of us is made in his image. And those of us who have heard the Father calling us and responded have been rid of our shame and guilt, and given great position and prestige as children of the King. While we are not worthy of worship as Jesus is, we are each worthy of dignity and honor, and can be conscious of this as our position through Christ.

Christ, however, in spite of his high position, doesn't *consider equality with God something to be used to his advantage.* More literal translations like the NASB express this as, *"did not regard equality with God a thing to be grasped";* in other words, this high status was not something he attempted to hold onto and assert over others.

Now **Christ descends to the lowest end of the see-saw of status: he** *takes the very nature of a servant.* This is a lot different than the false humility of obsequiousness, and it does not forget his intrinsic worth. Rather, it is a **choice** to descend to lower status, not for personal advantage (playing low to get high) but for the raising of others who had sunk from the status of image-bearers of the most high God to broken, lost, and helpless shadows of their original selves. He *humbles himself* by taking on their image and their very flesh, even to the point of death on their behalf.

We have even more reason **not to regard our high status as children of God something to assert or use to advantage:** it is not anything that we merited or claimed but simply who we now are because it was bestowed on us. We have been raised from humble beginnings. As Paul says in the verse quoted at the beginning of the chapter: *Think of who you were when you were called...*

We, the ones who have been raised to high status through his humble sacrifice, are now called to do the same on behalf of those around us. We are called not to stand proudly on the high status given to us, but like him, to descend so that others may be lifted up: *in humility value others above yourselves.* We are to look to their interests, rather than *selfish ambition or vain conceit.* **We, too, become the servants of those around us.**

Seeing Others Through the Lens of Christ

When I began to recognize the high status I possessed as a child of God, I understood how it gave me security in my relationship with the Father, but not yet how this eliminated shame or fear with other people. I asked a mentor, Hud McWilliams, how these two phenomena were related. After all, God may see me as righteous in Christ, but others are still likely to judge my flaws and failures! Am I meant, then, to live in a nice little me-and-God spiritual bubble, insulated from the painful give-and-take of relationships?

He pointed me to Romans 8:5-6: *Those who live according to the flesh have their minds set on what the flesh desires; but those who live in accordance with the Spirit have their minds set on what the Spirit desires.* **The mind governed by the flesh is death, but the mind governed by the Spirit is life and peace.** We read later in verse 16: *The Spirit himself testifies with our spirit that we are God's children.*

As the Spirit assures me of my high position with the Father, my mind is transformed so that I no longer have to take into my being the messages of shame that I receive from others and from *the flesh,* that part of me that is preoccupied with the knowledge of good and evil rather than the knowledge of God. And then, safe in his love, I can stop worrying about myself, as I embrace the life and peace that comes from a *mind governed by the Spirit.* I become free to forget myself, and to serve others with humility, as Jesus did.

Timothy Keller, in his booklet *The Freedom of Self-Forgetfulness,* says this: "Gospel-humility is not needing to think about myself. Not needing to connect things with myself. It is an end to thoughts such as, 'I'm in the room with these people; does that make me look good? Do I want to be here?' True gospel-humility means I stop connecting every experience, every conversation, with myself... [This is] the blessed rest that only self-forgetfulness brings."[16]

As we do this, we forego the way of being that looks at other people as objects, rating their relative worth to us. We relate to them as people who have intrinsic worth, through creation and Christ.[17]

In fact, embracing Jesus' way of humility is not simply forsaking the "I—It" way of being. It adds a new dimension to Buber's "I—Thou" ideal, as Christ stands between both.[18] Christ mediates our relationships, sharpens our view of the other, standing between us like the lenses in a pair of glasses so that we relate to them through him. **Then we begin to see other people as Jesus sees them and has made them to be.** "Spiritual love recognizes the true image of the other person which he has received from Jesus Christ, the image that Jesus Christ himself embodied and would stamp upon all men."[19]

And it is also worth us taking to heart what Gandalf says in *The Hobbit*: "You're a very fine person, Mr. Baggins, and I'm quite fond of you. But you are really just a little fellow, in a wide world, after all."[20] Not many of us were wise when we were called, or noble, or influential. But still we have been sent by God on a Quest to serve others, knowing that *God chose the foolish things of the world...*

Reflections:

Humility ascribes to others the worth we have been given.

"Now that she was left alone with the children, she took no notice of either of them… I expect most witches are like that. They are not interested in things or people unless they can use them; they are terribly practical."
— C.S. Lewis on the witch Jadis, *The Magician's Nephew*[21]

- How, when we see others as objects rather than people, do we behave like Jadis the witch? How does this lead to true evil?

Each of us tends to a general preference for either the "Better Than" or "Worse-Than" boxes in our status interactions with people, based on our upbringing and psychological leanings (though there will be exceptions in certain relationships). But **both are used to justify our wrong actions and attitudes toward the other person.**[22]

- When you think through your relationships with people, are you more likely to perceive yourself as Better-Than (superior, important, right) or Worse-Than (powerless, deficient, ill-fated)?
- What behaviors does this lead to for you personally? How does it relate to the self-protective habit of self-justification?
- How, in each of these, do we objectify the other person? How does it take away their worthiness as people in the image of God, and as fellow sons and daughters through Christ?

Now compare this with Christ's model of humility in Philippians 2.

- How is the Better-Than stance a caricature of true worth? How is the Worse-Than posture a twisted picture of true humility?
- What difference does it make, in taking the low position of humility, to know that you have a high position of worth as a child of God?
- What difference does it make, in recognizing this position of worth, that you did nothing to earn or deserve it? Why are we not to "hold onto" this worth, even though it is truly ours?
- How does recognizing that others also have worth, in their created image of God, and in the re-created image of Jesus, help you to see them differently and serve them with true humility? What behaviors might you see in yourself then? (Think of specific people…)

29 Faithful and True

The Lord said to me, "Go, show your love to your wife again, though she is loved by another man and is an adulteress. Love her as the Lord loves the Israelites, though they turn to other gods..."
[Hosea 3:1]

Counter-Cultural Commitment

Our culture does not prize loyalty. If someone displeases us, we "unfriend" them on our social networks. We drop people if we feel like we don't really click anymore, or if they take up with a partner we dislike. We shop around for the church that best suits our needs, and go somewhere else as soon as the kids don't love the youth group. Often, we go as long as we dare in dating relationships without making a commitment, and perhaps ditch it when the other person seems to be pressuring us for one. We only take the plunge of marriage when we are sure that this is the person that will make us happiest in life; if it turns out differently later, well, there's always a no-fault divorce...

So, when we read Hosea in our cultural context, it sounds crazy.

In the very first verses, we see God telling his prophet to make a thoroughly unsuitable marriage: *"Go, marry a promiscuous woman and have children with her, for like an adulterous wife this land is guilty of unfaithfulness to the Lord"* [Hosea 1:2]. It seems that the first child she bears is Hosea's, but the next two—a girl named "Not-Loved" and a boy called "Not-My-People"—are fathered by other men. Then she runs off with one of her lovers, and ends up sold into slavery. The word of the Lord comes to Hosea once again, in the verse at the top of the page, and Hosea goes out and buys his wife, bringing her back home.

Of course, God is demonstrating through his prophet his faithfulness to his unfaithful people. He is creating through Hosea a living picture of the anguish He feels at the adultery of Israel with their idols. (Since worship of Baal involved ritual prostitution, physical adultery was mixed up with this as well—see Hosea 4:14.) Sometimes in this book and other prophetic passages, God uses an alternate picture of a grieved Father with a wayward child:

When Israel was a child, I loved him, and out of Egypt I called my son.
But the more they were called, the more they went away from me.
They sacrificed to the Baals and they burned incense to images.

It was I who taught Ephraim to walk, taking them by the arms;
*   but they did not realize it was I who healed them.*
I led them with cords of human kindness, with ties of love.
To them I was like one who lifts a little child to the cheek,
*   and I bent down to feed them.* [Hosea 11:1-4]

But at the same time as Hosea the prophet is a picture of God's compassionate commitment to his inconstant people, he is also a real human being, suffering true pain and betrayal from his very human wife and her blatant infidelities. Surely God couldn't really ask a person to go through this, just to make his point? Surely God wants us to marry good people, have pleasant friends and supportive relationships? Surely he wouldn't call **me** to something like this?

But maybe he is. Maybe he does. Almost certainly, he is calling you to renew an uncomfortable commitment to someone who is in your life already. (Did that person just pop into your mind right now?) That is because not only does he use Hosea to model his brand of covenanted, committed love to us—he wants us to model our love for others on his own faithful love.

Psalm 89 celebrates this faithfulness in verse after verse: *I will sing of the Lord's great love forever; with my mouth I will make **your faithfulness** known through all generations. I will declare that your love stands firm forever, that you have established **your faithfulness** in heaven itself* [v.1-2]. These are just two of the seven times the psalmist uses the Hebrew word *emuwnah* in this psalm: a word literally meaning firmness or steadiness, but figuratively signifying faithfulness, fidelity, and truth.

The first part of the word, *em*, is also the Hebrew word for "mother," and conjures up the image of a mother's indestructible love for her infant: *Can a mother forget the baby at her breast and have no compassion on the child she has borne? **Though she may forget, I will not forget you!*** [Isaiah 49:15].

In the same way we are meant to have *emuwnah*—faithfulness, truth—in our own relationships. We tend to think of truth as an objective reality somewhere outside our persons—like the Platonic ideals. But the Hebrew conception of Truth was always based in the faithful Person of God. Parker Palmer notes that this is the basis of Jesus' teaching as well:

> "**[Jesus']** **call to truth is a call to community** – with him, with each other, with creation and its Creator. If what we know is an

abstract, impersonal, apart from us, it cannot be truth, for **truth involves a vulnerable, faithful, and risk-filled interpenetration of the knower and the known.**"[23]

Faithful Families

Since we began with Hosea, let's first explore what this means in our families. We're not all meant to go out and marry prostitutes, are we?

Probably not. But it does mean realizing that God does not call us to marry someone for the **primary** purpose of gaining our own happiness and fulfillment, but rather for building each other up in the "better or worse." He may even occasionally call a person to marry someone more for the other's good than their own. I know several remarkable cases of this:

- John, an English businessman, married a destitute Thai woman while he was working in that country, to save her from a life that could easily have ended in prostitution or slavery—even though they could not speak the same language. When we met them in Geneva, they had been happily married for over 20 years (and had learned how to communicate).

- Bartek, a Polish carpenter in our Brussels church, felt thankful for God's blessings in his life, and asked Him for a new challenge. A week later, an African woman asked him if he would marry her widowed sister and adopt her son. Even when it became clear this woman had AIDS, Bartek, believing God had sent him to care for them, moved from Brussels to Togo and married her.

- My own grandfather married my grandmother, his former high-school sweetheart, when she had been diagnosed with tuberculosis and given one year to live, so that he could care for her. In the end, she outlived him by about ten years, and cared for him during his terminal cancer.

None of these make sense in our self-focused society. But maybe that says more about our society than about them: *Because your sins are so many and your hostility so great, the prophet is considered a fool, the inspired person a maniac* [Hosea 9:7].

It is true: few of us are called to situations such as these. But many of us find ourselves facing questions of fidelity when a spouse is or seems to be no longer the person we married. Still, we know people who rise to this challenge too. My husband's mentor, Paul Petrie, cared for his quadriplegic wife, Rebecca, for the rest of her life after she fell down the stairs.[24] And the president of our Bible College, Robertson McQuilkin, quit his prestigious job to stay at home for the next fifteen years with his wife, after Alzheimer's made her fearful to be with anyone but him.[25] Others we know, like Hosea, have made the long journey back to trust after adultery or the mental/emotional unfaithfulness of pornography addiction.

This is not to say that there can never be divorce or separation. Over the last several months, I have been helping a disabled woman who finally left her abusive partner: setting up a separate bank account, finding new housing, etc. This is because fidelity, in the end, has to work both ways. We see this in Hosea, as God allows the Israelites to experience the consequences of their unrepentant infidelity to him. Hosea does the same, for a time; and when he invites his wife back, it must be her choice to come and remain faithful. In the same way, it is not just or right to allow my friend's partner to continue to abuse and oppress her—and it is actually more loving **to him** to put a stop to his destructive behavior.

At the same time, faithfulness calls us not to bail just because things are rocky. It calls us to face the conflict, to work on communication, to find resources to meet needs. It does not call us to be Lone Ranger heroes, and to try to fill these gaps ourselves. Rather, it calls us to lean into community and vulnerability before God and others, so that they can help us stay faithful.

That's what I saw with Paul and Rebecca, as they managed Rebecca's disability with the help of live-in volunteers. That's what I see with Adam and Caroline, the couple who adopted a challenged Ukrainian orphan, as they relate to their family and church. These friends are open and honest, and surrounded by others, both family and friends, who are faithful to them as they are faithful to their families. And they in turn are a blessing to those around them.

Committed to (not Consuming) Christian Community

This brings up our commitment to our church, our Christian community. When we first got married and became members of our church in Virginia, the pastor, Tom Kenney, asked us, "How has our church disappointed you so far?" We were surprised, but pleased to be asked. It hasn't, we replied. "Don't worry, it will," Tom said.

This is because the church is made up of people and people are the most annoying, exasperating, and dangerous creatures on the planet.

If it were just about the programs—the sermons, the worship songs, the facilities, and so on—it wouldn't be so hard to find the church that was perfect for you. But people make it almost impossible. They have differences of opinion about Bible study methodology, about drinking alcohol, about ways to educate your kids, about the color of the carpet in the nursery... And they can be strange.

When we were working at Crossroads Church in Geneva, we used to notice that God would graciously send us strange people—not a lot, but some—to help us to work on our own sense of grace. Some of these had mental problems. There was Diana*, the odd lady who wore a red clown wig and danced in the back of the church sometimes. There was Sandra, a sweet, slightly slow woman who waited patiently till everybody was finished talking to Carlton on Sunday morning, and then settled in for a nice 20-minute conversation when everyone else had driven away. (Except for me and the kids, sitting in the car and not-so-patiently waiting.) There was Terry, a homeless man who wore a coat, scarf, and balaclava to church even in the summer, played a harmonica tunelessly during services, and got the idea that God wanted him to live in the church building. (Carlton had to tell Terry that God had not mentioned the plan to him.)

And this is not to mention all the different nationalities, denominations and personalities that had gathered there in Geneva. Sometimes, not surprisingly, this led to conflict. Were all of these odd people part of the Truth that God wanted us to know and understand? Or should we, as so many of us do, shop around for a church full of people who most fit our own views, our own race, our own politics, our own visions, our own socio-economic background?

Romans 12:10 is talking about **actual people** when it says, *"Be devoted to one another in love."* In *Life Together,* Dietrich Bonhoeffer talks about our search for the perfect Christian community as a "wish-dream"—and a sin. Christian community, he argues, is something that we are given as a gift by God, not something we are meant to discover or create. If Christ stands between me and my brothers and sisters as mediator, I must see them as he sees them, and love them as Christ does. He states: "Those who **love their dream of a Christian community more than the Christian community itself become**

---

* Names in this paragraph have been changed.

destroyers of that Christian community even though their personal intentions may be ever so honest, earnest, and sacrificial."[26]

Maybe the church you are in already is the church you are meant to be in. Maybe you are meant to lean into relationship with your brothers and sisters, even with those you find critical, boring, contrarian, unreliable, air-headed, depressing, happy-clappy, or just plain odd. Maybe in this commitment we will find the community transformed into a purer image of Christ's body with its varied members, rather than a sanitized club of like-minded strangers.

Strangers to Whom You are Sent

In our section on "tent living," we already talked about being open to strangers to whom God is sending you. We cannot make a commitment to every one of these. Perhaps we touch their lives only for a short time. But other times, we might sense the Spirit sending us to make a commitment to one of these strangers, people who are not (or not yet) part of our Christian community.

This may come about because of a sense of compassion that God puts in your heart for their situation, or because they seem an answer to a prayer you prayed, or because they are part of a neighborhood or context you are praying for. They might be "people of peace," people who welcome you into their lives, and show openness to the Gospel. But they might also be an enemy that you feel called to love and pray for. It seems to me that each of us needs at least one person like this in our lives, to demonstrate God's kindness and faithfulness to them and to become more like Him.

One Sunday shortly after the Brussels attacks, a Syrian refugee named Moussab walked into our worship gathering. He had met a visiting street pastor at the makeshift memorial in town who had talked to him about Jesus, and given him the name of our church. Jonathan, one of our leaders, happened to sit next to him, and spent the whole evening unpacking what was going on for Moussab. Since then, Jonathan has welcomed Moussab home for meals, involved him in his prayer group, helped pay for him to come on our church retreat, met his friends, even taken him on vacation to his family home in France. He has continued to unpack the Gospel with him, to encourage him as he lives out baby faith in a new place and relates to other refugees, and to include him in community in every way possible. If you asked Jonathan about it, he would just likely just shrug in his Gallic way and say, "It's normal." But to those of us surrounding them, we can see how God has sent Jonathan to be a faithful friend to a foreigner in our midst.

As we have already seen, there are vulnerabilities in such a relationship, as with any other commitment. But when God calls you to commit to someone, he also provides the means to see it through. Everyone would have considered it normal for Jerry and Elizabeth, the couple whose Egyptian friend turned out to be a spy, to detach from his wife and blame her as well. Instead, they shared her pain and loss from the moment she found out through the court hearings of her husband's secret life. As they helped her with kids and house through the difficult months of preparing to move back to her family in another state, they also worked with her through their mutual feelings of betrayal. And they continue to deepen their relationship with her, as well as her extended family, through phone calls and visits.

Faithfulness and fidelity are not fashionable concepts in our society. But they, more than any belief or doctrine or creed, demonstrate the Truth of God, his compassion and goodness to his wayward children. As we commit ourselves to others, we can rejoice in God's commitment to us:

> I will betroth you to me forever;
>> I will betroth you in righteousness and justice,
>> in love and compassion.
> **I will betroth you in faithfulness** [emuwnah]
>> and you will acknowledge the Lord...
> I will plant her for myself in the land;
>> I will show my love to the one I called 'Not my loved one.'
> I will say to those called 'Not my people,' 'You are my people';
>> and they will say, 'You are my God.'" [Hosea 2:19-20,23]

Reflections:

God's loving faithfulness enables our own.

What is the key to faithfulness? Not gritting our teeth and determining to get through, but what we saw in the previous chapter: **seeing the other through the lens of Jesus and his faithful love for them—and for us.** This is what powers us to persevere in loving a person who is different, difficult or disabled—and in doing so, receive God's blessing.

Consider this quote from Robertson McQuilkin, about his years of caring for his wife with Alzheimer's: "No one ever needed me like Muriel, and no one ever responded to my efforts so totally as she. It's the nearest thing I've experienced on a human plane to what my relationship with God was designed to be: God's unfailing love poured out in constant care of helpless me."[27]

- What is your response to this quote?
- Why is faithfulness such a counter-cultural move in our time?
- Who is the person God brought to your mind as the one to whom you need to re-commit in faithfulness? Someone in your family? In your Christian community? Someone in need?
- How can you re-frame your view of this person/these people in order to see them more as Christ does? (How can you avoid looking at them from a Better-Than or a Worse-Than perspective?) How might a new recognition of God as faithful to you empower you to see and serve them differently?
- What will it look like to make this commitment? What behaviors will it entail? How can you lean into community to help you in your commitment to be faithful to this person?
- Are you facing a case where you need to love someone by calling limits on a sinful way they are behaving (as Hosea did with his wife)? What is your situation? How is this also a way of being faithful to them (rather than simply co-dependent)? What other faithful relationships do you have that could support you as you do this?
- Who is someone outside your family or Christian community that God might be calling you to make a commitment to for a time?

30 Debt Forgiveness

And forgive us our debts, as we also have forgiven our debtors.
[Matthew 6:12]

You Deserve It!

Try searching "I deserve the best" quotes online. You will be rewarded with a screen full of image tiles filled with words like these:

- "Respect yourself enough to know that you deserve the very best."
- "You deserve to be with somebody who makes you happy, somebody who doesn't complicate your life, somebody who won't hurt you."
- "If you feel like you deserve better, it's because you do."
- "Say it with me: I deserve to have my needs met."

We have heard words like these so many times—from mentor figures in movies, from self-actualizing characters in TV shows, from feisty independent women in chick-lit, from self-help gurus and TV preachers—that they sound like wisdom to us. Of course I deserve the best. Of course my needs should be met. Of course I shouldn't be hurt, or have my life complicated.

The problem is, this philosophy can kill off any true relationship you would ever seek to have, with God or other people.

The Anatomy of Peace identifies this ("I-Deserve") as their fourth box of self-deception. When I am in this box, I see myself as meritorious and right, but also a mistreated and unappreciated victim. The other person is seen as mistaken, offensive or abusive, and ungrateful for all I am and do.[28] In essence, I feel **entitled** to a lot of things from someone else: respect, love, fair treatment, attention, my way...

But wait—if I truly have worth, as a child of the King, don't I deserve to be treated like one? Lots of the "I deserve" quotes tie these ideas together, such as: "Know your worth. Know the difference between what you're getting and what you deserve."

Maybe these two things **would** tie together if our worth as children of God depended on our earning or deserving that position. But it doesn't. Our worth is given to us as a free gift. Our divine image is a divine gift of creation, not an achievement. Our guilt and shame are clothed in Christ's righteousness, not the filthy rags of self-effort we try to pass off as righteousness. We are justified by Jesus, not by our own judgment of what we deserve. And therefore, we are entitled to nothing. It is all by grace.

All of the boxes of self-deception described in *The Anatomy of Peace* have one goal: the justification of one's selfish attitudes and actions towards another person. As one character says about the I-Deserve box: "The more sure I am that I'm right, the more likely I will actually be mistaken. My need to be right makes it more likely that I will be wrong! Likewise, the more sure I am that I am mistreated, the more likely I am to miss ways that I am mistreating others myself. **My need for justification obscures the truth.**"[29]

Forget the Repayment Plan

Jesus gives us a clear example of this in his well-known parable of the Unforgiving Servant [Matthew 18:21-35]. Peter kicks it off with a question: *"Lord, how many times shall I forgive my brother or sister who sins against me? Up to seven times?"* (This is pretty generous, for most rabbis only allowed for three offenses before forgiveness was rescinded.) Jesus tells this story in response.

A servant has racked up a debt of ten thousand bags of gold to his master. But **each one** of these bags was worth 20 years of a day laborer's salary (like the talents in the Matthew 25 parable we looked at earlier). So he has somehow accumulated 200,000 years' worth of debt! (What on earth did he **do** with all of it? We have to wonder.) It is a crazy amount, and even crazier is the fact that he begs the Master, *"Be patient with me, and I will pay back everything!"* (What kind of reality is he living in? Does he really want to embark on a repayment plan lasting hundreds of millennia?) But the Master takes pity on him and cancels the whole debt.

Then, he meets another servant who owes him a hundred silver coins: around three month's wages. Most of the times I have heard this parable retold, the teller has likened this debt to about $20; but as you can see, the other guy actually owes him a considerable amount. Imagine how you would feel toward someone who owed you a quarter of your yearly salary! It is only when compared to the insanely enormous debt forgiven the first guy that such a debt would look like a pittance. Still, he grabs the other servant demanding payment, and cannot hear the echo of his own words when the man chokes through his stranglehold, *"Be patient with me, and I will pay back everything!"*

It is with this in mind that we must pray, *forgive us our debts, as we also have forgiven our debtors.* Sometimes we substitute the word *trespass,* with its connotation of stepping over the line, for this word *debt* in the Lord's Prayer. But the original Greek word, *opheilema,* means "that which is owed; that which is justly or legally due"—in other words, a *debt.*

We owe God our obedience, to not "trespass" his commands. But we also leave undone things we should have done—more liabilities.[30] And perhaps more than anything, we live only a tiny percent of our lives mindful of his presence and worshipful of his glory, focusing instead on our own comfort, our own rightness, our own losses and lacks—and the entitlements we credit to our accounts. We rack up debt to God every second of the day. And yet when we come to him, admitting our failure and our inability to pay, he writes off the debt for the sake of Jesus, who paid it in our place.

For if anyone was entitled to say "I Deserve," it was Jesus. But we have already seen that he didn't hang on to all of that [Philippians 2:6]. Instead, he justified us when we could never hope to justify ourselves. His justification of us, instead of obscuring the truth, shows up who we are: wayward kids brought back after wasting our inheritance, no longer clothed in shame but in the shoes of a freeman and the robe of a son. And then he gives us a ring embossed with his ensign, with which we can sign bills of humility and forgiveness to be credited to his account, to his unlimited riches of righteousness.

"No One Owes Me Anything"

Thus, we are meant to follow his example, and write off the debts of others. Because **he paid for these debts, just as he did for ours**.[31]

A couple of years ago I taught on the Lord's Prayer. While looking for resources to help us understand the petition about *forgiving our debts,* I ran across a video dramatizing the story of a young woman who was raped by a co-worker at a business conference. It had ruined her life: she lost her job, broke up with her boyfriend, and hid in the house as she suffered the effects of PTSD. The one thing that fueled her life was anger towards her rapist. Then one day at church, the pastor spoke on the Parable of the Unforgiving Servant, and this thought formed in her head: "No one owes me anything." She went home and began forgiving everyone she could think of that she felt had wronged her—including her rapist. He was never charged for what he did to her. But she was set free from the debt of his sin, in a deeper way than he was, by having forgiven him.[32]

I wept as I watched this video. And ever since, that woman's words have echoed in my mind, as a reminder when I am standing on entitlement:

"No one owes me anything."

When I release the debts of others, I release myself. I release myself from scorekeeping, from scrutiny, from excuses, from tit-for-tat trades. I release myself from bitterness, from anger, from replaying the offense ad nauseum. I release myself from the monstrous sin of grasping at a petty sum when I myself have been acquitted from gargantuan deficit—even if in human terms the offense is as serious as rape.

On the other hand, when I imprison others for the debts they owe me, I imprison myself inside a tiny box as well. We see this both in the parable and the Prayer: God's forgiveness of us is contingent upon our forgiveness of others. We ask for God's forgiveness in the prayer based upon the fact that we **have already** forgiven the debts of the other. And when the servant who has been forgiven the colossal debt throws his debtor in jail, he finds himself landing there right alongside him.

Is this teaching that we can lose our salvation by not forgiving others? I'm not sure of all of the theological ramifications here. What I **am** sure of—and this is the important thing—is that we cannot **experience** the forgiveness of God if we are holding others to account for their debts. When we say, "I Deserve," we are setting ourselves up as judge and jury, using our knowledge of good and evil to exact payment from our fellow. In that moment, we have separated ourselves from God's grace and made ourselves god.

Two-Way Repentance = Reconciliation

As the quote said earlier, "The more sure I am that I am mistreated, the more likely I am to miss ways that I am mistreating others myself." When my focus is on the wrongdoing of others towards me, I whitewash everything that I have done wrongly towards them to make their actions stand out in contrast.

Why do we not realize that we also offend other people? Don't we recognize that we could not be in **any** relationship were it not for the grace extended to us by our mates, our friends, our children, our communities? We may not owe as much as to God, and we may owe differing amounts to different people, but once we start playing the debt-accounting game, we will find ourselves always on the wrong side of it.

More wise words from Bonhoeffer: "If my sinfulness appears to me to be in any way smaller or less detestable in comparison with the sins of others, I am still not recognizing my sinfulness at all. ... How can I possibly serve another person in unfeigned humility if I seriously regard his sinfulness as worse than my own?"[33]

I am terrible at apologizing, as my husband will tell you. I want to be right all the time, or at least seen to be right, and even in my apologies can usually fit in some justification for my offense. Like most people, I would much rather be right than forgiven! But if I must be forgiven daily by God, I probably also need ask daily forgiveness from others as well. (Especially Carlton.)

Just as humility is not wallowing in shame or hiding in a Worse-Than box, neither is confession. It is not meant to be about promises of self-atonement (*"Be patient with me, and I will pay back everything!"*), or sneaky victim statements that try to secretly raise our status (*"I only did it because..."*). It recognizes that even our good intentions may have bad outcomes. As both parties are able to see themselves as sinners and see the other through a Christ-lens, reconciliation will be redemptive, and the relationship will grow even **because of** the offense as they turn back toward God and each other.

Reconciliation, unlike forgiveness, requires two people. It is something to pray for and work towards, but we cannot control the will of the other. The great thing about forgiveness, however, is that you can choose to offer it yourself, of your own free will.

Or rather, should we say, out of the riches of Christ's righteousness. For when he pays our debt, he does not just bring us back to zero in our righteousness accounts, so that we have to work to replenish them. Rather, he deposits the riches of his righteousness that we can spend on others, including the means to cover the debts that they owe us. In this way, we pass on the grace of Jesus and live debt-free lives.

> Let no debt remain outstanding, except the continuing debt to love one another, for whoever loves others has fulfilled the law. [Romans 13:8]

Reflections:

Release the debts owed you, and find freedom.

How do you hold on to entitlement with others?
- "I deserve to be made happy, to be satisfied…"
- "I deserve to be loved more, better, in my way…"
- "I deserve your respect, your trust, not to be questioned…"
- "I deserve to do only fulfilling/interesting tasks I choose…"
- "I deserve my time, my rest, my pleasures, my freedom…"
- "I deserve to do only my share, not what I think is your job…"
- "I deserve an explanation, an acknowledgement you offended me, an apology I deem as sincere…"
- What are other entitlements you feel toward another person?

What does it look like in practice when you feel entitled?
- Do you confront or attack the other person, and demand from them the thing you feel you deserve?
- Do you bottle up resentment, and then let it burst out when they attack you, or when the pressure becomes too much?
- Do you use passive-aggressive means to make them pay?
- How is your demeanor toward the other? Sarcastic? Silent? Cold? Critical? Contemptuous? Angry?
- **How well does this get you what you think you deserve?**

Think of someone you are holding something against.
- Meditate on the debt forgiven you by God. (Make a list?)
- Now think of their debt as also paid by Jesus. Now, **you** can cover their debt out of the inexhaustible riches of Jesus credited to your account. They do not owe you anything.
- Are you able to let go of your entitlement? Do you feel free? If not, maybe you have not truly grasped **your** forgiveness…

Does this mean that we cannot address the ways in which others hurt us? Of course not. But it does mean that we come to them having already forgiven them, and not demanding what we deserve. Rather, we acknowledge our own fault (in our attitudes and unforgiveness, if not in action). Then we bring the faults of others to their attention **for the sake of their growth, and the reconciliation of the relationship**, not because "I deserve" something. This is only possible if we will constantly remember: **"I have been forgiven much—no one owes me anything."**

risking resurrection

(or, crosses and coracles)

31 Tempted to Crossless Christianity

Then Jesus said to his disciples, "Whoever wants to be my disciple must deny themselves and take up their cross and follow me. For whoever wants to save their life will lose it, but whoever loses their life for me will find it." [Matthew 16:24-25]
Read Matthew 16:13-27.

From Cornerstone to Stumbling Stone

The breathtaking swiftness of the fall must have confused Peter very much. Only minutes earlier, Jesus had called him blessed for his heaven-inspired statement of Jesus' identity: *"You are the Messiah, the Son of the living God"* [Matthew 16:16]. Jesus followed this by giving his outspoken disciple a new name—Peter, the Rock—and by proclaiming that his confession would be the cornerstone for a new community. When his rabbi and Master further stated that he was giving Peter the keys to his new kingdom, it must have been a very heady moment for this former fisherman. We can tell this because of the extreme presumption of what he did next.

He rebuked his Rabbi.

This was unheard of in first-century Judaism. A disciple literally walked behind his rabbi as they went along the road, bodily demonstrating his commitment to follow in the rabbi's footsteps. The disciple did not ever teach in his rabbi's presence; indeed, some sages thought that doing so merited God's judgment.

That Peter rebuked Jesus may have been due, however, not only to an improper wielding of the new authority granted him, but also because Jesus with his very next words had begun to demolish every one of Peter's ideas of what being the Messiah meant: *From that time on Jesus began to explain to his disciples that he must go to Jerusalem and* **suffer many things** *at the hands of the elders, the chief priests and the teachers of the law, and* **that he must be killed** *and on the third day be raised to life* [v.21].

But... the Messiah was meant to be a victorious ruler! One who defeated the oppressors of the people—not a criminal crucified as so many would-be Jewish messiahs had already been. No wonder Peter responded with such vehemence against this idea: *"Never, Lord! This shall never happen to you!"* [v.22]. And he was probably only giving voice to the dismay felt by all of Jesus' disciples.

For wasn't this the whole point of following the Messiah: to learn God's holy ways and so receive his comfort and protection? To restore the nation and rule under Jesus in the *shalom* of God? To be kept safe and set free to live long, prosperous, peaceful lives in the promised land, without fear of death?

But it was not the way of the Rabbi Jesus. He knew about himself what Hebrews 2:14-15 tells us: *Since the children have flesh and blood, he too shared in their humanity so that **by his death he might break the power of him who holds the power of death**—that is, the devil—and free those who all their lives were held in slavery by their fear of death.* In Peter's rebuke, Jesus recognizes not simple insubordination, but a Satanic temptation to turn away from his calling to the Cross.

And so he turns to face Peter, and rebukes him in turn: *"Get behind me, Satan! You are a stumbling block to me; you do not have in mind the concerns of God, but merely human concerns"* [v.23]. In these words, Peter heard himself reduced from The Rock, uttering the cornerstone confession of the new kingdom, to a roadblock placed by the devil to trip Jesus up.

Temptation to Reject the Cross

It was not the first time Jesus had faced such a temptation. At the very beginning of his ministry, Satan himself had met him in the desert and offered him the world's kingdoms without the cross [Matthew 4:8-9]. Jesus resisted this temptation with the same vehemence as he does Peter's: *"Away from me, Satan!"*

How strong was the temptation to resist the cross, even for Jesus, can be seen in the fact that Satan tempts him one last time as he hangs in exposure and agony. The chief priests and elders stand at the foot of the cross and mock him, saying: *"He saved others, but he can't save himself! He's the king of Israel! **Let him come down now from the cross, and we will believe in him.** He trusts in God. Let God rescue him now if he wants him, for he said, 'I am the Son of God'"* [Matthew 27:42-43]. It was a last-ditch attempt by the devil to get him to reject the path of suffering and death for proofs of earthly power and authority. After all, he had prayed only the night before, *"My Father, if it is possible, may this cup be taken from me..."* [Matthew 26:39]. But Jesus stays where he is, the embodiment of *"yet not as I will, but as You will."*

If rejecting the cross was a temptation for Jesus, how much more is it for us?

Like Peter, we too can be dismayed by Christ's Cross. It seems defeatist to some people, and barbarous to others. Richard Niebuhr famously described the liberalism of his day in these words: "A God without wrath brought men without sin into a Kingdom without judgment through the ministrations of a Christ without a Cross."[1] Still others deny the Cross by twisting it into a symbol of political power or prosperity, the very temptation Jesus resisted in the desert with Satan; as he told Pilate, *"My kingdom is not of this world. If it were, my servants would fight to prevent my arrest"* [John 18:36].

But perhaps we most demonstrate our inability to accept Christ's Cross when we refuse to follow Jesus to the cross ourselves.

Take Up Your Cross and Follow Me

When Jesus tells Peter, *"Get behind me!"* he is reminding him of the path all good disciples should tread—in the footsteps of their rabbi. Peter had forsaken that path and presumed to rebuke Jesus and revise his mission. Jesus sends him back to the place of following, listening, imitating.

And this imitation would not just be in life, but also in death. Jesus tells Peter and the rest: if the Master would take up the cross, his disciples must do the same. That is the context of the verses at the beginning of this chapter, verses that have been central to the theme of our discussion all along.

Just as the idea of a Christ on the Cross was unthinkable to Jews looking for a victorious military ruler, the idea that people would deliberately follow Jesus into suffering and death goes against the basic premise of most religions throughout the ages. The general idea has usually been that I would offer worship and sacrifice to the gods so that they in return would protect my crops, protect my money, protect my family, protect my life. Fear of death is the fuel of idolatry.

In earlier chapters, we explored the masks worn by this fear-driven idolatry in our times. The philosopher Peter Kreeft notes: "For our culture, the cardinal problem of human life is to conform objective reality to the wishes of Man... This relates to our **ignoring of death** through the connecting link of **a demand for comfort, security and control**."[2] Rather than appeasing supernatural forces for our protection, we rely on our own self-protective devices, thus banishing the bogeyman of death from conscious thought as much as possible.

It does not work. The fear of death enslaves us whether we face it or not.

But as we already seen, Jesus came to *free those who all their lives were held in slavery by their fear of death* [Hebrews 2:15]. In fact, he came to give us the freedom and power to lay down our own lives as he did.

Remember Bonhoeffer's principle that the simple understanding of Jesus' commands must not be driven out by a more spiritualized interpretation? This temptation is never greater than with these words: *"Whoever wants to be my disciple must deny themselves and take up their cross and follow me."* We too easily reduce this disturbing, solemn charge to a nudge toward patience in heavy traffic or with an annoying person like garrulous Aunt Agatha.[3] The thought of real suffering, much less actual physical death, rarely or barely enters our consciousness as the context of this commandment.

When it does begin to sink in, we may find ourselves as dismayed as Peter. How can Jesus call us to make a choice to put our arms around death, the very thing we have most feared all our lives, and carry it with us as we follow him? St. Augustine considers this conundrum: "A question not to be shirked arises: whether in truth death is good to the good. For if it be, how has it come to pass that such a thing should be the punishment for sin? For the first men would not have suffered death had they not sinned. How then can that be good to the good which could not have happened except to the evil?"[4]

Following Jesus Through Death's Door

The answer to this paradox has to do with the fact that we are **following** Jesus into death, and that in **his** death, he redeems this ultimate evil into something ultimately good for his followers. Peter Kreeft explains this in his Christian philosophy of death, *Love is Stronger than Death*:

> "All death is a door. Jesus' death, for a Christian, is a special door. All death is a sacrament, the primary sacrament in every person's life. Jesus' death for a Christian, energizes these other deaths, opens the door of death, wins through to heaven for man, transforms death from a hole into a door, from a door to nonbeing into a door to being, from a door to hell into a door to heaven. **The early Christians called the day of their death *dies natalis*, birthday.**"[5]

Without this redemption of death, we are right to fear it, for it makes a mockery of our lives, morphing them to meaninglessness. The Preacher mourns this in Ecclesiastes 8:3,5: *This is the evil in everything that happens under the sun: the same destiny overtakes all. The hearts of people, moreover, are full of evil and there is madness in their hearts while they live, and afterward they join the dead... For the living know that they will die, but the dead know nothing; they have no further reward, and even their name is forgotten.*

But the Preacher also proclaims: *He has made everything beautiful in its time. He has also set eternity in the human heart...* [3:11]. Now, the doorway into eternity, created by Jesus through his Cross, can make even death beautiful, as it becomes our re-birth in resurrection. In the birth process, both mother and baby go through a grueling physical ordeal. But the end makes all that pain worthwhile for both. So Christ becomes, in effect, both our brother and our mother in the resurrection process, willingly going through the labor of death to rise again and bring us to birth in new life: *For the joy set before him he endured the cross, scorning its shame...* [Hebrews 12:2].[6]

Because of Christ's Cross, we pass through our death like babies being born into a new reality in which life, growth and freedom exist in a form we could not have imagined in the womb of this world. We pass through death's door into a New Creation, a world made new, reborn just as we are. We find ourselves released from all that hindered us here—disability, sadness, sin and evil—and set free to be completely who we were made to be, in perfect relationship with our Creator, and in Him, with each other.[7]

Thus, rather than death draining meaning from life, resurrection gives meaning to our death through new life. This is why Paul calls our faith *"futile"* without it; why he urges us, *"If only for this life we have hope in Christ, we are of all people most to be pitied"* [1 Corinthians 15:17,19]. It is why he can proclaim, quoting the prophets of old: *"Death has been swallowed up in victory." "Where, O Death, is your victory? Where, O Death, is your sting?"* [v. 54b-55].[8]

Even we as Christians can settle for a futile type of faith, if we succumb to the temptation of believing in crossless Christianity for ourselves. If our faith is only that God will keep me safe, heal me, prosper me and never let anything bad happen to me, it is not truly faith at all, but idolatry wearing a Christian mask, still living in slavery to fear of death. Only through embracing the cross—our own cross—

can we find that the sting of death has been nullified, taken for us by Jesus on his Cross.

Peter, as he listened to his Master's disturbing directive, could not have imagined that he and his brother disciples would follow him with joy to their own crosses, as all but one of them died the death of a martyr. He could not yet have contemplated saying, with the future apostle Paul: **For to me, to live is Christ and to die is gain** [Philippians 1:21]. But Jesus, with the assurance of a Leader who knows that he is taking his followers to somewhere better than they know, though the way be hard, assures them that *whoever wants to save their life will lose it, but **whoever loses their life for me will find it**.* And even if we with Peter find this a baffling paradox, may we, like him, commit ourselves to get back behind our Master and follow him on his journey through death to resurrection.

Reflections:

Meditate a few moments on Matthew 16:24-25 (the verses at the beginning of the chapter). Then consider: how are **you** tempted towards "Crossless Christianity"?

- Do you tend to reduce Christ's call to *take up your cross* to an injunction to patience in irritating circumstances (or something similar)? Have you ever thought about it in terms of following Jesus into actual suffering—even death? What are your reactions when you consider this? What does it mean to you that Jesus says this is how you will *find your life*?
- How do you think about death? Do you think about it at all? When you do, what emotions does it bring up?
- What are ways you might treat God or Christianity as an idol to save you from *fear of death*? Do you expect God to always keep you safe? To expel all suffering from your life? To guard you from tragedy? What "bargains" might you make with God to guarantee your continued security and prosperity? How do you respond when God seems to fail these expectations or bargains?

Follow Jesus through death's door—to find eternal life.

C.S. Lewis observes: "If we thought we were building up a heaven on earth, if we looked for something that would turn the present world from a place of pilgrimage into a permanent city satisfying the soul of man, we are disillusioned, and not a moment too soon."[9]

- Consider St. Augustine's conundrum on p. 206. Why is this an important question? Why must we deal with it? How does death, as a final annihilation, drain meaning from life?
- How does the resurrection reverse this? What does your future resurrection mean to you? How might it fuel your own boldness, your willingness to follow in Jesus' footsteps?

Imagine yourself as a child in the womb.
- Why might you not want to leave? What could be your fears? What beyond imagination is waiting for you in the world outside?
- How is this parallel to our experience with death? What are some wonderful things you know are waiting for you there? (Not to mention what you could not even imagine…) How might this remove *fear of death* and create anticipation of your "birthday"?

32 Walking on the Water

Therefore, I urge you, brothers and sisters, in view of God's mercy, **to offer your bodies as a living sacrifice,** *holy and pleasing to God—this is your true and proper worship. Do not conform to the pattern of this world, but be transformed by the renewing of your mind. Then you will be able to test and approve what God's will is—his good, pleasing and perfect will.* [Romans 12:1-2]
Read Matthew 14:13-33.

Peter and That Boat

Only a little time before Peter's declaration of Jesus as Messiah an unforgettable incident occurred that probably contributed to its expression. After a remarkable day in which the disciples had assisted Jesus in the miraculous feeding of several thousand hungry people, their Master sends them ahead in a boat while he goes alone up a mountain to pray. In the dark before dawn, riding swift waves that had carried them far toward the opposite shore, Peter and his buddies perceive a human figure coming toward them on the water—and conclude in terror that it must be a ghost. (The fear of death, it seemed, was stalking them across the lake...) Jesus, on hearing them cry out, immediately says, *"Take courage! It is I. Don't be afraid"* [Matthew 14:27].

What happens next is equally remarkable. Peter says, *"Lord, if it's you, ask me to come to you on the water."* What on earth possessed him to do this? True, he had that day seen Jesus provide in abundance for his followers. And now Peter was seeing him demonstrate his mastery over nature before his very eyes. Even so—where would Peter have gotten the idea that Jesus would want **him** to walk on water as well?

Perhaps it was the idea of following, so ingrained into the Jewish model of discipleship, that made him think: If Jesus wants me to follow his footsteps, even across the water, he will make it possible for me to do so. So he asks, and Jesus says, *"Come."* And Peter walks on the water, just like his Master.

Of course, as we all know, he only goes a little way before he starts focusing on the flood instead of following. And Jesus catches him and saves him before he drowns, saying, *"You of little faith... why did you doubt?"* [v.31].

Peter, I think, gets a lot of flak from preachers chiding him for having been distracted by the waves instead of keeping his eyes on Jesus. But I wonder how many of **them** would have gotten out of that boat in the first place, had they been there? The other eleven seem to have just sat rocking in the boat, never even considering the possibility. The *little faith* of Peter to follow his Rabbi, imperfect and full of doubts as it was, was more than theirs.

Think of the impact of this day's experience on Peter. His Master draws huge crowds, so mesmerized by his words that they don't even leave to find food. And then he feeds them all! He walks on the waves, and then calls Peter to follow in his death-defying wake. And when Peter falters, his life is saved by his amazing Rabbi! Truly, with influence and power like this, he must be none other than the Christ, come to rescue his people from their oppression.

No wonder he is ready to say, *"You are the Messiah, the Son of the living God."*

Perhaps he recalled the words of Isaiah 43:2:

> *When you pass through the waters, I will be with you;*
> *and when you pass through the rivers,*
> *they will not sweep over you.*
> *When you walk through the fire, you will not be burned;*
> *the flames will not set you ablaze.*

Peter must have imagined their band riding through the Roman ranks, untouchable, as Jesus with his power over the forces of nature calls down lightning from heaven upon them. He must have foreseen Jesus feeding the fighting hordes that would gather around them, taking care of their every need as he meted out miraculous manna to his victorious army. Peter himself, the Rock, would become a renowned warrior, like one of David's mighty men—perhaps even the Messiah's right-hand man. He must have envisioned Jesus as a latter-day Moses, bringing his people safely, unscathed, through the sea, as the waves engulf their oppressors. They would be invincible.

So no wonder he was confused when Jesus talked about suffering and being killed. When he directed his disciples to take up their own crosses and follow. Obviously, Jesus had the power to protect and save them. So why was he adopting this fatalistic posture? Why would Jesus save Peter from a watery grave only to lead him to a cross?

The Safety Paradox

Maybe we can identify with Peter. Don't we experience this same kind of cognitive dissonance when we try to harmonize the apparent promises of safety in Scripture with Jesus' call to die?

I would imagine that all of you reading this book can recall at least one incident in which you were aware of God's protective hand having kept you or someone you love safe from injury or death. Perhaps you have experienced miraculous healing. Or you have had the sense that some "coincidence" prevented you from having been in a place where death was certain, a sense that you escaped with mere scratches from mortal circumstances through His provident protection.

During the Brussels attacks, two missionary friends of ours were in the departure hall of the Brussels airport when the terrorists' bombs went off. Both of them were knocked out in the explosions. When they came to, they found themselves surrounded by dead bodies. They had been in the forefront of the blast—and yet they were virtually unhurt. God, in his sovereign mercy, clearly protected them in a place where they should have died.

Scripture, too, is full of stories like this. Daniel in the lions' den. David fighting Goliath. The three boys in the fiery furnace. Esther daring death for her people. These are the stories we love from Sunday School, tales of faith-filled heroes risking their lives and escaping death through God's protection, as Peter did when he stepped out of the boat. It would be easy to look at these stories— modern and Biblical—and conclude that followers of God should lead a charmed existence in which those who truly believe will always be kept safe from suffering and death. (If this were true, this book would be very easy to write, for I could just exhort you to renew your faith, take the dares, and chalk up any difficulty, loss, or tragedy you face to your own lack of belief.)

But in Jesus' challenge to risk, he tells you, definitively, that you will save your life **only** by losing it. And this means embracing the risks when Jesus says "Come"—not because you are positive that you will never face death as you do, but because you trust that you will be kept safe **in death** as well as in life. If the *fear of death* that enslaved us is gone, then to pass through the door into resurrection life is as much safety as is being spared.

The safety we experience in following Jesus is both relative and absolute. It is **relative** in that our physical safety is dependent, at any given moment, on what God's will is for that time of our lives. If there is still more he wants us to learn here, more he wants us to accomplish for our good and his glory, more places and people to which he wants to send us—then death cannot touch us. But when in his all-wise Providence he sees fit to "call us home," then our lives here are complete, even if we would not yet have deemed our work done.

Until that day, you can never lose this earthly life before the time God has set for you. Jesus, betrayed in the Garden, says to his captors: *"I told you that I am he. If you are looking for me, then let these men [the disciples] go."* John comments on this: *This happened so that the words he had spoken would be fulfilled: "I have not lost one of those you gave me"* [John 18:8-9]. Jesus had a mission for these men, and they would fulfill it. Our missionary friends in the airport can take heart that He still has purposes on this earth for them to fulfill, for they are still here, still alive in the place he has sent them.

On the other hand, our safety is **absolute** in that even if we suffer, even if we die, our essential selves are secure in his hands.

> *When I am afraid, I put my trust in you.*
> *In God, whose word I praise—in God I trust and am not afraid.*
> **What can mere mortals do to me?** [Psalm 56:3-4]

All that can be taken from us are the things we **have,** not the things we **are.** We can lose our eyesight, our possessions, our family, our homes—our sanity, even. Many of these things can be taken from us by wicked people. But the essence of who we **are**—our identity as children of God, and the character attained through choices to follow the Master—can never be taken from us. Jesus tells us, *"Do not be afraid of those who kill the body but cannot kill the soul"* [Matthew 10:28]. In fact, as we take up our cross and follow Jesus into suffering and death, who we truly are will be revealed more fully.

And Jesus reminds us that even the things we **have** and have given up for his sake will be regained in the Resurrection: *Truly I tell you,* ***at the renewal of all things,*** *when the Son of Man sits on his glorious throne... everyone who has left houses or brothers or sisters or father or mother or wife or children or fields for my sake* ***will receive a hundred times as much and will inherit eternal life*** [Matthew 19:28-29]. In the New Creation, nothing good is ever lost.

Living as a Sacrifice

We only get to physically die once. But we are called to daily practice for this dying by (as the Romans text at the beginning of the chapter tells us) *offering [our] bodies as a living sacrifice.* This is not a one time for all deal, a single surrender. It is constant, ongoing. In Luke 9:23, Jesus' Disciple Directive reads: *"Whoever wants to be my disciple must deny themselves and take up their cross **daily** and follow me."*

The problem with living sacrifices, I heard a preacher say, is that they can keep getting off the altar. We can pick up the cross or step out of the boat. But then we are easily distracted and discouraged when the weight feels too heavy, or the waves look threatening. This is why we have to keep making a **daily** choice to die to ourselves; to say, *Thy will be done,* and be done with our will. Peter didn't realize that the risky business of walking on water was going to be his life's pattern when Jesus said, *Come.*

But just as these little deaths help us practice for the big one that is coming to us all (whether we embrace it or not), so they also help us live little resurrections that are sculpting who we are, the essential person that is created out of choices to follow Jesus. Just as through physical death our bodies will one day be resurrected, so through these daily deaths to our own will and way we will find that instead of being *conformed to the pattern of this world,* we are being *transformed by the renewing of our minds.* **Our minds are being gradually resurrected, transformed just as our bodies will be.** This change begins here, in this world, fitting us for the next one where it will be complete.

When you make the choice to die to "I Deserve" and dare to forgive the person who wronged you (as Jesus forgave you), you embrace the opportunity to find freedom from bitterness. When you lay on the altar your legitimate desire for a future spouse, and say *"Not my will, but yours,"* you clear the way to begin to appreciate people of the opposite sex as they are, instead of judging them in relation to you as possible mates. When you step out on the water and engage in mission where God is sending you, you make it possible to find peace as you perceive Jesus' prevenient presence in that place.[10] Then, as you embrace the choices to dare and to die, you discover more of God's will revealed to you—*his good, pleasing and perfect will.*

We, of course, don't do it perfectly. We easily lose our focus on Jesus, and fear the waves. We freak out, and think, *What made me think I could do this?* But Jesus is there in that moment to catch us, to remind us that we need never doubt him, to keep us truly safe—and fuel our next faith footsteps.

The word *sacrifice* means, "to make something holy." As we offer our bodies daily as living sacrifices, embracing the risks to which God calls us, he also transforms us more and more into something holy, sacred to him and reflecting his glory. Take these words to heart:

> *If we live, we live for the Lord; and if we die, we die for the Lord.* **So, whether we live or die, we belong to the Lord.** *For this very reason, Christ died and returned to life so that he might be the Lord of both the dead and the living.* [Romans 14:8-9]

Reflections:

We come more alive
as we embrace daily death.

Remember this verse? *For we know that if the earthly tent we live in [our body] is destroyed, we have a building from God, an eternal house in heaven, not built by human hands... For while we are in this tent, we groan and are burdened, because we do not wish to be unclothed but to be clothed instead with our heavenly dwelling, so that what is mortal may be swallowed up by life* [2 Corinthians 5:1,4].

Consider the "Safety Paradox" we discussed on p. 213.

- Have you ever experienced a sense of God's delivering you, or someone you loved, from death? What happened? What do you sense he was sparing you (or them) for? How are you differently "sent" as a result?
- How does it encourage you to know that you cannot die until God's purposes for you are fully accomplished? How might this transform your view of the time you have left?
- And how does it encourage you to know that even in death your life is not lost—that you are absolutely safe? To know that who you are is preserved and purified in death? And that all you value most on earth is restored to you in the New Creation? How might you live in light of this?

How does it look for you to practice dying daily as a *living sacrifice*?

- What difference does it make for you to know that as you die daily you will also experience "small resurrections"—in the *transformation of your mind*? Does this change anything in your perspective about risk and self-denial?
- What are you being called to die to **today**? A negative attitude toward someone? Self-deceptive justification of your actions? A legitimate desire still unfulfilled? A retreat from courage into comfort and safety? Trying to control your circumstances? Self-reliance? Self-protective behaviors?
- How might your mind be transformed as you lay yourself on the altar, step out of the boat, take up your cross? How could you make it a habit to approach each day like this?

We can rely on Jesus, the Holy One who sacrificed himself, to finish his work and make us new: *For by one sacrifice he has **made perfect forever** those who are **being made holy*** [Hebrews 10:14].

33 The Struggle to Stand Firm

*"Simon, Simon, Satan has asked to sift all of you as wheat. **But I have prayed for you, Simon, that your faith may not fail.** And when you have turned back, strengthen your brothers." But he replied, "Lord, I am ready to go with you to prison and to death." Jesus answered, "I tell you, Peter, before the rooster crows today, you will deny three times that you know me."* [Luke 22:31-33] **Read Luke 22:14-62.**

Trading Your Cloak for a Sword

The disciples didn't get it when Jesus said, *"That's enough!"*

Their Master had been telling them (in the verses above) that the crisis he had previously predicted was upon them. He even goes so far as to remind them of their expedition to the *lost sheep of Israel*, when they took no purse or bag or extra sandals, but were welcomed and provided for wherever they went [Matthew 10:6]. Now, he tells them, they will be facing hostility rather than hospitality: *"But now if you have a purse, take it, and also a bag; and if you don't have a sword, sell your cloak and buy one"* [v.36]. This is because their Leader has been labeled a criminal; Jesus describes himself as the Suffering Servant from Isaiah 53, the One *"numbered with the transgressors."*

But the disciples get fixated on the fact that he has told them to purchase swords. At last, the revolt is come! *"See, Lord, here are two swords,"* they say. And he replies, *"That's enough!"* [v.38]. But he doesn't mean that two swords are sufficient, as they seem to think. (How could all of them be protected by such a paltry number of weapons, anyway?) Rather, "the Jews, when a companion uttered anything absurd, were wont to use this phrase."[11] Jesus, frustrated with his disciples' inability to understand the kind of spiritual struggle they faced, even now, is cutting off the conversation.

However, for Peter, who apparently owned one of the swords, Jesus' pronouncement was a license to kill. When a party armed *with swords and clubs* arrives with Judas, the disciples ask, *"Lord, should we strike with our swords?"* [v.49]. Peter, not waiting for the answer, swings to slice off the head of the high priest's servant, but the man ducks sideways. All Peter manages to sever is his ear.

Immediately Jesus' non-aggressive intentions become evident: *But Jesus answered, "No more of this!" And he touched the man's ear and healed him* [v.51]. John tells us that he directly rebukes Peter: *"Put your sword away! Shall I not drink the cup the Father has given me?"* [18:11]. Jesus further challenges the arresting group: *"Am I leading a rebellion, that you have come with swords and clubs?"* [Luke 22:52].

Then, they let go the disciples as Jesus asks, and lead him to die.

What kind of war was this?

Imagine the turmoil in Peter's mind—thoughts and emotions churning like wheat being sifted. He was ready to fight and die in battle. But Jesus appeared to have given up without any fight at all. Was he, Peter, ready to go out like that—not with a bang, but a whimper? It appeared meaningless, fatalistic. And thus, instead of courageously fighting, he ends up lurking around, cowardly denying he even knows Jesus when a lowly servant girl asks him. Three times.

Fight or flight: the two basic human responses when faced with danger. Anger or fear. Attack or hide. Retaliate or collaborate. But is there another way? There is. Jesus had told it to his disciples already.

Stand Firm to Win Life

That last week, he spoke to them of wars and earthquakes and famines, of coming dangers and difficult times. And then Jesus says:

*"But before all this, **they will seize you and persecute you.** They will hand you over to synagogues and put you in prison, and you will be brought before kings and governors, and all on account of my name. And so you will bear testimony to me. **But make up your mind not to worry beforehand how you will defend yourselves.** For I will give you words and wisdom that none of your adversaries will be able to resist or contradict. You will be betrayed even by parents, brothers and sisters, relatives and friends, and they will put some of you to death. Everyone will hate you because of me. But not a hair of your head will perish. **Stand firm, and you will win life.**"* [Luke 21:12-19]

Here we see the safety paradox clearly stated: **They will put some of you to death... But not a hair of your head will perish.** The way to win this kind of life that death cannot kill is to *stand firm*, to persevere, not to give up, not to give ground. This is not the kind of militant, muscular Christianity that is out to attack and destroy the people who oppose it. Neither is it a groveling, apologetic belief that seeks to appease the opposition. Rather, it is recognition that persecution and opposition are the norm in this present age, and a choice to be faithful and persevere in the face of it.

And so **"Stand Firm!"** becomes the motto of the apostles as they move out into a world ruled by the Enemy. They use it to urge others:

- *Be on your guard; **stand firm in the faith**; be courageous; be strong.* [I Corinthians 16:13]
- *Whatever happens... **stand firm in the one Spirit,** striving together as one for the faith of the gospel without being frightened in any way by those who oppose you.* [Phil. 1:27]
- *You too, **be patient and stand firm,** because the Lord's coming is near.* [James 5:8]

The same Jesus values we examined in relation to people around us—vulnerability, humility, faithfulness, forgiveness—should characterize also our perseverance in the battle against evil. We recognize that we will likely be wounded, that suffering in this world is inevitable and gains meaning only by standing firm. We do not overestimate our own power or courage to stay the course on our own, but link arms with comrades who will stand beside us. We trust our Defender for our protection, rather than our own strength. And we renew our commitment each day by taking up the cross again.

Here is the most famous biblical image of standing firm: *Finally, **be strong in the Lord** and in his mighty power. Put on the full armor of God, so that you can **take your stand** against the devil's schemes... Therefore put on the full armor of God, so that when the day of evil comes, **you may be able to stand your ground, and after you have done everything, to stand. Stand firm then,** with the belt of truth buckled around your waist...* [Ephesians 6:10ff].

It is in this text that we learn that even though people may be the face of opposition and persecution, that they are not really the enemy: *For **our struggle is not against flesh and blood,** but against the rulers, against the authorities, against the powers of this dark world and **against the spiritual forces of evil** in the heavenly realms* [v.12]. This is why we can be vulnerable, humble, and even forgiving towards our "enemies" at the same time as we remain faithfully committed to standing firm. It is why Jesus can say, *"Love your enemies and pray for those who persecute you"* [Matt. 5:44]. The real enemy is not them; it is behind them. Remember: *Once you were alienated from God and were enemies in your minds because of your evil behavior* [Col. 1:21]. They are as worthy—or unworthy—of redemption as you.

Also in this text, we finally understand what kind of sword Jesus wanted his disciples to strap on: *Take... **the sword of the Spirit,** which* *is the word of God* [v.17]. Most of the metaphors in the text depict defensive armor: *belt of truth, breastplate of righteousness, shield of faith, helmet of salvation.* But this is an offensive weapon that makes it possible to take back ground from the Enemy. And there is one more in the arsenal: **Pray in the Spirit on all occasions** *with all kinds of prayers and requests. With this in mind, be alert and always keep on praying for all the Lord's people* [v.18].

Prayer was the weapon Jesus used on behalf of his disciples, and especially Peter, when the Enemy was *sifting him like wheat.* He prayed that Peter's *faith would not fail.* He urged Peter to use this weapon for himself too, in the Garden: *"Get up and pray so you will not fall into temptation"* [Luke 22:46].

But Peter, too tired to use his weapon, did fall into temptation.

When You Have Turned Back

Peter's self-reliance, his confidence in his battle skills, quickly turns to fearful self-protection when belligerence fails. He follows Jesus to the High Priest's courtyard, but fails to stand firm there. Three times he disowns knowing Jesus, even calling down curses on himself to convince the company. Luke tells us that on the third denial, while he was still speaking, the cock crowed, and Jesus turned to look straight at Peter.

No wonder he went out and wept bitterly. He had pledged to die or go to prison with his Master, to follow in his footsteps till the very end. And look how quickly he had failed to stand firm.

But Jesus' prayer for Peter was that his *faith would not fail.* It would falter, yes, but it would not utterly fail. Though in Peter's time of persecution—mild, maybe, compared to what he would face later in life—he had turned his back on the battle, Jesus would give him the chance to rejoin his comrades in arms. This sifting of Satan would result in removal of the chaff from the wheat.

Standing firm, it turns out, is a long-haul game. There will be failures on the way—sometimes even huge ones, like this. But Peter had learned, when he called out for help while sinking in the waves, that restoration is possible when faith falters. As long as faith endures, failure may even strengthen it by weaning us from self-reliance and self-protection, goading us to grab the hand of Jesus, and giving us the humility and empathy to encourage other falterers.

In fact, Jesus himself seeks out Peter after his resurrection and restores purpose to him, asking him to reaffirm his love for him three times, and telling him to *"Feed my sheep"* [John 21:15-17]. In this purpose is the answer to Jesus' prayer for Peter before his denial, that **"when you have turned back,** *[you will]* **strengthen your brothers."**

And this is what we see him doing in the rest of the New Testament. He still has some missteps (like giving in to those who wanted to discriminate against Gentiles). But the overall pattern is of a man who is standing firm in faith and strengthening his brothers in the face of human and spiritual opposition:

- He uses the *sword of the Spirit*, the Scriptures, to explain the Gospel to his fellow Jews, and three thousand become disciples of Jesus [Acts 2].
- He is put in jail for speaking of Jesus, and when released by an angel, goes straight back to preaching. And when the authorities order him to cease and desist, he answers them, *"We must obey God rather than human beings!"* [Acts 5:29]
- He ventures into Samaria, the hated enemy of Judea, to pray for new believers to receive the Holy Spirit [Acts 9]; then to a Roman centurion—an oppressor he had dreamed of conquering—to bring the Good News to him [Acts 10].

Eventually, he becomes a missionary to Rome itself, the center of the occupying empire. While there, he writes letters of encouragement to the Christian community, now suffering Jesus' predicted persecution. Perhaps thinking of his own time of sifting and failure, he writes: **Be alert and of sober mind.** *Your enemy the devil prowls around like a roaring lion looking for someone to devour.* **Resist him, standing firm in the faith,** *because you know that the family of believers throughout the world is undergoing the same kind of sufferings* [I Peter 5:8-9].

And in the pressure of the day, he holds up the vulnerable, humble, faithful example of his Master, calling them to follow him:

But **if you suffer for doing good and you endure it,** *this is commendable before God. To this you were called, because Christ suffered for you, leaving you an example, that* **you should follow in his steps...** *When they hurled their insults at him, he did not retaliate; when he suffered, he made no threats. Instead, he entrusted himself to him who judges justly* [I Peter 2:20-21,23].

Reflections:

Courage = resisting evil, enduring to the end.

In *The Lord of the Rings,* Tolkien's epic of good and evil, Faramir says: "War must be, while we defend our lives against a destroyer who would devour all. But I do not love the bright sword for its sharpness, nor the arrow for its swiftness, nor the warrior for his glory. **I love only that which they defend.**"[12]

How are you being called to stand firm?

- In what ways does *the devil seek to devour* you? How does he try (or succeed) to make you falter, fail and despair? What lies, stratagems, and attacks do you need to *stand firm* against?
- Are you able to fully accept Jesus' restoration in your failures? How could those same failures make you more reliant on him? How could you re-write your failures, and Jesus' forgiveness of them, as a means to faith? What difference would it make to take a long-haul view of *standing firm*?
- Who are your comrades in this battle? How do you see yourselves *standing firm in one Spirit* and *striving together* [Phil. 1:27]? In what practical ways do you support and encourage one another to stand firm and be courageous? (If you feel like you are alone in the battle: who could come stand beside you?)
- How do your failures give you grace toward others? How could they help you *turn back* and *strengthen your brothers*?

Hebrews 12:3 says: **Consider him who endured such opposition from sinners, so that you will not grow weary and lose heart.**

- Do you face *opposition from sinners*, as Jesus did?
- How much of this is due to faults you must confess, and not spiritual opposition? We can deceive ourselves about this... As Peter reminds us: *How is it to your credit if you receive a beating for doing wrong and endure it?* [1 Peter 2:20]
- What does true spiritual opposition from people look like for you? How are you likely to respond—retaliation or conciliation? What would it look like to *stand firm* instead?
- How does it help your perception of enemies to know that they are not the true enemy, but rather the spiritual forces behind them? How does this influence your responses to them? How could Jesus' example serve as a model for you?

34 The Cross, The Cell, and The Coracle

*Jesus said, "...when you are old you will stretch out your hands, and someone else will dress you and lead you where you do not want to go." Jesus said this to indicate the kind of death by which Peter would glorify God. **Then he said to him, "Follow me!"** Peter turned and saw that the disciple whom Jesus loved was following them... When Peter saw him, he asked, **"Lord, what about him?"** Jesus answered, "If I want him to remain alive until I return, what is that to you? **You must follow me."** [John 21:18-22]*
Read John 21:15-25.

Red, White and Green

Saint Patrick's Irish converts had a problem. They had no martyrs.

Uniquely in Christian history, the fifth-century conversion of Ireland had happened without bloodshed. And their apostle had brought with him accounts of the martyrs of old: people like Peter who, when sentenced by Nero to a cross, asked to be crucified upside down because he was not worthy to die in the same way as his Master. Or like the disciples Andrew, Philip, Bartholomew, Thaddeus, and Simon, who were also crucified. Or stories about James, who was beheaded; Matthew, who was stabbed; and Thomas, killed in India by a spear. Clearly, when Jesus said to his followers, *"Whoever wants to be my disciple must deny themselves, and take up their cross and follow me,"* he meant it literally. So what were the Irish to do?

Their solution was a new kind of martyrdom—two kinds, in fact. Here they are, described in a Celtic homily from the seventh century:

> "Now there are **three kinds of martyrdom which are accounted as a Cross** to a man, white martyrdom, green martyrdom, and red martyrdom. White martyrdom consists in a man's abandoning everything he loves for God's sake... Green martyrdom consists in this, that by means of fasting and labor he frees himself from his evil desires, or suffers toil in penance and repentance. Red martyrdom consists in the endurance of a Cross or death for Christ's sake."[13]

The Green martyrdom—*green* symbolizing the land of the Emerald Isle—consisted in joining a monastic community. Here monks lived in a cluster of individual cells centered around communal buildings. These new communities popping up all over Ireland (a land with no towns or cities at the time) attracted both those taking vows and laypeople to live together in a rhythm of life governed by work and prayer.

The White martyrdom, initiated in the century after Patrick by St. Columba, consisted in self-imposed exile from Ireland as a missionary to the ends of the earth. In Columba's case, that was Iona, an island off the coast of Scotland. Monks would set themselves adrift without oars in small coracles, little boats of wicker and hide, to go to whatever land the Spirit blew them—all over Europe (and perhaps, in the story of St. Brendan, even to North America). "All who followed [Columba's] lead were called to the white martyrdom, they who sailed into the white sky of morning, into the unknown, never to return."[14]

I, too, can relate to the Irish dilemma. For I do not face death daily for my faith; in fact, I have barely faced death at all. I have not yet lost any of my closest family members or friends, and I would say that my life is far more characterized by comfort than by suffering—especially when compared to my brothers and sisters in other parts of the world. Indeed, it has made me quite reluctant to write this section of the book: how can I speak of the disciple's call to die meaningfully when my own experience of death is so small?

The Irish encourage me. For Jesus' call to the Cross applies whether one is hiding from persecutors in a cave in Cappadocia, or living in comfort in an apartment in Belgium. We are both called to follow in Jesus' footsteps and die daily—even if martyrdom looks different for each of us.

The Follow-ship of Peter and John

Jesus made this clear on the day he restored Peter. The disciples, at a loss after the resurrection, had returned to their old life of fishing. But after a miraculous catch of fish reminiscent of their first calling, they find Jesus cooking them breakfast on the beach. After eating, it appears that Jesus and Peter took a walk together. In this conversation (quoted at the beginning of this chapter), Jesus gives his ashamed disciple the opportunity to reaffirm his love and commitment, entrusts him with a new mission—and reveals the way in which he would die for God's glory.

And then, he says to Peter, *"Follow me!"*

At the Last Supper, Peter had asked Jesus, *"Lord, where are you going?"* Jesus replied, *"Where I am going, you cannot follow now, but* you will follow later." *Peter asked, "Lord, why can't I follow you now? I will lay down my life for you"* [John 13:36-37]. Now, on the beach, Peter seems to understand that in his cryptic words, Jesus is talking about his death in the future, and he does not respond with his earlier bravado. He understands, in a much deeper way than he did that first day on the shore of Lake Galilee, the commitment that Jesus demands when he calls him to follow.

But, as he has done in earlier moments of deep revelation, he takes his eyes off his Master, and turns around to notice John behind them. (Following them, actually, just as Jesus asked Peter to do.) And Peter asks, *"Lord, what about him?"* Does he ask because he is afraid? Because he hopes to have his friend for company on the road to the cross? Or is it just the human tendency to compare oneself with another and make sure we're all being treated fairly?

So at this late date, Jesus has to correct Peter once more. He tells Peter it is none of his business what happens to John—his business is to follow, even if Jesus wants John to stay alive until his return. Then John, who is writing the story many years later, adds this touchingly humble note: *Because of this, the rumor spread among the believers that this disciple would not die. But Jesus did not say that he would not die; he only said, "If I want him to remain alive until I return, what is that to you?"* [21:23]. John, in fact, does become the only one of the Twelve not to die the death of a martyr. Instead, tradition tells us that he died of old age in exile on the island of Patmos—a kind of White Martyrdom.

I am glad for the example of John. Not because he reassures me I can be a real disciple without the Cross (he does not), but because he shows that Red Martyrdom is not the only path one can take to follow Jesus to the Cross. When Jesus calls us to follow him, he calls us on different paths and I am not meant to judge the path of another—I am meant to faithfully follow him on the path of self-denial and radical dependence on which he is leading **me**.

There are many places around the world—North Korea, Iran, India, Syria, and Sudan, to name just a few—where our brothers and sisters **are** facing Red Martyrdom. It is our responsibility and privilege to honor them and pray for them, for the strength and faith to stand firm in the face of persecution.[15] Theirs is an arduous path, and whatever small self-denials I embrace daily cannot compare with it. But rather than causing me to breathe a sigh of relief and embrace my comforts, or to feel like a second-class Christian because I happen to live in a "safe" place, their experience and example should encourage me, like the Irish, to take seriously the question of what it means to *take up my cross* in my own context. In fact, as Christianity in the West loses its cultural acceptance and influence, and opposition to our faith begins to rise, we may find that these practices are good preparation for *standing firm*.

A New Monasticism

In defining the three kinds of martyrdom—the Cross, the Cell, and the Coracle—the Celtic saints gave us clues to ways in which the path of discipleship could be pursued through a form of monasticism that substituted the daily "deaths" of self-denial for physical death. Dietrich Bonhoeffer comments on the monastic movement: "Here, on the boundary of the church, was the place where the awareness that grace is costly and that grace includes discipleship was preserved... Monastic life thus became a living protest against... the cheapening of grace."[16]

However, traditional monasticism still left out large categories of those who would profess to follow Jesus, such as the layperson and the married, and created a special group of "super-disciples." How could the former discover paths for taking up their own cross and following Jesus? Bonhoeffer said in a 1935 letter:

> "The renewal of the church will come from **a new type of monasticism**, which only has in common with the old an uncompromising allegiance to the Sermon on the Mount. It is high time people banded together to do this."[17]

This comment has sparked a movement to explore deeper paths for Christ-centered discipleship in the last few decades, paths that include aspects of the Cell and the Coracle and can be practiced by Christians in all life-situations:

- **The Cell:** This is the disciple's **inner journey with God**, where he/she is alone before the Creator, to seek His face. It involves disciplined daily prayer rhythms, contemplative prayer and Scripture meditation, personal examination and intentional spiritual formation, perhaps in accountability to a "soul friend."
- **The Coracle:** This is the disciple's **journey out to engage and serve the world in mission**, together with his/her community. It involves caring for creation in the place one is planted,

venturing out to the margins of society and offering hospitality to the stranger, sharing a common life with fellow pilgrims and helping the needy, and following the wind of God to the people and places he sends you.[18]

Even if the terminology of "new monasticism" is not personally appealing to you, the necessity of developing deep discipleship is one that Jesus impresses on us all: of daily following Jesus, embracing his will for our lives, regardless of the risk. It is not a formula or program. It is not membership in an organization or institution. It not a bargain we make with God to keep us safe and comfortable. It is nothing less that the complete commitment of all we have and all we are to him, to use and to keep and to take and to send for his glory.

Where the Tide Takes You

For me, the image of a coracle—casting off wherever the winds and waves of the Spirit may lead—embodies the idea of risky faith, of self-denying discipleship that dares death. With a coracle, my path across trackless seas can never be exactly the same as yours, even if we arrive at the same destination or stop in the same ports. You will experience different waves and weather than I will, just as Peter and John followed Jesus across different waters.

Frederick Buechner says, "Faith is not being sure of where you're going, but going anyway. A journey without maps."[19] Each of us, in our coracles, is dependent upon the winds and tides and currents being directed by One who is Master of the Universe. You can trust him that, even in tempests, he sees the whole weather system and exactly where you will make landfall. At the same time, he is with you on the journey where he sends you, in your little craft with you. He never sends you without accompanying you. And so your coracle also becomes your cell, where you can be still and know that he is God. You can find rest in the midst of the storm, knowing his transcendence over every circumstance, his presence near to you.

As Nietzsche said: 'He who has a *why* to live can bear almost any *how*.' In other words, however difficult, scary, or painful our circumstances are, we can endure them if we have a deeply-held purpose that gives meaning to our life. The old catechism question reminds us what this is:

What is the chief end [purpose] of man?
Man's chief end is to glorify God and enjoy him forever.[20]

It is this purpose that can give you the courage to step into your little boat and push off from the beach. If you know Him as the most powerful and glorious Being there is, but also the pleasure of His ever-presence, you will find the risk of going where he sends you to be worth it, no matter the danger.

And then, maybe you can begin to relate to Paul when he says:*I eagerly expect and hope that I will in no way be ashamed, but **will have sufficient courage** so that now as always Christ will be exalted in my body, whether by life or by death. **For to me, to live is Christ and to die is gain*** [Philippians 1:20-21].

Reflections:

Follow Jesus courageously
on your own unique faith journey.

Peter continues today to encourage his fellow followers to stick to the path of faith, provisioned by the power and presence of Jesus: *His divine power has given us everything we need for a godly life through our knowledge of him who called us by his own glory and goodness... For this very reason, make every effort to add to your faith goodness; and to goodness, knowledge; and to knowledge, self-control; and to self-control, perseverance; and to perseverance, godliness; and to godliness, mutual affection; and to mutual affection, love* [2 Pet 1:3,5-7].

What path is Jesus calling you to follow?

- Do you find yourself confronted more by opposition or comfort in your life? How do you find yourself challenged by the Celtic idea of an "alternate martyrdom"? (And maybe take a moment to pray for those who **are** facing Red Martyrdom.)
- How is your life defined by **the Cell**: disciplines of discipleship that develop an inner journey with God? What are some new disciplines of prayer, meditation, or devotion that you sense the Holy Spirit calling you to? Set some goals to implement these in your life. Who might be a "soul friend" that you could be accountable to for these practices?
- How is your life defined by **the Coracle**: practices of missional servanthood to those around you? (Some of these are in the section "Traveling Light.") How could your faith be turned more outward in your neighborhood? How is God sending you to dare something new for him? How is he calling you to face a situation he has put in your path with faith and grace?
- Take some time to meditate on the path of discipleship outlined above by Peter. How do these relate to the practices of the Cell and the Coracle that you have been considering?

Peter continues: *So I will always remind you of these things, even though you know them and are firmly established in the truth you now have. I think it is right to refresh your memory as long as I live in **the tent of this body**, because I know that I will soon put it aside, as our Lord Jesus Christ has made clear to me* [2 Peter 1:2-14]. May we, with Peter, continue steadfast, as we look forward to the time when we put aside these tents for the home God is building for us!

35 Ready to Risk

For in the day of trouble
  he will keep me safe in his dwelling;
he will hide me in the shelter of his sacred tent
  and set me high upon a rock. [Psalm 27:5]

A Dangerous World

When we look around our world, we see many dangers. Here are things that have happened while I have been working on this book:

- an Ebola epidemic in West Africa,
- disastrous flooding in India and Malawi,
- deadly earthquakes in Nepal and Italy,
- severe drought in Brazil,
- economic collapse in Greece,
- deliberately-caused plane crashes in France and Egypt,
- race riots in the United States,
- drug wars in Mexico,
- major terrorist events in France, Germany, Belgium, and Turkey,
- and millions of refugees risking their lives to get to Europe.

And this is not to mention the major conflicts going on in Syria, Iraq, Afghanistan, Nigeria, Somalia and Ukraine, among others.

Why should we be surprised at these things?

Jesus said to his disciples: *"Nation will rise against nation, and kingdom against kingdom. There will be great earthquakes, famines and pestilences in various places, and fearful events and great signs from heaven"* [Luke 21:10-11]. The disciples would see this in their own lifetimes, as the Romans destroyed Jerusalem itself. And these troubles have continued throughout the two millennia since Jesus made this prophecy.

True, some times and places seem more troubled than others. The latter half of the twentieth century was remarkably calm and prosperous for the West, but recent events have proven that none of our security measures can guarantee complete and lasting safety. We may also be entering a new troubled time for the people of God, with the demise of Christendom in the West and the loss of a Christian consensus. As the disciples would see a rise in persecution along with the *fearful events* Jesus prophesied, we too may see our faith in the West come under more pressure than it has faced in centuries.

Dietrich Bonhoeffer said during one of history's troubled times:

"There is no way to peace along the way of safety. **For peace must be dared, it is itself the great venture and can never be safe. Peace is the opposite of security.** To demand guarantees is to want to protect oneself. Peace means giving oneself completely to God's commandment, wanting no security, but in faith and obedience laying the destiny of the nations in the hand of Almighty God, not trying to direct it for selfish purposes. Battles are won, not with weapons, but with God. They are won when the way leads to the cross."[21]

As we face the coming days, take to heart Gandalf's words to Frodo:

"I wish it need not have happened in my time," [Frodo says]. "So do I," said Gandalf, "and so do all who live to see such times. But that is not for them to decide. All we have to decide is what to do with the time that is given us."[22]

Pictures of Living By Faith in the Face of Fear

And for the time that is given us, God calls us to live by faith, boldly. He calls us to follow him into risk, whether it is facing the great unknown to which he is sending you, or facing the difficult situations he has sent to you.

We have looked in this book at a number of metaphors to help us understand the kind of bold and risky faith to which we are called. Let's review them now, to try to grasp the different aspects of it:

Lions. We are not called to be safe—we are **called to be dangerous**. The Spirit empowers us to put fear aside, even in the face of true danger, and to live boldly.

- *The wicked flee though no one pursues, but the righteous are as bold as a lion.* [Proverbs 28:1]

Little Teapots. We are all vessels made by a Master, created individually with artistic virtuosity. We are cleansed of everything that would make us unsuitable for serving the Master's guests. And then he prepares in us the good works he will pour out through us to a thirsty world in need of

provision and renewal. We are **called not to sit safe on a shelf, but to be used in his service, in the ways he has designed us and designed for us.**

- *For we are God's workmanship, created in Christ Jesus to do good works, which he has prepared beforehand for us to do.* [Ephesians 2:10]
- *But we have this treasure in jars of clay to show that this all-surpassing power is from God and not from us.* [2 Cor. 4:7]

Bags of Gold. We have been entrusted with generous resources from the Master, resources of wealth, wisdom, abilities, relationships, and many others. We are **called to gamble these resources for our Master's good, investing them so that they will gain and grow.** We must not try to bury and protect them, for in doing so we call the Master a miser, a "hard man" who is out to take from us instead of inviting us to share in his happiness.

- *His master replied, "Well done, good and faithful servant! You have been faithful with a few things; I will put you in charge of many things. Come and share your master's happiness!"* [Matthew 25:21]

Mighty Mountains. We are **called to fear God only,** humble before the One who holds the mountains in the palm of his hand, trembling at the foot of Infinite Everest. When we do, he transforms our fear of Him to trust as we come to know his great works on behalf of those he loves, and casts out our fear of any created thing. And so we are **called to risk, safely roped into him as the Rock,** daring the heights he sends us to, and crossing the crevasses he opens before us.

- *The fear of the Lord is the beginning of wisdom, and knowledge of the Holy One is understanding.* [Proverbs 9:10]
- *"Do not tremble, do not be afraid.*
  Did I not proclaim this and foretell it long ago?
  You are my witnesses. Is there any God besides me?
  No, there is no other Rock; I know not one." [Isaiah 44:8]

Castles & Tents. This mighty God **calls us to abandon the fortified castles** we have created for ourselves, **choosing instead to live in vulnerable tents.** In these, we are protected because he himself tents with us, and dwells in the center of our camp—in fact, he moves in with us. In doing so, he **calls us in our temporary tents to make our homes a reflection of the time when he will make his home with us forever.**

- *By faith [Abraham] made his home in the promised land like a stranger in a foreign country; he lived in tents, as did Isaac and Jacob, who were heirs with him of the same promise. For he was looking forward to the city with foundations, whose architect and builder is God.* [Heb. 11:9-10]

Righteous Robes. When a clearer view of God begins to erase our fear, we can relate to the people around us differently. Rather than self-promotion and self-protection, God **calls us to live in vulnerability and humility, faithfulness and forgiveness toward others.** We can remove the masks we wear before others, and show our true faces, confident that the robe given to us by our Father covers our shame. Then, endowed with the resources of Christ's righteousness, we are free to serve and to forgive others, just as Jesus faithfully humbled himself to serve and forgive us.

- *The son said... 'Father, I have sinned against heaven and against you. I am no longer worthy to be called your son.' But the father said to his servants, 'Quick! Bring the best robe and put it on him. Put a ring on his finger and sandals on his feet.* [Luke 15:21-22]

Crosses & Coracles. The safety God grants us is absolute, so that even if we are killed we do not perish, but are resurrected to eternal life. Therefore Jesus **calls us to follow him to the Cross** and embrace it as he did, dying daily to ourselves in rehearsal for the time we are

reborn. He **calls us to board our coracle and allow the wind of the Spirit to blow it where he wills,** and to step out on the water as he says come. And in this present life we are **called to stand firm against evil,** knowing we will remain until the good works he created for us are completed.

- *Then [Jesus] said to them all: "Whoever wants to be my disciple must deny themselves and take up their cross daily and follow me. For whoever wants to save their life will lose it, but whoever loses their life for me will save it.* [Luke 9:23-24]

I hope that each of these images will embolden your faith, and help you to live like lions in this present age.

A Tent on a Rock

The picture that most gives me courage as I face this dangerous world is that of a tent on a rock, described in the quote from Psalm 27 at the beginning of this chapter. (It is why I have chosen it for the cover illustration.) For it is based in the character of God, and it is in that we will find the courage to risk our calling.

It is in standing firm on the Sovereign, Transcendent Creator God who holds all things in his loving hands.

> In believing in his Providence in the face of scarcity.
> In trusting his Renewal when everything here seems to be going to hell.
> In firmly roping ourselves into him in trust and stepping out to rescue those who have no anchor but themselves; in offering to share our cables with those whose ropes have become frayed and weak.
> In knowing that, secured in this way, no fall, even from such a height, can result in ultimate death.

It is in embracing the vulnerability of the Immanent, Incarnate Christ who *pitched his tent among us.*

> In releasing our guilt and shame because of him.
> In recognizing the redemption and adoption we have received, the renewal that is taking place in us.
> In allowing him to indwell our hearts and our homes in such a way that they become pictures of the place that he has gone ahead to prepare for us, that we may be with him and his Father always.

It is in the juxtaposition of these two facets of God that we find the faith to risk.

> Far above and near around.
> Immense and intimate.
> Powerful and vulnerable.
> Strong and loving.
> Able and willing.

It is really no risk to trust him.

Notes

Section 1: Designed to Dare

[1] I rewrote this chapter (which previously had dealt with the US response to the Ebola epidemic) on the day after the March 22, 2016, attacks in Brussels. Some of these predictions have come true, both in Brussels and internationally.

[2] This is a prayer that I pray every day. It is part of the Midday Prayers in the Office of Celtic Daily Prayer published by the Northumbria Community. You can order their prayer books through their website, www.northumbriacommunity.org.

[3] The primary reference in Ephesians 2:10 is to the masterpiece God is creating of his people as a whole, in his Body. The verses following this are a discussion on how Christ's sacrifice has led to the reconciliation of Jews and Gentiles, and all of the pronouns in this chapter are plural. So, Biblically, the primary masterpiece in view here is not each individual but the Body as a whole. However, there are enough other Scriptures relating to God's creation and recreation of the individual for his purposes to think that this verse may also be legitimately applied to the case of individual believers as well. (Cf. Psalm 139, Isaiah 49:5, Jeremiah 1:4-10, among others.)

[4] You can see a picture of this on the Chrysler Museum's website (www.chrysler.org), by searching their collection with the keywords "Façon de Venice Goblet."

[5] The context of these verses is Paul's contrasting how Timothy should teach and behave as a pastor/teacher with the example of false teachers that have crept into the church. I have chosen to use The Message version here, because it helps clarify the rather confusing phrase in the NIV, "*Those who cleanse themselves from **the latter**,*" in v. 21. It is clear from the wider context that Paul is instructing Timothy both as a teacher to *correctly handle the word of truth,* to *avoid godless chatter,* and not to *be quarrelsome,* but *kind* in his instruction; and as a believer to *flee the evil desires of youth and pursue righteousness, faith, love, and peace.* Peterson in *The Message* implies at least these latter goals in his translation of this short section.

[6] In my earlier book, *Rest: Living Sabbath Every Day,* I examine these works of God more fully as part of an exploration of what Hebrews 4:10 means when it says, *Anyone who enters God's rest also rests from their works, just as God did from his.* You can find this in the first section of the book, entitled, "Resting in God's Completed Works."

[7] I have explored both of these somewhat more fully in the last section of the above-mentioned *Rest,* entitled, "Working Restfully." However, these concepts are deep enough to warrant a book in themselves!

[8] Need is basic to the human condition. Sometimes we act and think as though we are meant to outgrow need (like children outgrow their parents), but dependence is always the basic posture of the creature toward the Creator. Just as a child learns to love its parents in deeper ways than looking to them to meet its need, we also learn

affection and desire for God—but it is need that is our first connection to him. And we might also state that sin not only arises when people try to meet their needs apart from God, but that, in fact, sin can be **defined** as meeting our needs apart from depending on God. (This also deserves a book of its own!)

Section 2: Five Habits of Self-Protective People

[1] This neighborhood, Schaerbeek, became well known to TV news viewers in the wake of the Brussels bombings when the site where the bombs were made was located in an apartment there—in a building about 400 meters from our present flat.

[2] A helpful book regarding healthy boundaries and where they are needed, written from a Christian perspective, is *Boundaries* by Henry Cloud and John Townsend (Zondervan, 1992).

[3] Clip from TLC show *Extreme Couponing*: a video entitled "Photo of the Haul." Accessed 3/15/15: http://www.tlc.com/tv-shows/extreme-couponing/videos/photo-of-the-haul/.

[4] This is another show from TLC. Clips from this show may be seen on tlc.com.

[5] Dietrich Bonhoeffer, *The Cost of Discipleship,* 1937. Translation by R.H. Fuller, (SCM Press Ltd, 1959; Touchstone Press, 1995), 175.

[6] Bonhoeffer, *Discipleship,* 178 [emphasis mine].

[7] Dietrich Bonhoeffer, *Life Together,* trans. John W. Doberstein (Harper & Row, 1954), 34, 36.

[8] Bruce Dawe, "How to Go On Not Looking" (1964). The whole poem is worth looking up and pondering, in its extended metaphor of a no-longer-successful circus performing to an empty house. Dawe quite often deals with such themes. Both this poem and "The Not-So-Good-Earth" (1966, quoted later in the chapter) were contained in *The Penguin Book of Australian Verse* (Penguin Australia, 1972; 387, 388) which I wore out as a teenager.

[9] If you are interested in the medical details of oxytocin's effects on stress reduction, read "Self-soothing behaviors with particular reference to oxytocin release induced by non-noxious sensory stimulation" (Kerstin Uvnäs-Moberg, Linda Handlin, and Marie Petersson, in *Frontiers in Psychology,* 12 January, 2015). All of the effects that I have noted in this chapter are documented here.

[10] See note 8 on the Bruce Dawe poems above.

[11] This is also his lead-in to the diatribe concerning the rich that we looked at in Chapter 7, Stockpiling Resources. James 5:4-6 goes on to say: *Look! The wages **you failed to pay** the workers who mowed your fields are crying out against you. The cries of the harvesters have reached the ears of the Lord Almighty. You have lived on earth in luxury and self-indulgence. You have fattened yourselves in the day of slaughter. You have condemned and murdered the innocent one, who was not opposing you.*

[12] For a deeper, fuller discussion of this heinous tendency, especially among evangelicals, read Chapter 2, "Single-Minded Obedience," in Dietrich Bonhoeffer's book, *The Cost of Discipleship.*

Section 3: The Only Thing We Have To Fear

[1] There are dozens of references to this concept in the Old Testament. One example to consider is 2 Chronicles 19, where Jehoshaphat admonishes his appointed judges: "Now let **the fear of the Lord** be on you. Judge carefully, for with the Lord our God there is no injustice or partiality or bribery" [v.7], and then addresses the Levites and priests: "You must serve faithfully and wholeheartedly in **the fear of the Lord**" [v.9]. In the New Testament, the term "God-fearing" is mostly found in Acts: to refer to the Diaspora Jews gathered at Pentecost [2:5]; to Cornelius [10:2,22]; to Gentile converts to Judaism in Pisidian Antioch [13:26,50]; and to Greek Gentiles who followed the One True God in both Thessalonica and Athens [17:4,17].

[2] From The Open Door, 1902, re-published by Doubleday in 1957.

[3] C.S. Lewis, The Pilgrim's Regress, in The Timeless Writings of C.S. Lewis (Inspirational Press, 1933, 1943), 134.

[4] Bruce Schneier, "Close the Washington Monument," blog post on Schneier on Security, December 2, 2010.

[5] Michael Meade [quoting an unnamed Irish poet], "Go Toward the Roar," blog post on The Huffington Post, September 19, 2011. This is a great post about facing one's fears.

[6] This skit aired on Season 6 of Mad TV (Fox) in 2001, and may be viewed on YouTube.

[7] It is hardest for us to do this **when our greatest fears seem to have come true,** as with Job. We question God: Why? Like Job, we demand answers. The philosopher Peter Kreeft helps us understand that when God appears as Questioner in Job's pain, he himself becomes Job's Answer: **"The danger of truth is that it gets obscured by truths...** Thus, God does not answer Job's questions; God answers Job instead... Just as Jesus constantly answers the questioner instead of the question... so **here God answers Job's deepest heart quest:** to see God face to face; to see Truth, not truths; to meet Truth, not just to know it. Job is satisfied with the only answer that could possibly have satisfied him, in time or in eternity, the only answer that can satisfy us in time or in eternity: **the Answerer, not the answer.**" Peter Kreeft, Three Philosophies of Life, Book Two: "Job: Life as Suffering" (Ignatius Press, 1989).

[8] The full text of Jonathan Edwards' "Sinners in the Hands of An Angry God," preached July 8, 1741 at Enfield, Connecticut, may be read online on several websites, including Christian Classics Ethereal Library. It is a sermon that is still studied today as an example of the preaching of the Great Awakening in North America at the time.

[9] From The Book of the Sparkling Stone, written by Ruysbroeck not far from Brussels in Groenendael Priory in the latter half of the 14th century. (This quote is from Kindle Edition of the 1915 translation by Evelyn Underhill.)

[10] C.S. Lewis, The Great Divorce (Harper Collins, 1946, 1973), 75. The quote goes on to say: "All that are in hell choose it. Without that self-choice, there could be no hell. No soul that seriously and constantly desires joy will ever miss it. Those who seek find. To those who knock it is opened."

[11] Andrée Seu Petersen, "Faith is the Thing," in WORLD Magazine, February 21, 2015.

[12] If you want to learn more about these four heroic people, read the following

biographies and memoirs:

- *The Confession of St. Patrick,* by St. Patrick (public domain; text online)
- *No Greater Love,* by Mother Teresa (New World Library, 2010)
- *The Hiding Place,* by Corrie Ten Boom (originally published 1971)

Section 4: Finding Your Fortress

[1] In case you wish to know who these people are: Edward Coke was an English jurist [1552-1634]; James Otis was an American lawyer [1725-1783]; and Alexander Chase is a contemporary American journalist.

[2] Julian of Norwich, *Revelations of Divine Love,* trans. Grace Warrack (1901). Online: https://jesus.org.uk/sites/default/files/media/documents/books/others/revelations-of-divine-love.pdf.

[3] Julian of Norwich, *Revelations.*

[4] N.T. Wright comments in *Simply Jesus* on how the Incarnation established Jesus as the New Temple: "How does God normally forgive sins within Israel? Why, through the Temple and the sacrifices that take place there. Jesus seems to be claiming that God is doing, up close and personal through him, something that you'd normally expect to happen at the Temple... the place on earth where God's presence intersected with human, this-worldly reality... When Jesus healed people, when he celebrated parties with all and sundry, when he offered forgiveness freely to people as if he were replacing the Temple with his own work—in all these ways it was clear, and he intended it to be clear, that this wasn't just a foretaste of future reality. This *was* reality itself. This was what it looked like when God was in charge." — N.T. Wright, *Simply Jesus: A New Vision of Who He Was, What He Did, and Why He Matters* (Harper Collins, 2011), 79 & 105. This book is well worth reading if you want to understand this matter more deeply.

[5] David may also have been thinking of the time when the priest Ahimelek gave him and his men bread and a sword at the Tabernacle, when he was fleeing Saul [see 1 Samuel 21].

[6] C.S. Lewis, *The Four Loves* (Harcourt Brace Jovanovich, 1960), 80.

Section 5: Traveling Light

[1] Cambridge Dictionary of American Idioms (2006).

[2] From the *Targum Neofiti,* as quoted in *Targums and the Transmission of Scripture into Judaism and Christianity,* by Robert Haywood (BRILL, 2010), 30. Targumim were Aramaic paraphrases of the Hebrew Scriptures by rabbis that additionally expanded and commented on them. Few Jews accept them as authoritative; but they do help us to see the texts through the eyes of people much closer in time and culture to them than we are.

[3] Not coincidentally, Ezekiel tells us that the primary sin of Sodom was that it was *arrogant, overfed and unconcerned; they did not help the poor and needy* [15:49]. Perhaps this anti-definition might help us locate the "righteous" in our own cities.

[4] The "Tic-Tac-Go" exercise is something that we have learned from Stan Rowland, the founder of Community Health Evangelism (CHE) and its urban equivalent,

Neighborhood Transformation. You can find out more about their ministry at www.chenetwork.org. (Oh, and for my British friends: "Tic-Tac-Toe" is the same as "Noughts & Crosses.")

[5] Bonhoeffer, *The Cost of Discipleship*, 82.

[6] Larry Dixon, "A Theology of Sexuality." Chapel message delivered at Columbia International University on 8 April, 2015.

[7] Christian Smith and Hilary Davidson, *The Paradox of Generosity: Giving We Receive, Grasping We Lose* (Oxford University Press, 2014), 1.

[8] Smith & Davidson, *Paradox of Generosity*, 8.

[9] The story of Madison Holleran, a university athlete at the University of Pennsylvania who committed suicide on January 17, 2014, was famously reported in an article entitled "Split Image," published May 7, 2015 on ESPN's website espnW. Including her story as an example here is in **no way** intended as any reflection on her parents, whom I do not know and refuse to judge—only on the fragility of many students entering university today. Reading her story, however, was part of what triggered my own biblical research into fear and risk, as my concern was raised about the epidemic of anxiety among young people. I pray that the insights in this book could help parents and their children to think through some of the deep spiritual issues surrounding this fear disease, and prevent more stories like Madison's.

[10] Hara Estroff Marano, *Psychology Today*; November 1, 2004.

[11] Hannah Rosin, *The Atlantic*; April 2014.

[12] Quoted in "Who Owns the Problem?" by Terri Lobdell, *Palo Alto Weekly*; November 18, 2011.

[13] Judith Locke, Marilyn Campbell & David Kavanagh, "Can a parent do too much for their child? An examination by parenting professionals of the concept of overparenting." *Australian Journal of Guidance and Counseling*, 2012.

[14] The animated Pixar movie *Inside Out* is an insightful story demonstrating the value of not trying to exclude sadness from the lives and memories of children, and how painful experiences are also crucial to the process of maturing.

[15] "Toddler 'strangled to death' in freak accident when his head got trapped between gates that were meant to stop him going downstairs," 23 October 2013, Daily Mail Online; http://www.dailymail.co.uk/news/article-2473055/.

[16] Alan Hirsch, "Defining Missional," in *Leadership Journal*, Fall 2008. For more in-depth explanations, read Hirsch's book, *The Forgotten Ways: Reactivating the Missional Church*, Brazos Press, 2009 (5th edition).

[17] I discuss further some of these ideas of simultaneous rest and activity, as well as Sabbath observance, in my book, *Rest: Living Sabbath Every Day* (2014).

[18] Stories and quotes from Judges 6 (Gideon), Exodus 4 (Moses) and the book of Jonah. Especially note Jonah's reason for not wanting to go to Nineveh (Jonah 4:2-3): *"Isn't this what I said, Lord, when I was still at home? That is what I tried to forestall by fleeing to Tarshish. I knew that you are a gracious and compassionate God, slow to anger and abounding in love, a God who relents from sending calamity. Now, Lord, take away my life, for it is better for me to die than to live."*

Section 6: Willing to Be Wounded

[1] Mary Gilmore (1865-1962), "Never Admit the Pain," in *The Penguin Book of Australian Poetry* (Penguin Australia, 1972), 87.

[2] I consider Brené Brown to be my soul sister in encouraging people toward courage in their daily lives. (She has certainly encouraged me.) What I am attempting to do in this section from a biblical perspective, she demonstrates from a fully researched social science perspective. The full title of this book is *Daring Greatly: How the Courage to be Vulnerable Transforms the Way We Live, Love, Parent and Lead* (Portfolio Penguin, 2013).

[3] Brown, *Daring Greatly*, 33-34.

[4] Brown, *Daring Greatly*, 37.

[5] C.S. Lewis, *The Four Loves*, 121.

[6] Dietrich Bonhoeffer, *Ethics*, trans. Neville Horton Smith (Macmillan, 1955; Touchstone, 1995, Kindle Edition), in Ch. 1, "The Love of God and the Decay of the World," 24.

[7] This is one of the "boxes of self-deception" discussed in *The Anatomy of Peace*, which we will look at again in the next chapter.

[8] Brown, *Daring Greatly*, 64.

[9] Genesis 37:3: *Now Israel loved Joseph more than any of his other sons, because he had been born to him in his old age; and he made an ornate robe for him.* The meaning of the Hebrew term translated *ornate robe* is uncertain; the traditional "coat of many colors" reflects the Septuagint translation (Greek version of the Old Testament). More recent scholarship suggests that the Hebrew indicates "a long robe with long sleeves." In the agrarian culture of the time, someone wearing a robe like this would not do dirty manual labor.

[10] C.S. Lewis, ed., *George MacDonald: An Anthology*, (Macmillan, 1978), 8.

[11] Troy Cady is a good friend of mine who runs a non-profit called PlayFull [www.playfull.org] that helps people (adults included) use play to nurture healthy relationships and create thriving organizations. They are based out of Chicago – check them out!

[12] *The Anatomy of Peace: Resolving the Heart of Conflict,* by The Arbinger Institute (Berret-Koehler Publishers, 2006, 2008). While this is not a "Christian" book, the principles in this book are strongly biblical, and have been extremely influential in my own life, enabling me to perceive and repair some of the brokenness in my relationships. The "Better-Than Box" diagram can be found on p. 108; the "Worse-Than Box" on p. 120.

[13] *Anatomy of Peace*, 108 [emphasis mine].

[14] This philosophy is at the basis of *The Anatomy of Peace*. You can find it explained briefly there on pages 79-80. It was originally expressed in Buber's book *Ich und Du [I and Thou]*, published in German in 1923 and first translated into English in 1937.

[15] C.S. Lewis, *The Weight of Glory and Other Addresses* (Walter Hooper, ed.; New York: Touchstone, 1996), 45.

[16] Timothy Keller, *The Freedom of Self-Forgetfulness: The Path to Christian Joy* (10Publishing, 2012, 2014), 32.

[17] It is worth revisiting here the Bonhoeffer quote we looked at earlier in chapter 8, "Planning and Controlling": "Human love constructs its own image of the other person, of what he is and what he should become. It takes the life of the other person into its own hands. **Spiritual love recognizes the true image of the other person which he has received from Jesus Christ,** the image that Jesus Christ himself embodied and would stamp upon all men." [*Life Together,* 36.]

[18] Buber himself talks about God as the Ultimate "Thou," and suggested that practicing an "I-Thou" attitude toward others as a way of life would lead us to him: "One who truly meets the world goes out also to God." I am suggesting, as Bonhoeffer does, that the reverse is even more deeply true, and that our honest face-to-face experience with God is what makes it truly possible to have an "I Thou" relationship with others.

[19] Bonhoeffer, *Life Together,* 36.

[20] J.R.R. Tolkien, *The Hobbit* (Allen & Unwin, 1937, 1972), 279.

[21] C.S. Lewis, *The Magician's Nephew,* (Collier Books, 1955, 1970), 72.

[22] *Anatomy of Peace,* 137.

[23] Parker J. Palmer, *To Know as We are Known: A Spirituality of Education* (Harper Collins, 1983, 1993, Kindle Edition), 48.

[24] I highly recommend Rebecca Petrie's book, *Falling Into Grace* (Gabriella Press, 2009) describing her journey after her fall and paralysis. Rebecca died only a couple of years ago. She was a joy to all who knew her, and a mighty prayer warrior whom we miss greatly.

[25] You can also read this inspiring story in Dr. McQuilkin's book, *A Promise Kept* (Tyndale, 1998). My husband and I were attending the university when Muriel McQuilkin was diagnosed, and he resigned a little after our graduation.

[26] Bonhoeffer, *Life Together,* 27.

[27] Robertson McQuilkin, quoted by Gary Thomas, in *A Lifelong Love: How to Have Lasting Intimacy, Friendship and Purpose in Your Marriage* (David C. Cook, 2014), 171.

[28] The "I-Deserve" box diagram is on p. 111 of *The Anatomy of Peace.*

[29] *Anatomy of Peace,* 112.

[30] Think about the link with the other half of the line in the Prayer: *as we forgive those who trespass against us* versus *as we forgive our debtors.* What proportion of the things that we find hard to forgive in others are the things that they have **not** done, that we wish they had done but didn't? Often, these things left undone in our human relationships form a far more significant part of the "debt" we hold against them than the actual offenses committed against us.

[31] My Reformed friends might take issue with this, citing the Calvinist doctrine of Limited Atonement. But I think that even if your theology states that Jesus died only for the elect (and therefore would not have "paid the debts" of unbelievers), you might agree that **we** are not the ones who determine the identity of the elect.

Mustn't we treat all around us as someone for whom Christ has died? And therefore we are to forgive, as Christ would if they repented.

[32] The YouTube link for this video, entitled "The Unmerciful Servant", at the time I watched it (February 2014) was: https://www.youtube.com/watch?v=923VwqKq5vM. It was made by Chris Marcus, whose website is www.christophermarcus.com.

[33] Bonhoeffer, *Life Together*, 96-97.

Section 7: Risking Resurrection

[1] H. Richard Niebuhr, *The Kingdom of God in America,* (Wesleyan University Press, 1937, 1983), 193.

[2] Peter Kreeft, *Love is Stronger than Death*, (Ignatius Press, 1992, Kindle edition), Ch. 2, sec. 5, "Death as a Stranger: The Modern Post-Christian Ignoring of Death".

[3] Since my maiden name is Cross, I have been the subject of many a joke based on this verse. Most of them suggest my long-suffering husband as the subject of this command.

[4] Augustine, *The City of God*, Book 13, Ch. 3.

[5] Kreeft, *LISTD*, Ch. 5, sec. 2 [Kindle edition].

[6] This conception of Jesus as our mother may seem a little odd to us, but what I am expressing is not a new idea, nor some politically correct attempt at gender equality in the Godhead. Julian of Norwich, in her *Revelations of Divine Love,* long ago spoke of Christ, the second person of the Godhead, as the mother who "by virtue of his passion, death, and resurrection joins us to our substance." But if the idea offends you, you are welcome to disregard it.

[7] Kreeft, in his book *Love is Stronger than Death,* explores this concept much more fully from a philosophical point of view. I recommend this beautifully written book to anyone interested in grappling with how Christians should think about death, as he explores the five "masks" worn by Death: the Stranger, the Enemy, the Friend, the Mother, and the Lover.

[8] The originals of these quotes read as follows in the NIV:
- Isaiah 25:8 ... *he will swallow up death forever. The Sovereign Lord will wipe away the tears from all faces; he will remove his people's disgrace from the earth. The LORD has spoken.*
- Hosea 13:14 *I will deliver this people from the power of the grave; I will redeem them from death. Where, O death, are your plagues? Where, O grave, is your destruction?*

[9] C.S. Lewis, *Weight of Glory*, 51-52.

[10] Please pardon the plethora of P's.

[11] Joseph Henry Thayer, *Thayer's Greek Lexicon* (1889); Entry for *hikanos* (Strongs G2425). Retrieved from blueletterbible.org. Thayer notes that this was a phrase used in the Septuagint translation of Deuteronomy 3:26, when God becomes angry with Moses begging to see the Promised Land he had been forbidden to enter, and says *It is enough!* (I was also amused by the archaic phrasing of this Thayer quote.)

[12] J.R.R. Tolkien, *The Two Towers* (Houghton-Mifflin, 1954,1994), 656.

[13] Quote retrieved 10/15/16 from http://orthodoxinfo.com/general/history1.aspx.

[14] Thomas Cahill, *How the Irish Saved Civilization* (Doubleday, 1995, Kindle edition), in chi 6: "What Was Found." This is a fascinating account of how these "martyrdoms" of the Irish transformed Europe through re-evangelization, as well as the preservation and spread of literature and literacy.

[15] I would encourage you to become or stay informed on this; numerous organizations have websites devoted to how we can pray for and support the persecuted Church around the world. Open Doors (opendoors.org) publishes an annual Watch List with prayer points for the countries in the world where persecution is most severe.

[16] Bonhoeffer, *The Cost of Discipleship,* 46.

[17] Extract of a letter written by Dietrich Bonhoeffer to his brother Karl-Friedrick on the 14th of January, 1935. I first encountered this quote through the Northumbria Community and you may read it on their website: www.northumbriacommunity.org/who-we-are/introducing-the-community/.

[18] My husband and I have been deeply influenced on our own journey by the Northumbria Community, a Trinitarian "new monastic" community based in the northern part of England. These principles are part of their ethos.

[19] Frederick Buechner, on AZQuotes.com.

[20] *The Westminster Shorter Catechism,* Question 1.

[21] Bonhoeffer, "Peace Speech" at Fano, Denmark, 28 August 1934.

[22] J.R.R. Tolkien, *The Fellowship of the Ring* (Houghton-Mifflin, 1954, 1994), 50.